Independent Politics
How American Disdain for Parties Leads

D0208734

The number of independent voters in America increases each year, yet they remain misunderstood by both media and academics. Media describe independents as pivotal for electoral outcomes. Political scientists conclude that independents are merely *undercover partisans*: people who secretly hold partisan beliefs and are thus politically inconsequential.

Both the pundits and the political scientists are wrong. The authors show that many Americans are becoming embarrassed of their political party. As a result, Americans deny to pollsters, party activists, friends, and even themselves their true partisanship, instead choosing to go "undercover" as independents.

Independent Politics demonstrates that people intentionally mask their partisan preferences. Most importantly, breaking with decades of previous research, the book argues that independents are highly politically consequential. The same motivations that lead people to identify as independent also diminish their willingness to engage in the types of political action that sustain the grassroots movements of American politics.

Samara Klar is an Assistant Professor of Political Science at the University of Arizona. She studies how individuals' social surroundings and personal identities influence their political attitudes and behaviors. Her work has been published in journals including the *American Journal of Political Science*, the *Journal of Politics*, and *Public Opinion Quarterly*, and has been supported by the National Science Foundation. She has been recognized with a Distinguished Junior Scholar award in political psychology from the American Political Science Association and a Burns Roper Fellowship from the American Association of Public Opinion Research. Klar earned a Ph.D. in political science from Northwestern University and also holds degrees from Columbia University and McGill University.

Yanna Krupnikov is an Assistant Professor of Political Science at Stony Brook University. Her research focuses on the way political communication affects public opinion and the way people express their political opinions through political actions. Krupnikov's work has been published in *American Journal of Political Science*, *Political Behavior*, and *Political Communication*, and has been supported by the National Science Foundation. She is a winner of the Midwest Political Science Association's Robert Durr Award and the award for Best Paper by an Emerging Scholar. Krupnikov earned a Ph.D. in political science from the University of Michigan and also holds degrees from the University of Toronto and Brandeis University.

Independent Politics

How American Disdain for Parties Leads to Political Inaction

SAMARA KLAR
University of Arizona

YANNA KRUPNIKOV
Stony Brook University

CAMBRIDGE
UNIVERSITY PRESS

CAMBRIDGE
UNIVERSITY PRESS

University Printing House, Cambridge CB2 8BS, United Kingdom

One Liberty Plaza, 20th Floor, New York, NY 10006, USA

477 Williamstown Road, Port Melbourne, VIC 3207, Australia

314-321, 3rd Floor, Plot 3, Splendor Forum, Jasola District Centre, New Delhi - 110025, India

79 Anson Road, #06-04/06, Singapore 079906

Cambridge University Press is part of the University of Cambridge.

It furthers the University's mission by disseminating knowledge in the pursuit of education, learning and research at the highest international levels of excellence.

www.cambridge.org
Information on this title: www.cambridge.org/9781316500637

© Samara Klar and Yanna Krupnikov 2016

First published 2016

A catalogue record for this publication is available from the British Library

Library of Congress Cataloging in Publication data
Names: Klar, Samara, author. | Krupnikov, Yanna, author.
Title: Independent politics : how American disdain for parties leads to political inaction /
    Samara Klar, University of Arizona; Yanna Krupnikov, Stony Brook University.
Description: New York, NY : Cambridge University Press, 2016. | Includes bibliographical
    references.
Identifiers: LCCN 2015031027 | ISBN 9781107134461 (hbk.) | ISBN 9781316500637 (pbk.)
Subjects: LCSH: Party affiliation – United States. | Political parties – United States. | Political
    culture – United States. | Mass media – Political aspects – United States. | Polarization
    (Social sciences) – United States. | United States – Politics and government – 21st century.
Classification: LCC JK2271 .K53   2016 | DDC 324.0973–dc23
LC record available at http://lccn.loc.gov/2015031027

ISBN   978-1-107-13446-1   Hardback
ISBN   978-1-316-50063-7   Paperback

Contents

Figures

Tables

Acknowledgments

In a way, this book stands as a testament to the importance of attending academic conferences – even conferences that take place in the middle of a particularly hot and humid Chicago summer. At the annual meeting of the International Society of Political Psychology in 2012, Samara presented work on political independents. At the very same meeting, Yanna presented work on social desirability. We were two young academics who knew of each other, but just barely. After our panel, we reintroduced ourselves to one another and casually chatted about our respective projects. Before we knew it, we had hit upon an intriguing idea: *Could it really be possible that Americans believe it socially desirable to tell other people that they are politically independent?*

This book is also a testament to the dangers of casually chatting with people at academic conferences, as this particular conversation led to a project that would consume the next several years of our lives.

After our first set of experimental results demonstrated that people did find political independence to be socially desirable, we realized that our seemingly simple question was much more complicated. What followed was a quest to understand what it is about American politics that drives people to hide their partisan identities and what the implications of these "undercover partisans" are for political parties, political action, and representation. Some fourteen original experiments, many written pages, and (approximately) thousands of e-mails, numerous phone calls, and several video chats later, our casual chitchat has led to this book. And our distant acquaintanceship has led to a fulfilling coauthorship and great friendship that will last for many years to come.

We loved working on this project, in large part because of the countless individuals who made it possible. In what follows we want to take the opportunity to thank everyone who generously gave us their time and thoughts. We consider ourselves very lucky to have the support of these individuals.

We would first like to thank David Magleby, an author of the groundbreaking book on independents that provides the strong base for our own work. It was a conversation with David that allowed us to pinpoint precisely what was important about our idea. David's ability to put our project into perspective was encouraging and his genuine enthusiasm was infectious. We are not sure if David knows how pivotal his feedback was to our ability to complete this book, so we are thrilled for this (additional) opportunity to thank him.

There are not enough words to properly thank Jamie Druckman. Jamie helped us navigate almost every stage of the book-writing process. We are tremendously thankful for Jamie's kindness, patience, and willingness to answer the countless questions we sent his way, no matter how naïve or complicated they might have been. We wish we could say that we'll leave Jamie alone now that the book is published but, unfortunately for him, we make no such promise.

We are grateful to Diana Mutz for providing extremely helpful advice about the process of writing a book and for generously relieving our anxieties with great food, conversation, and wine. We are grateful to Howie Lavine for sharing his expertise on self-monitoring and for his enthusiastic encouragement, to Michael Neblo for helping us consider the overall structure and narrative of the book, to Adam Berinsky for his suggestions about the framing of our argument, and to Ted Brader (upon whom we thrust the roles of guru and life-coach) for his patient support and brilliant advice.

During the 2014 meeting of the American Political Science Association, the following scholars graciously agreed to meet with us and offered us extremely valuable feedback on this project: Alan Abramowitz, Marc Hetherington, Shanto Iyengar, Joanne Miller, Steve Nicholson, and Markus Prior. These meetings were crucial to the completion of the manuscript.

Reading drafts (of anything) is difficult and time-consuming, so we are forever indebted to the people who selflessly put aside their own important projects so they could read (often multiple!) drafts of our chapters. Adam Seth Levine not only read our chapters and offered us thoughtful, careful feedback but also answered (even the most minor) questions. We are grateful not only for his help as a scholar but also for his friendship. It was Jon Caverley who initially suggested that this project could be a book. Proving that no good deed goes unpunished, Jon subsequently read our draft chapters. We are grateful not only for Jon's feedback but also for his assurance that we could actually write a book.

Critical to this book are our theoretical arguments – Chapter 2 – and we are lucky to have had Chris Weber read a draft of this particular chapter. Chris's thoughtful, detailed comments made this chapter tremendously better.

We have been lucky to surround ourselves with a true dream team of academic friends and mentors. We would like to thank the following people who contributed to various parts of this book, be it with incisive feedback, helpful data, or much-needed encouragement: Nichole Bauer, Matthew Baum, Emily

Beaulieu, Amber Boydstun, John Bullock, Sarah Cho, Jon Cohen, Morris Fiorina, Dan Galvin, Eric Groenendyk, Laurel Harbridge, Sunshine Hillygus, Leonie Huddy, Josh Kertzer, Matt Lebo, Milton Lodge, Joshua Meyer-Gutbrod, Brint Milward, Irfan Nooruddin, Spencer Piston, Jeff Segal, Chuck Shipan, John Sides, Rune Slothuus, Paul Sniderman, Mark Snyder, Stuart Soroka, and Chad Westerland.

We are grateful to those who attended presentations of various elements of this book and gave us helpful feedback: specifically, attendees at Northwestern University's Institute for Policy Research, Cornell University's Department of Government, the University of Arizona's Works in Progress Workshop, and Harvard University's Working Group in Political Psychology and at the annual meetings of the American Political Science Association, the Midwest Political Science Association, the International Society of Political Psychology, and the American Association of Public Opinion Research.

We are fortunate to have the support of the political science departments at Northwestern University, the University of Arizona, and Stony Brook University. We are grateful to these institutions for providing us with brilliant colleagues to consult for advice, generous resources to support our research, and great places to go to work each morning. Of course, we could not have completed this project without excellent research assistants: Kristen Ditsch (who conducted some background research well before the start of the project), Blake Findley, Eli Johnson, Janesh Rahlan, Jamie Welch, Breanna Wright, and Sara Yeganeh. Thanks also to the terrific students in Samara's "Methods of Political Inquiry" class in the spring semester of 2014 for their help with data collection.

Critical to this process was our editor at Cambridge University Press, Robert Dreesen, and the two very helpful reviewers who read our manuscript. We thank Robert for his enthusiasm, time, and care with this manuscript. We also owe sincere thanks to Brianda Reyes for her expert guidance throughout the production of this book.

Finally, we are deeply grateful to the people who support us the most. Samara would like to thank her parents, Lewis and Irene Klar, for their inspiring intellectual curiosity, their cheerful encouragement, and their love. They read many early drafts of this manuscript and without them many typos would surely remain. Samara thanks her loving and lovable family, Noah, Emma, Delilah, and Isaac, and Ilan, Noa, Yael, and Eitan, for all of their support. Most of all, she is grateful every minute to Yotam Shmargad for thinking so deeply about her work (and eagerly discussing it for hours during long hot walks in the summer), for sharing with her his brilliant wisdom and his affectionate love, and for putting their happiness before everything.

Yanna thanks her parents, Vulf and Svetlana Krupnikov. Most of what she has accomplished in life Yanna owes to their tremendous sacrifices, and this book is just one more example of something that would have been impossible without their love and encouragement. Yanna also thanks her grandparents, Khaim and Eugenia Kushkuley, for their support. Finally, she thanks John Barry

Ryan who read multiple (full) drafts of the manuscript and encouraged her to write the strongest version of the argument. Yanna also thanks John for his love, sharp sense of humor, excellent taste in music, and never running out of intelligent things to say about the world (she also forgives him for winning every board game they have ever played together).

In short, we could not have completed this project without these aforementioned individuals. We sincerely thank each one.

Independents in Name Only

"If you say you're a Democrat, that must mean you are a left-wing liberal with no personal responsibility. If you say you are a Republican, you must be a right-wing millionaire who doesn't care about others."

– Jennifer Cummins, Kentucky voter

"Whoever wins independent voters in Ohio, wins Ohio," Mitt Romney's political director told Fox News with forty-eight hours to go until Election Day 2012. Meanwhile in the Democratic camp, the party's Hamilton County, Ohio chairman stressed to the *Financial Times*, "We need a good, solid turnout among the independent voters."[1] During the 2012 presidential campaign, the American media published nearly 2,000 articles addressing the thoughts, ideas, and feelings of independent voters like Kentucky resident Jennifer Cummins, quoted at the beginning of this chapter. Pundits and political operatives proclaimed that persuading independents like Cummins to pick one party over the other would be the key to electoral victory.

The pundits and political operatives who believe that independents can be persuaded are wrong.

Political scientists have known for nearly half a century that Cummins, along with the vast majority of independents, have most likely already chosen a candidate long before Election Day.

"Voters are not 'declaring independence' from political parties. ... In fact, the American electorate is much more partisan than in the recent past," writes political science professor and blogger John Sides. The very same people who avoid

---

[1] Brett LoGiurato (November 12, 2012) "Why Winning The Independent Vote Can Actually Be A Bad Thing." *Business Insider*.

Barney Jopson (November 6, 2012) "Voters in Crucial Swing County Relish Influence." *Financial Times*.

partisan labels, scholars find time and again, are independent in name only. When asked, the majority of independents will admit that they lean toward one of the two major parties, and these "leaners" appear suspiciously partisan in practice (Hajnal and Lee 2010, p. 46). They vote consistently for one party as opposed to another (Keith et al. 1992; Magleby et al. 2011), they express attitudinal support for one party over another (Keith et al. 1992; Magleby et al. 2011), and their policy preferences and affective predispositions line up consistently with just one of the two parties (Iyengar and Westwood 2014; Magleby et al. 2011). For these reasons, political scientists have dismissed independents – like Jennifer Cummins – as politically inconsequential.

But the political scientists who believe independents are politically inconsequential are also wrong.

In this book we argue that both media and political scientists fundamentally misunderstand independent voters. At best, media view independents as objective observers of American politics. As we will show, media often portray independents as people who are not beholden to partisan allegiances, who listen to new information, who make careful political choices, and who, ultimately, vote for the party that makes the best case during a given campaign. At the very least, media portray independents as electorally unpredictable, which makes them more newsworthy than the ever-predictable partisans (Gans 1979; Boydstun 2013).

Political scientists, on the other hand, dismiss independents as nothing more than "undercover partisans."[2] As such, independents "consistently support only one party's candidates," explained Alan Abramowitz – a prominent voice on partisanship in America – in a 2014 *Politico* column entitled "The Partisans in the Closet: Political independents are (mostly) a figment of your imagination".[3] Indeed, this was precisely the conclusion of one of the most thorough investigations of independent voters to date: the 1992 book *The Myth of the Independent Voter*. Relying on an elaborate series of national surveys, the book's authors argued that the political preferences of independents are virtually identical to those of their partisan counterparts. "Independents," the authors concluded, "are not a bloc.... They are largely closet Democrats and Republicans" (p. 4).

Political scientists are right to suggest that independents are not persuadable blank slates, but to dismiss them as merely "undercover partisans" is to ignore the complexity of the democratic process. To assume independents are inconsequential for American politics is akin to a doctor telling a patient that since his

---

[2] This description is given to independents by the authors of *The American Voter*, Angus Campbell, Philip Converse, Warren Miller, and Donald Stokes. Other scholars have also referred to independents as partisans who are "in the closet" (e.g., Keith et al. 1992). Both terms suggest the same idea: people who have clear partisan preferences but opt to hide them. We use the term "undercover partisans" for consistency.

[3] Alan Abramowitz (January 8, 2014) "The Partisans in the Closet." *Politico Magazine.*

nagging cough won't instantaneously kill him, there is no reason to investigate its cause. If independents are nothing more than undercover partisans, why won't they identify with their own party? Why, when given the choice of Democrat, Republican, or independent, do they report that they are independents? *If there is nothing unique about these people politically, why are they so motivated to intentionally misrepresent their own partisanship?*

These questions lead to an even larger one: Do the motivations that lead people to conceal their partisanship – that is, to go undercover – have any broader consequences for American politics? Could the motivations that lead individuals to avoid partisan labels also lead them to change their behaviors in politically important ways? These are the questions that motivate this book.

We argue that independent voters are consequential for American politics in ways that neither journalists nor political scientists have predicted. In doing so, we tell a new story about independents and partisans in America. It is a story that should alarm both partisans and political parties. The endless conflicts and the seemingly insurmountable disagreements between parties have led many Americans to dislike partisans. As a result, people who hold clear partisan preferences have gone undercover. Going undercover means not only that people avoid revealing their partisanship but also that people refuse to engage in consequential political actions simply because these actions could make them appear partisan. Struggling to balance their hatred of partisans with their political preferences, undercover partisans create a Catch-22 for American parties: represent my interests at all costs, but don't bicker with the other party while doing it, and don't expect any help from me!

1.1 GOING UNDERCOVER

Our story begins with a puzzle. Since about the 1970s, a sizeable portion of Americans have avoided offering a partisan identification, instead reporting that they are independent. Yet, there exist virtually no demographic or even political differences between these independents and partisans. Independents look like partisans and partisans look like independents.[4]

In the summer of 2013, for example, 45.7 percent of the participants in the Pew Politics Survey picked "independent" as their initial identification. In Table 1.1 we provide demographic data for Democrats, Republicans, and independents. Independents as a group appear slightly less educated than Democrats, but they match the education rate of Republicans. Independents are less likely to regularly attend religious services than are Republicans, but they attend at similar rates as Democrats. On average they are closer in age to Democrats, but they are closer in racial makeup to Republicans. On the whole, there is nothing particularly distinct about independents.

---

[4] We focus on these particular demographic characteristics, as these are the characteristics that often drive participation and engagement in politics (Verba et al. 1995).

TABLE 1.1. *Demographic Characteristics of Independents and Partisans*

	Basic Demographic Characteristics (N = 1408)^			
	Independents	Democrats	Republicans	All
% Male	56.5%	40.6%	50.0%	49.9%
% with BA +	38.18%	44.49%	37.03%	39.6%
Avg. Age	50.1	52.3	56.4	52.3
% White	80.5%	44.49%	89.5%	76.3%
Regular religious attendance	35%	39.8%	48.7%	39.8%
% with income of 50,000+	50.9%	45.82%	50.36%	48.6%
	Additional Demographic Characteristics (N = 2104)*			
% Labor Union Connection	14%	15.9%	12.4%	14.2%
% Military Connection	25%	19.3%	26.2%	23.1%
% Currently Employed	49.2%	48.8%	47.4%	48.5%
% with children under 18	36.3%	34.9%	41.2%	37.2%
Where do you get your news:				
% from TV	48.1%	58.7%	55.5%	54.4%
% from radio	16.3%	15.2%	25.2%	18.5%
% from newspapers	30.6%	36.2%	26.9%	31.7%
% very interested in politics	44.5%	56.9%	47.1%	50.1%

^ Results from Pew July 2013 Political Survey: "Regular religious attendance" means the respondent attends religious services at least once a week.

* Results from the 2007 Washington Post Kaiser Family Foundation-Harvard University Survey of Political Independents: Labor union connection means the respondent or someone in the household is a member of a labor union; military connection means the respondent or someone in the household either serves in the military or is a veteran. Survey includes an oversample of independents, so results presented are weighted in order to compare across partisan groups.

A similar non-pattern emerges when we consider additional demographic characteristics, as well as non-ideological political factors (bottom of Table 1.1). Here we turn to the 2007 Survey of Political Independents, a survey conducted to explore independents as a group. The findings reveal that independents are just as likely as partisans either to be a member of a labor union or to live with someone who is a labor union member.[5] They are also just as likely to have some connection to the military – either through their own service or by living with someone who has served. Political scientists would predict that independents are slightly less interested in politics – and they are, but the actual differences are small.

The similarities between independents and partisans persist when we consider voting choices. In 2012, nearly 40 percent of independents said that they

[5] The Survey of Political Independents was conducted by telephone from May 3 to June 3, 2007. Independents were randomly selected for participation post-self-identification as "independent." Due to this oversample we use weights to compare across the parties. We do not use weights in the Pew 2013 survey. Plase see the web appendix for Chapter 1 for weighted results.

generally "leaned toward" the Democratic Party, and among them only 4 percent voted for Romney. About a third of independents, meanwhile, said that they "leaned toward" Republicans, and among them less than 7 percent voted for Obama. This pattern nearly replicates the behavior of voters who report that they are partisans. According to the American National Election Studies, just over 4 pecent of self-identified Democrats voted for Romney in 2012; among self-identified Republicans, just over 6 percent voted for Obama. Overall, in the 2012 presidential election – as in most prior elections – independents appeared to behave much like partisans. These patterns reinforce what many political scientists have long argued: there exist almost no differences between partisans and independents.

So why are these people independent?

1.2 "I DON'T LIKE POLITICAL PARTIES"

The idea that there are so few discernible differences between partisans and independents may be comforting to some researchers. If independents are "a bit bashful about admitting it, but partisan nevertheless" (Wolfinger 1995, p. 184), then the fact that more than a third of Americans eschew partisanship is largely politically inconsequential.

Yet the similarities between independents and partisans are puzzling. If these two groups are virtually identical along characteristics that are politically important, why do some group members identify as partisans and others as independents? And if the lack of discernable differences is due to the fact that independents are simply undercover, *why are they undercover*? Indeed, the idea that individuals – who by all accounts have no explicit reason to do so – are avoiding partisanship should leave both scholars and political elites uneasy. As we will argue and demonstrate in this book, the superficial similarities between partisans and independents mask a series of critical, and politically consequential, differences.

In the 2007 Survey of Political Independents, self-identified independents were presented with a list of reasons why someone might choose to be an independent, and they were asked to select the reasons for their own decision to cast partisanship aside. Some of the reasons in the choice set provided to respondents by the survey reflected an idealized view of independents ("*I vote for candidates, not parties*"), others suggested a more practical reason for opting out of partisanship ("*I am not comfortable with either the Republican or Democratic Party*"), while still others spoke to a general avoidance of politics ("*I'm not very interested in politics*"). Respondents were first asked to answer whether something was a reason for why they are independent; if they answered affirmatively, they were asked a follow-up question to determine whether this was a major or minor reason for their independent identification.

Figure 1.1 displays the patterns of reasons provided. The white bars represent the proportion of people who selected a response option as a reason for

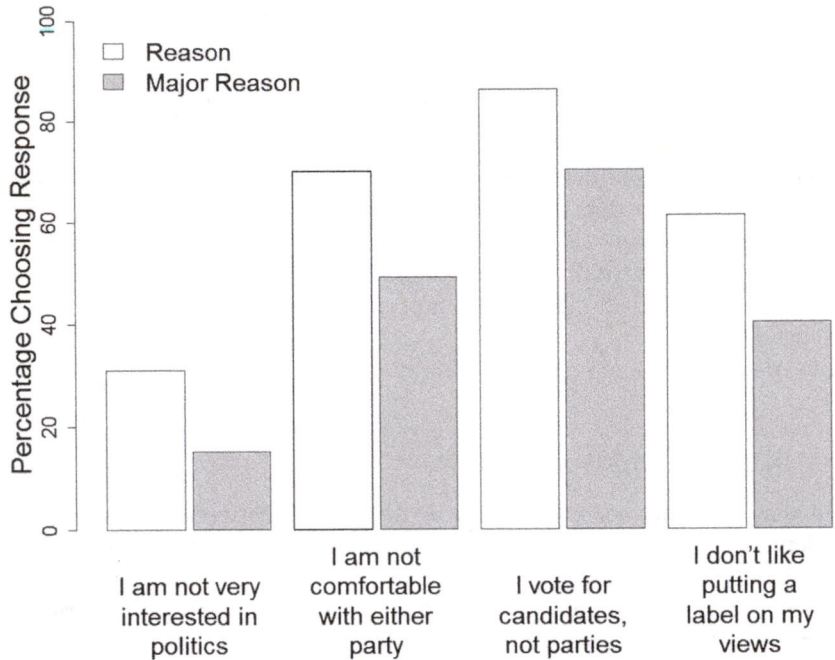

FIGURE 1.1. Reasons Why People Select Independent.
Data from the 2007 Washington Post Kaiser Foundation Harvard University Survey,
$N = 2104$.

being independent and the gray bars show the proportion of respondents who subsequently reported that a particular response option is a *major* reason for their independent identification. Nearly 70 percent of independents reported that they are not comfortable with either of the two parties, while 61 percent reported that they simply do not like party labels. In contrast, very few independents explained that being an independent is driven by their lack of interest in politics. Selecting independent, at least at first glance, seems to be an exercise motivated by avoiding labels, rather than by a disinterest in politics.

An even more interesting pattern emerges when we break with convention and allow people to *explain* their partisan identities in their own words. Unencumbered by the constraints of survey questions, we gave a group of ordinary Americans the chance to tell us – under the cloak of anonymity – as much or as little as they wanted about why they selected a particular partisan category.[6]

[6] Responses from open-ended items in a 2014 study conducted via the Internet with a nationally representative set of adults using Survey Sampling International (SSI). Although SSI is a non-probability sample, other scholars have used SSI to collect not only experimental but also survey data (Iyengar and Westwood 2014). These open-ended responses were obtained by

The explanations most partisans offered reflected most of the factors that we have long known to contribute to partisan identification. Republicans and Democrats alike mentioned their ideological connections to a given political party: "I chose to affiliate myself with the Republican Party mostly because of fiscal policy," explained one participant. Another supported the Democrats because the Democrats "seem to be more for the middle and low income people and not the upper class. Republicans are for the rich and not for the poor." People spoke about family history and a tradition of partisan affiliation. "When I got married my husband was Republican, so I guess I went with him, that is the reason I am with the Republican Party," explained a participant. Still others noted that their identities had led them to a party; one participant explained a preference for Democrats as follows, "I am an African American follower when it comes to politics for the race."[7]

What the independents offered, however, was far more complex. Some described selecting independent as a means of avoiding a direct affiliation to either party. "Belonging to a herd is not my style," explained one participant (who also noted wanting a "none of the above" option to the partisanship question). "I do not want to be affiliated with a certain party," explained another. Another participant noted that they "don't want to be associated with either party." This participant would later go on to explain that the Democrats have "gone off the rails." And one simply concluded, "I don't like political parties."

For others, the choice of "independent" represented rising above what they perceived to be traditional political machinations and persistent political problems. "I am independent because anything else would make me feel I was contributing to disunity," offered one participant. Another noted, "if current government Democrats and Republicans [are] what we have to choose from then I will be independent."

"I am very tired of the fighting between both the Republican and Democratic political parties," explained one participant. "I think that there is a need for balance and compromise, and so I am an independent," concluded another.

These anonymous responses reflect the way independents present themselves to media. Shortly before the 2012 election, CNN was among the numerous media outlets that allowed independents to tell their own stories and discuss why they turned away from partisanship. In this series, a number of people

providing individuals with unlimited space to explain their partisan identifications. We discuss this sample in Appendix A1. Please note that the open-ended responses have been edited for spelling and grammar. We provide the verbatim versions of the responses in the web appendix to Chapter 1.

7 Of course, people cannot always successfully explain their own motivations or may provide a well-thought-out justification for a choice that was based on impulse or made "without awareness, effort or intent" (Pronin 2009, 2). In our case, however, the public explanation for selecting the independent identification is also quite important and informative. Put another way, people's justification for their identification as independent can help illuminate their perceptions of partisanship in American politics.

who described themselves as politically independent walked CNN journalists through the reasoning behind the "independent" label.[8]

We opened this chapter with Kentucky resident Jennifer Cummins's explanation to CNN for why she identifies as independent. Similarly, Omekongo Dibinga of Washington, DC explained, "I don't like being labeled. I've been labeled a lot of things in my life." Roger Cantillo, a New York voter who had only recently traded in his Democratic affiliation for independence, invoked a more practical approach: "It's just unfortunate that there's a lot of gridlock, and people are playing both sides."

What is notable about individual explanations of independence – offered by both our anonymous participants and the CNN interviewees – is that they also underscore the idea of independence as a *positive trait* relative to the less desirable partisan affiliation. North Carolina voter Mary Helen Yarborough, for example, reported, "I feel better as an independent. I feel like it's a more honest position." Similarly, one of our anonymous participants explained that being independent is just "common sense," while another wrote that being independent means being "more open to the truth." When Arizona voter Bretton Holmes claimed independents are voting as "free thinkers," he made this point even more directly. Independents, these explanations suggest, break the mold. They break with the "dogma" of partisanship, as Texas independent Jim Mitchem called it. Independents in their own words appear to think of themselves as a political scientist's ideal voter: rational, thoughtful, and fair.

And so a pattern finally emerges: partisan labels are negative and oppressive. Identifying with a party is akin to affiliating oneself with disagreement, fighting, and gridlock. Being independent is different; being independent is positive; being independent is constructive; being independent is *American*.[9]

1.3 THE SOCIAL VALUE OF INDEPENDENCE AND ITS CONSEQUENCES

The possibility that there is a benefit – *a social value* – to identifying as an independent holds the key to answering the questions we posed at the beginning of this chapter. Political independents, we suggest, are viewed more positively than are partisans: independents are perceived as "free thinkers" who are "more open to the truth" and able to set aside the "dogma" of partisanship. The belief that political independents are in some way superior intersects with people's existing motivations to make the best impressions they can on others (Schlenker

[8] Christina Zdanowicz (November 2, 2012) "Neither Republican Nor Democrat: Why I'm an Independent." CNN.com. The quotes included are part of this article. A number of the participants in the CNN story also recorded their own videos with fuller explanations of their independent identifications.

[9] Indeed, as Mary Helen Yarborough tells CNN, beng independent is "more American ... America was born on the theme of independence, and I find that being a committed independent is therefore truer to our national pride."

and Weigold 1989; Goffman 1967; Holtgraves 1992). This desire to portray a positive political image is further magnified when people are led to believe that negative traits are associated with partisanship. Driven by a natural need to make a positive impression and believing that being openly partisan is likely to make a terrible impression, people retreat undercover. This reluctance to associate with a party, however, is not limited to just rhetorically identifying as independent. More importantly, these same motivations can lead people toward an avoidance of political *actions* that betray any partisan preference.

There are numerous ways in which individuals may receive negative cues about partisans, thus motivating them to avoid partisanship altogether. This information might come from family and friends or it might come from media and partisan politicians themselves. This information need not directly state that partisanship is negative. In fact, as we will show, media coverage of partisan disagreement – something that has become a news staple (Levendusky 2009; Mattes and Redlawsk 2014) – associates partisanship with a series of negative traits, such as stubborn inflexibility, bitterness, closed-mindedness, and anger. These are characteristics that individuals generally perceive in a negative manner both politically and socially (Kinder et al. 1980; Rodríguez-Bailón et al. 2000; Hardy and Jamieson 2005; Oltmanns et al. 2005). When people believe that partisanship is associated with these types of traits, they go undercover and opt to identify themselves as "independents."

Put more broadly, our approach demonstrates that there is a critical component to partisanship that few scholars have previously considered: the *expression* of partisanship. As we will show throughout this book, people may have stable and consistent partisan identities and preferences, but their willingness to *express* these identities can fluctuate. Our goal is to consider the political forces, conditions, and motivations that drive these fluctuations. Ultimately we find that Americans' systematic, deliberate, and often frequent choices to self-identify as "independent" signal serious consequences for partisanship and, in turn, for political parties.

1.3.1 The Partisan Consequences of Going Undercover

By focusing on what motivates individuals to avoid partisanship, our work stands as one of the first systematic examinations of *why* American partisans go undercover and what this means for American democracy.[10] Although scholars have reasoned that people who identify as independents may have an overall different connection to the party than do those who identify as partisans (Magleby et al. 2011; Miller and Shanks 1997), to date there has been little empirical or theoretical examination of the individual processes or broader

---

[10] Discussing the research presented in *Myth of the Independent Voter*, Magleby et al. (2011, p. 258) note, "In *Myth*, we stopped short of adducing causes for *why* individuals in the electorate identify as independents rather than as partisans."

political conditions that motivate individuals to report that they are independent.

Beyond identifying these motivations, our work challenges some of the most deeply held conclusions in research on political partisanship and political behavior. Through an elaborate series of novel experimental and observational studies, we demonstrate that independence is not simply a "myth" – rather, it is a paradox. Contrary to what journalists and pundits suggest, people who call themselves independents are not pure blank slates – they are unlikely to swing between the two parties depending on the election.[11] These people have consistent partisan preferences that lead them to the same party's candidates in most elections.

Even more importantly, we also break with decades of political science research. Independents may not differ from partisans in their ideological profiles or political choices, but they *are* unique. Determined to present themselves in the best possible way, these Americans represent an unusual breed of voter – ones who would rather undermine their own partisan preference than damage their perceived social image. The undercover partisan refuses to openly identify with a party, all the while holding their preferred party to an impossibly high political standard.

1.3.2 The Behavioral Consequences of Going Undercover

Not only do our findings have key implications for understanding why people avoid partisanship; our book is also the first to show that the same motivations that lead people to identify as independent have profound consequences for political behavior. In particular, the conditions that motivate people to go undercover also lead people to avoid political actions that publicly display their partisanship, actions such as advocating for a party when chatting with a friend or coworker, wearing a political button, posting a campaign sign, or even sharing a message from a political party with their social network. A decline in these types of behavior is consequential, as public displays of partisanship are often the simplest – and most persuasive – forms of political participation.

Advocating for the importance of this type of citizen communication, James Stimson writes that politicians, parties, and campaigns need people "with the personal attributes of good salesmen" (Stimson 1990, p. 354). Stimson suggests that political actors need ordinary people to sell them to other ordinary people. Public displays of partisanship, then, become "sales techniques." Research shows that these types of sales pitches by ordinary people can have profound

---

[11] This is not to suggest that there is no evidence of people who describe themselves as independent swinging between parties. Indeed, Campbell et al. (1960) show some evidence of this pattern in *The American Voter*. This is simply to acknowledge that these swing voter characteristics are unlikely to be the norm, and people who identify as independents show a greater tendency to consistently vote for the same party than to move between parties.

effects on the behaviors of others. People convert their preferences to votes "within a particular social context rather than in social isolation" (Beck 2002, p. 330). Indeed, people often mold and change their political views to be more like their friends and discussion partners (Lazer et al. 2010; Klar 2014a). Citizen-to-citizen communication can even shift how people vote: the more people discuss politics with advocates for the other party, the more likely they are to cross party lines (Beck 2002). Even more starkly, Beck et al. (2002) found that citizen-to-citizen conversation has a greater impact on people's political choices than do the national media. In short, when people sell politics, their social circles seem to buy it.

The Internet has only magnified the power of selling politics. In a study of 61 million Facebook users, Bond et al. (2012) tracked the effects of "social contagion," showing that the political "statuses" people post to their Facebook pages have an effect not only on their in-network "friends" but also on the friends of these Facebook friends. Stieglitz et al. (2012) point to similar patterns on Twitter, noting that the possibility that a political message can be "re-tweeted" – or shared with additional Twitter users in increasingly broader networks – exemplifies Twitter's position as a powerful platform for the spread of citizen-to-citizen discussion (Stieglitz et al. 2012).

Relying on these new forms of Internet communication, both the Democratic National Committee (DNC) and the Republican National Committee (RNC) encourage their supporters to promote the party through public displays of partisanship. In fact, the parties even provide guides on the best ways a person can sell the party. In 2014, for example, the RNC launched "Victory 365" a website dedicated to encouraging citizen-to-citizen communication. Engaging in things like "sharing messages on social networks" and "recruiting your friends," the RNC suggests, can "grow our party and win elections."[12]

These forms of participation are simple, but they necessitate a public display of partisanship. Whether a person displays a sticker, posts a status on Facebook, or even suggests to a friend that he should vote for a particular candidate, these actions require some public acknowledgment of a partisan preference. To successfully "sell" the party, a person must publicly acknowledge having a connection to a party (Beck et al. 2002). Unwillingness to identify with a party not only means an increase in undercover partisans but also suggests that the citizen as a political "salesperson" is in jeopardy.

Considered through the lens of political participation, then, undercover partisanship is not merely an inconsequential quirk shared by more than one-third of American voters. Rather, "going undercover" is the by-product of a deep disdain for partisanship – a disdain so profound that it leads many Americans to alter their day-to-day behavior. In this book, we demonstrate that the conditions that increase the rates of independent identification also diminish

---

[12] The website is www.gopvictory365.com and was launched as part of the 2014 congressional campaign by the RNC.

people's willingness to discuss partisan politics with others, to take overtly partisan actions, to engage in social networks that discuss politics, and to display their political preferences in an array of ways. The more that people care about what others think of them, the more likely they are to shy away from engaging in any partisan behavior – even when these behaviors may give them a political voice (Verba et al. 1995) or benefit the party they (secretly) support.

We return to these behavioral implications throughout the book. We demonstrate that the motivations that lead people to identify as independent also lead them away from taking the types of actions that can often best promote their partisan interests. Moreover, we consider political behavior in a broader perspective. The media often suggest that contemporary politics are marked by more partisanship than ever, and as a result, ordinary people are more willing to publicly fight on behalf of their preferred party. This argument stands in stark contrast to the results we present in this book. Parties, as we argue in later chapters, must now work harder than ever to encourage their supporters to take even the most minimal and costless forms of political action.

1.4 PLAN OF THE BOOK

This book relies on a diverse series of empirical tests to trace why and when individuals avoid partisanship and what this means for American politics. We begin in Chapter 2 by theorizing *why* partisans might go undercover and *when* they are most likely to do so. We consider long-term historical patterns in American politics, including evolving perceptions of independents among the American public. Relying on novel research from across the social sciences, we argue that as people learn that partisanship is associated with negative traits, they grow to believe that it is personally damaging to identify as a partisan. We show that over time there has been a considerable increase in the amount of information that suggests a relationship between partisanship and these negative traits. In particular, we connect these messages about negative traits to coverage of partisan disagreement. We show that the media are increasingly focused on covering the parties in such a way that amplifies disagreement. Even when disagreement can be considered civil and even when parties do attempt to compromise, the media continue to create a narrative of an antagonistic relationship marked by a profound, insurmountable gulf between the parties.

In Chapter 2 we also introduce an important psychological construct that can help explain *who* is most susceptible to masking their partisan preferences. Finally, we explain how the same motivations that lead people to identify as independent also have strong, heretofore unexplored consequences for political action. The theoretical contribution we advance in Chapter 2 sets the foundation for the empirical tests we present in the remainder of the book.

The last decade has introduced numerous methodological innovations to political science, and our empirical approach makes use of these innovations. New techniques in participant recruitment allow us to overcome geographic limitations and reach diverse groups of Americans. Technological advances allow us novel means of capturing people's thoughts and opinions and allow us to track how they imagine the political reality around them. We rely on innovative experimental approaches that give us the opportunity to observe whether our participants take real, costly political actions. These experimental approaches allow us to test our predictions in ways that would have been impossible just two decades ago.

In Chapter 3 we present a series of experimental studies to demonstrate the social desirability of identifying as an independent. We show the types of political coverage that exacerbate this perception. We then reinforce our experimental findings with a case study of a key political misstep and show how one candidate's error drove voters away from his whole party. Overall, the evidence in this chapter suggests that the way Americans express their partisanship is highly dependent on the impressions they are seeking to make, the extent to which making positive impressions is important to them, and the broader political context. Chapter 3 directly tests the mechanisms at the heart of our theoretical argument.

We begin to present a broader set of results in Chapter 4. Moving away from perceptions of independents, we consider how people feel about partisans. Relying on three new experiments, we demonstrate that Americans discriminate against both Democrats *and* Republicans, while placing independents on a pedestal. Among our findings are those suggesting that people believe that partisans are physically unattractive and that many would avoid living in the same neighborhoods as partisans.

In Chapter 5 we take on the behavioral implications of going undercover. An aversion to partisanship may change what people say, but does it change what they do? What makes this chapter particularly unique is that it relies on a series of studies in which respondents are required to take real political actions. Through these studies we reveal the most damaging implications for American politics: social norms in favor of independents lead Americans to conceal their partisanship to the detriment of the party that they, in fact, support. Breaking with previous research on partisanship and political participation, this chapter shows that undercover partisans stand as obstacles in the way of grassroots politics in America.

After demonstrating why Americans go undercover and how this decision affects their political behavior, we turn to a series of tests that focus on Americans' day-to-day political engagement. In Chapter 6 we leave the experimental lab and turn to nationally representative survey data of Americans. We show that people who are more concerned with the impressions they make on others are also significantly more likely to identify as independents. Furthermore, they are less likely to take actions that might reveal their true partisan preferences.

To this point, our results hint that a great chasm exists in American politics between what Americans *say* they want from politicians and what they *really do* want. In Chapter 7 we examine this chasm. First, we employ a nationally representative survey of Americans in which we ask partisans and independents to tell us, in their own words, what they want from government. The independents, to no surprise, call for compromise. We then hold their feet to the fire with experimental studies that reveal how undercover partisans react when their preferred party engages in bipartisan cooperation. We show that undercover partisans are a nightmare for the American political party: they hate partisan disagreement, but they also hate when their preferred party gives up anything for the sake of compromise.

At a time when political parties are asking for more from their members at the grassroots level, undercover partisans pose a critical and unpredictable challenge. Undercover partisans, we suggest, shun partisan participation yet nonetheless demand stronger leadership. In Chapter 8 we conclude by discussing how our work fits within broader research on partisanship. We also address alternative explanations by considering how our work fits within contemporary arguments about polarization and political participation in America. Although certainly some segments of the populace have grown more polarized and partisan, we show that many other people are fleeing undercover. Moreover, we argue that suggested increases in political participation are overstated – rather, parties have to work harder than before to promote political action. People may have preferences for a party, people may even strongly believe in the superiority of a particular party, but American politics is leading them away from the *expression* of these partisan preferences. In turn, this hesitancy to express partisanship has consequences for political parties.

2

Inside the Mind of an Independent Voter in America

> "I am no bird; and no net ensnares me: I am a free human being with an independent will."
>
> – Charlotte Brontë, author, from the novel *Jane Eyre*

Everyone wants to make a good impression. As a result, we tend to modify our behaviors – for example, by pretending to like something we actually do not like at all just for the sake of impressing the people around us. The desire to make a good impression is so pervasive that even we, the authors of this book, are not immune to it. We began this chapter with a quote from the classic novel *Jane Eyre*, written by Charlotte Brontë. Many people respect Brontë's work, and, deep down, we felt that opening our second chapter with a quote from *Jane Eyre* would lead readers to form a better impression of us. Secretly, though, the passage we really wanted to open with is from an episode of the television show *Friends*. Rachel – one of the characters on the show – claims that her favorite movie is *Dangerous Liaisons* because she does not want to admit that her favorite movie is actually *Weekend at Bernie's*. Much like Rachel's concern about the negative judgments associated with loving *Weekend at Bernie's*, we too worried that opening with a reference to *Friends* would leave a negative impression of us (even though we do believe that *Friends* makes for a better opener to this chapter than Brontë).

The problem for American political parties, as we will discuss in this chapter, is that the parties want to be respectable, like *Dangerous Liaisons*, but they are really more like *Weekend at Bernie's* – something that one might secretly support but would rather not associate with publicly. The presence of independents, we argue, goes hand-in-hand with the perception that being a partisan is not something to be proud of. As a result, people are reluctant to behave in any way that might lead others to identify them as supporters of political parties.

In this chapter, we make our way through a series of political puzzles. Previous scholarship has concluded that independents are merely undercover partisans, but we move beyond this conclusion. We consider what it is about American politics that motivates partisans not only to report that they are independent but also to avoid forms of political participation that may be perceived as partisan. To do so, we weave together three separate threads: the role of independents in post–New Deal American politics, the American political context today, and individual psychology.

We first consider what we know about independents and, more importantly, what we still do not know. Next, we broaden our perspective and turn to evidence from psychology and sociology to understand why people might turn away from partisan politics. Beginning with the way parties are portrayed in modern American politics, we look at how people balance their own political preferences with what they believe others expect of them. This chapter sets the foundation for a refrain that we will often return to throughout this book: the label "independent" is merely the tip of the iceberg – it is what lies beneath that should worry American political parties.

2.1 INDEPENDENTS IN AMERICA

2.1.1. The Birth of the Independent Survey Respondent

Although mentions of independents in American politics date back to the early years of the twentieth century (Bryce 1929), the story of modern scholarship on independents begins in much the same way as the story of the modern political survey. In 1948, a team of survey researchers at the University of Michigan launched a series of large-scale surveys of ordinary Americans. The survey questions covered attitudes about a variety of political topics – from policy issues to presidential approval – and, of course, partisan preferences. The collected data produced the most intricate portrait of Americans' political attitudes to date and ultimately formed the basis for a book aptly titled *The American Voter*, published in 1960.

What made *The American Voter* foundational was its attention to how ordinary voters make political choices. The book's authors, Angus Campbell, Philip Converse, Warren Miller, and Donald Stokes, were particularly interested in studying why individuals identify with a particular party. As a result, *The American Voter* devoted a good deal of time to exploring how people describe their attachments to a party, an approach that has since come to be categorized as "the Michigan model" of politics. At the heart of the Michigan model is the idea that when people classify themselves as members of a party they do so because they have some sort of important connection to that party. This argument introduced one of the most enduring ideas of American politics: a person's partisanship is whatever they say it is.

To capture partisanship, the surveys in *The American Voter* relied on a question that researchers use to this day: Generally speaking, do you usually think of yourself as a Democrat, a Republican, an independent, or what? People who report that they are Democrats and Republicans are asked a follow-up question to determine whether they are strong supporters of the party. People who report that they are independents are asked whether they "lean" toward a particular party. By asking independent voters if they lean toward a party, Campbell and his colleagues were the first to point out that many independents can, in fact, hold partisan preferences.[1]

The *American Voter* made no bold claims regarding independent voters, but rather left the question of their underlying motivations unanswered. Were they simply hiding their partisan attachments?[2] Or could independents be genuinely untethered to either one of the political parties? *The American Voter* was agnostic on these points, and ultimately the authors left open the possibility that independents could be consequential for American politics. Some thirty years later, however, a different group of scholars would take a much less charitable approach.

2.1.2 Questioning the Role of Independents

In the years after the publication of *The American Voter*, the number of political independents continued to increase. When political scientists first began measuring independents in the mid-twentieth century, roughly a fifth of Americans identified as such (from a high of 22% in 1952 to a low of 15% in April 1956).[3] By the mid-1980s, 35 percent of Americans self-identified as independent – the first time in American history that people identifying as independents outnumbered people identifying with one of the parties (Wattenberg 1986, p. 23).

The growth in independents over these decades did not go unnoticed by either media or by academics. Rather, with uncharacteristic agreement, both pundits and political scientists saw the rise of independents as a signal of a new political dawn. Partisanship, scholars suggested, was becoming "a more casual matter than it ever before has been before" (Ladd 1985, p. 23). The increase in independents was argued to create a fertile ground for third parties (Abramson et al. 1983; Campbell 1979) and for "free-floating politics" with no partisan anchors (Pomper 1976, p. 130). The rise of independents – and the idea that parties were weakening – also led to research on the "dimensionality" of partisanship. This line of scholarship questioned whether people's political beliefs fit

---

[1] As Campbell et al. (1960) explain, Berelson et al. (1954) also hint that there is something unusual about independent voters. In particular, Berelson et al. (1954) write, "the classic 'independent voter' of high interest and low partisanship is a deviant case" (26–27). Notably, however, Berelson et al. (1954) focus more on moderates than independents.

[2] These were the people who Campbell et al. called "undercover partisans" (p. 123).

[3] *The American Voter* analyzed the years 1952 to 1958; the distribution of independents across these years was as follows: 22% in 1952, 18% in 1953, 22% in 1954, 15% in April of 1956, 24% in October of 1956; 21% in 1957; 19% in 1958. See Campbell et al., table 6–1 for the full distribution of partisanship across these years.

on a bipolar political scale of ideology, instead suggesting that people's political views were multidimensional (Katz 1979; Weisberg 1980; though see Green 1988 for an alternative perspective) Taken together, this work suggested that American partisan politics was on the precipice of a change fueled by independents.

In 1992, with nearly 40 percent of Americans identifying as politically independent, a team of six researchers – Bruce Keith, David Magleby, Candice Nelson, Elizabeth Orr, Mark Westlye, and Raymond Wolfinger – published a book exploring the political opinions and preferences of these people. Far from the ambivalent conclusions laid out by *The American Voter*, this new look at independents questioned the very idea that they were in any way significant to the American political landscape. Not only were independents politically inconsequential, Keith et al. concluded, but, in fact, they were not even independent. The book title, *The Myth of the Independent Voter*, said it all.

Much of the argument in *Myth* rests on the two-stage partisanship question first introduced in *The American Voter*. *Myth* begins with the idea that when asked if they "lean" toward a party, most independents say yes. People who lean are known as "leaners," while people who do not lean are called "pure" independents. Prior to *Myth*, many scholars did not differentiate between leaning and pure independents (see for example Luskin et al. 1989; Norpoth 1987; Franklin 1984; Feldman and Conover 1983). In contrast, the authors of *Myth* argued that leaners and pure independents were different. "Pures" were small in number and highly disengaged from politics. Leaners, however, appeared to behave just like partisans. Tracking a variety of political opinions and outcomes, Keith and his coauthors showed that independents who lean toward the Democrats are in most ways politically indistinguishable from people who report that they are Democrats. Similarly, independents who lean toward the Republicans are, for all intents and purposes, just like "real" Republicans.

The conclusion of *Myth of the Independent Voter* was unambiguous. On the very last page of the book, the authors wrote:

As citizens, we take heart in our findings that the surface-level increase in independents does not portend a decline in political stability, the decay of the political system, nor any of the other unwelcome developments heralded by some scholars. In fact, we might go as far as to say that it portends very little. (p. 203).

In the decades since the publication of *Myth*, the idea that independents are nothing more than undercover partisans has become deeply entrenched in scholarship on political partisanship. Political scientist Jeremy Pope summed it up as follows:

This finding has become so widely accepted in political science that it is difficult to overstate its importance. When the media and political scientists speak about partisans now, they often explicitly include leaners in their accounting. … Despite some dissenters, few if any of the efforts of political scientists to correct media misperceptions have been as successful (Pope 2012, p. 1)

Recent scholarship supports the notion that leaners behave much like their partisan counterparts (see for example Abramowitz 2010, Pope 2012). Indeed, Magleby, Nelson, and Westlye (three of the original authors of *The Myth*), demonstrate in a 2012 piece entitled "Revisiting the Myth of the Independent Voter" that little has changed about leaners since the original book was published.

These conclusions raise the question, did we learn all there is to know about the political consequences of independents more than two decades ago?

2.1.3 Revisiting Independents

Let us begin with what we know about independents. We know that, when given the opportunity, many (indeed most) independents report that they lean toward one of the two parties. We also know that "leaners" tend to vote for their preferred party just as consistently as do partisans. Finally, we know that since the 1970s the number of leaning independents in our electorate has been increasing steadily.[4]

The list of what we know about independents, however, pales in comparison to what we do *not* know about them. First, not all political scientists agree that independents are not genuine. Warren Miller – one of the authors of *The American Voter* – had doubts that independents were merely undercover partisans (Weisberg 1993). Political scientist Morris Fiorina, whose work has shaped the way political scientists view the two parties, continues to argue that independents are attitudinally different from partisans (e.g., Abrams and Fiorina 2014). Research on campaign advertising shows that people who describe themselves as independents – including leaners! – are more responsive to negative advertising than are partisans (Ansolabehere and Iyengar 1995). And Klar's (2014) analysis of what motivates individuals to engage in politics demonstrates that independents (yes, leaners too!) are driven by an attachment to an independent identity. In short, as Fiorina (2012) notes, the motivations that lead people to identify as independent are far from agreed upon. "This is a subject that cries out for more research," Fiorina wrote about independents in the 2012 article entitled "If I Could Hold a Seminar for Political Journalists ... " (p. 7).

In order to understand the political implications of independents we must change our lens. Rather than focusing on what differentiates independents from partisans, we must step back and consider why and when the label "independent" is most likely to be used. *Why* would a person with a clear partisan preference want to report that he or she is an independent? Even some of the authors of *The Myth of the Independent Voter* have renewed the call to solve this particular mystery, writing nearly two decades later that, "In *Myth*, we stopped short of attributing causes for *why* individuals in the electorate

---

[4] Increases in the number of leaning independents are apparent using ANES data from 1970 to 2012; we plot these increases in Figure 2.3 of this chapter.

identify as independents rather than as partisans" (Magleby et al. 2011, p. 258).

Certainly, as Magleby et al. (2011) underscore, there have been speculations as to why people hide their partisanship. Maybe, as political scientists Warren Miller and J. Merrill Shanks mused, partisan identification is like religion, and independents are parishioners who have strayed from the flock – people who have lost their "sense of oneness" with the other believers (Miller and Shanks 1996, p.121).[5] Perhaps independents want to assert their individuality in order to build up their self-esteem (Dennis 1988, 1992). Each of these ideas is a plausible explanation for describing oneself as independent. But, given that approximately 40 percent of the electorate call themselves "independent," we can say with equal certainty that we need to know much more.

A lack of any systematic argument as to why people report that they are independent also means that we know very little about the broader consequences of this phenomenon. To begin with, are some people more likely than others to hide their partisanship? Does something about American politics motivate citizens to disguise their partisanship? Could independents be a signal of broader political patterns? Put another way, is the possibility that some people misrepresent themselves as independent an isolated malady, or is it just one symptom of a much more serious disease spreading through American politics?

In order to separate the symptom from the disease, we need to understand whether the forces that lead people toward the label "independent" can also change other ways in which they interact with politics. To date, research has only focused on the people who identify as independent and, in turn, whether these people support one particular party over another. This is a point that James Stimson (1993) emphasized in his review of the *Myth of the Independent Voter*:

But the "independent voter" is not only a matter of voting behavior – perhaps not even primarily so. The topic lies at the intersection of issues of voting, party systems, and political parties generally. It is about how politicians campaign and then govern, what elections mean, and more. The empirical basis in the book is voting alone. Thus, its suggestions that misunderstanding the "myth" has major implications for parties and party systems remain only suggestions. I wish the authors had ventured further away from the survey data to explore those implications. (p. 495)

Two decades after *Myth*, as the percentage of people reporting they are independent has increased, it has come time to answer Stimson's call.

2.1.4 Where Do We Go From Here?

We use a new lens to examine not only political independents but also political partisanship as a whole. Capitalizing on the considerable scholarly and

---

5 We also draw this point from Magleby et al. (2011) in their discussion of why people go undercover.

methodological advances of the past two decades, we take a more holistic view of the decision to describe oneself as "independent." What makes our approach unique is that we peek behind the curtain or, in this case, under the cover. We identify the broader political conditions that push people away from revealing their partisanship. We also isolate the types of people who are most likely to identify as independent while harboring partisan preferences. Most importantly, we explain that the same mechanisms that lead people undercover also produce other consequential shifts in political behavior. The choice to say, "I'm independent" when asked about one's partisanship is, as we have suggested, just the tip of the iceberg.

Our arguments hold implications not only for the study of independents but also for the study of political partisanship, political participation, and the fate of parties in American politics. Relying on a new theoretical approach and leveraging recent methodological advances in political science, we reveal implications that previous scholarship did not uncover.

2.2 PARTISANSHIP AS IMPRESSION MANAGEMENT

We have a colleague who at parties and other social events will engage in spirited discussions about the critically acclaimed hit television show of the moment. If one were to judge simply by these conversations, this colleague has seen most – perhaps even all – of the television shows that will eventually be nominated for top entertainment awards. But our colleague harbors a secret: he has not watched a single one of the shows he is discussing. Why does he engage in – and even at times initiate – these conversations? Why not simply admit to his conversation partners that he has not yet watched a particular show? Because, as our colleague explained to us, he feels that to confess that he has not seen the show may negatively affect how others perceive him. To make the most positive impression, this colleague instead pretends to have seen something he has not.

Our colleague is not alone. Americans are so deeply concerned with making positive impressions that Emily Post, the godmother of American manners, has spent over half a century advising people on what they should and should not say and do in various settings. Etiquette rules aside, people routinely adjust their opinions and behaviors to make the most positive impression they can on others. This process is called *impression management*.

Impression management is a part of human nature. Psychological (Schlenker and Weigold 1989) and sociological (Goffman 1959) theories suggest that people work every day to present themselves in a manner that will be pleasing and impressive to others (Goffman 1967; Holtgraves 1992). Impression management often also has an element of "self-glorification" – the need to be on the positive end of a comparison to another person (Brown and Gallagher 1992; Schlenker and Weigold 1992). If we are judged by how we behave, what we say, and what we wear, then the goal is to present an image that is most likely to be judged in a positive way. Similarly, if we imagine we are going to be compared to another person, we want to be perceived as (even ever so slightly) better than that other person.

But how do we know what is *positive* and *impressive*? How does our colleague, for example, know that he will make a more positive impression if he pretends to have seen *Arrested Development*, than if he admits that he has not watched a single episode? The answer lies in perceived social norms. Broadly defined, social norms can refer to either what is commonly done or, alternatively, to what is commonly approved and disapproved (Shaffer 1983). These norms are sometimes attributed to broad cultural standards: a guest, for example, would make a terrible impression on a Russian host simply by showing up with a bouquet containing an even number of flowers.[6] Other times, however, these perceived social norms are unique to a particular person (or group of people). Not all people, for example, will agree with our colleague that watching television shows makes a positive impression; some might argue that a more positive impression could be made by claiming that one does not own a television at all.

Perceived social norms arise from beliefs about how others behave or what others think. The information people receive on a regular basis, be it through social networks, the media, or simple daily observations, help people assess the types of opinions and behaviors that will make the best impressions on others. The belief that a certain type of behavior will be more valued or accepted by others around us even has a name: social desirability.[7] People gather cues from their broader social environment, although their beliefs about what is desirable need not be tethered to their immediate social context. This means that people can come to view certain behaviors as socially desirable even if their peers and social circles do not actually engage in these behaviors.

This need to make a positive impression based on what we *think* other people think,[8] as Zaller and Feldman (1992) explain, leads us to "consciously misreport attitudes in order to avoid embarrassment" (p. 601). Our colleague pretends that he has seen popular television shows because he believes this will be impressive to others. A person who believes that most people dislike smokers may report that he does not smoke, even as he hides a pack of cigarettes and *even if there are other smokers in the room*. And, in a much more pivotal example, people who harbor negative views toward racial minorities will often deliberately lie about those views because they understand that racial prejudice is judged harshly (Berinsky 1999, 2002, 2004; Berinsky and Lavine 2012; Feldman and Huddy 2005; Gilens et al. 1998; Krysan 1998; Heerwig and McCabe

---

[6] A bouquet containing an even number of flowers by Russian norms signify a sad event (in particular, death).

[7] Social desirability is often codified by cultural standards such as in issues of race and politics. Other times, it may be more specific to individuals' own social circles or interactions.

[8] This may mean people individually, or the aggregation of people as a society.

2009; Huddy et al. 1997; Kane and Macaulay 1993; Kuklinski et al. 1997; Mendelberg 2001; Reeves 1997; Sniderman and Carmines 1997; Streb et al. 2008; Terkildsen 1993).

This idea leads us to the over-arching argument that will fuel most of the chapters of this book:

People who misrepresent their partisanship do so because they believe that openly identifying as a partisan will make a negative impression on others,

If you believe that most people perceive *both* Democrats and Republicans in a negative light, then the best way to ensure that others do not form a negative impression of you is to hide your partisanship – even if you've spent a lifetime supporting one of the two parties.

We can take this argument a step further. As we note earlier, impression management is motivated by a need to avoid making a negative impression, but it also contains an element of self-esteem and self-flattery to the process: we don't want to be just like other people, we may also want to be *better* than other people (Schlenker and Weigold 1992).[9] When people believe that partisanship is associated with negative traits, they may also believe that the best image they can project is a nonpartisan one. This means that even when a person is aware that he is surrounded by Democrats, he may describe himself as an "independent" because he believes that being independent is not only the best way to make the most positive impression but also the self-description that positively distinguishes him from the others (Brown et al. 1988; Schlenker and Weigold 1992).

Of course, not all people who call themselves independents are deliberately misrepresenting their partisanship to impress other people. Certainly there are people who may be "true" independents: people who have no clear political affiliation. We do not deny their existence. Moreover, some people who identify as independent may actually *believe* that they have no partisan affiliation, making their avoidance of partisanship an implicit, rather than an explicit, process. Our goal, however, is to clarify the motivations and conditions that can lead people down the path of avoiding their partisanship either through the "independent" label or in other ways. By solving this piece of the independent puzzle, we can begin to track the implications that the growing ranks of independents hold for American politics.

---

[9] It is important to differentiate impression management from conformity. While impression management may under certain conditions take the form of conformity, under other conditions, people may actually deliberately avoid conformity to make a positive impression. Moreover, even as people engage in impression management they want to maintain some adherence to their sense of self (Cialdini and Goldstein 2004). A Republican who recognizes that everyone around her is a Democrat and that being honest about her partisan affiliation will make a negative impression may find it loathsome to associate with the opposing party. In this case, identifying as an independent allows our Republican to maintain her sense of self *and* make the most positive impression.

2.2.1. The Role of Self-Monitoring

We started this chapter with the assertion that everyone engages in impression management, but the extent to which this occurs varies from one individual to the next. Let us return for a moment to our colleague who pretends to have seen television shows that he, in fact, has never watched. As our colleague admits, he pretends to have seen these shows because he believes that doing so will make a more positive impression on others. Ultimately, our colleague's behavior stems from two factors. First, the opinions of others are important to him and, second, he is willing to modify his behavior in order to engage in this charade.

Of course, not everyone is like our colleague. Indeed, most readers could easily come up with a friend (or even two or three) who seems unconcerned about the way he or she is perceived by others. This friend fits in to a group of people who seem fully aware that their behaviors may be judged disparagingly but to the outside observer show little interest in changing their behaviors to make better impressions. Unlike our colleague, these types of people would freely admit that they have not seen the television shows other people seem to enjoy, even as they realize this admission may lead others to perceive them in a somewhat more negative light.

The idea that some people are more concerned about making a good impression than are others is something that psychologists have recognized since about the 1970s. Psychologists call this concept *self-monitoring*: the extent to which people amend their behavior so as to improve the impression they may make on others (Snyder 1979; Lavine and Snyder 1996; Gangestad and Snyder 2000). A concept brought to the forefront by psychologist Mark Snyder, self-monitoring captures the extent to which people engage in impression management.

Self-monitoring can be considered along a continuum. The more a person self-monitors, the more he molds and adjusts his behavior, often concealing his true feelings in the process. By contrast, the less people engage in self-monitoring, the less likely they are to adjust their behaviors (Gangestad and Snyder 2000). Those who are higher self-monitors, act and speak in ways that they believe will be perceived as more socially positive and socially desirable (Lippa 1978; Weber et al. 2014).[10] Low self-monitors, on the other hand, "express it as they feel it" rather than "monitoring, controlling, and molding" their expressions to fit the situation (Snyder 1974, p. 527). Low self-monitors may be just as aware of what is socially desirable, but they are less willing to change their behaviors or alter the way they express their thoughts to fit that norm. Rather, the "behavior of low self-monitors is principally guided by the desire to express their own inner dispositions, including their personal values,

---

[10] For ease of discussion, in much of his work, Snyder separates people in to two groups: high and low self-monitors. While we follow suit, it is important to note that not every person is a constant high or low self-monitor in every situation. For this reason, Snyder often describes the concept as a "differentiation characteristic": on average, some people engage in more self-monitoring, while others engage in less.

attitudes, and affective states" (Lavine and Snyder 1996; p. 585). As a result, low self-monitors, as Weber et al. (2014) describe, "manifest a greater consistency between their private beliefs and attitudes and public actions than do high self-monitors" (p. 66).

Although scholars from a wide variety of disciplines have identified how self-monitoring affects things such as friendships, individual decision-making, education, leadership, management, consumer decisions, and even romantic relationships, scholars have also explored how this trait can help to explain political behavior (Lavine and Snyder 1996; Berinsky 2004; Berinsky and Lavine 2012; Weber et al. 2014). Given the strong American cultural norm of racial equality, for example, the more that people engage in self-monitoring, the more they misrepresent their attitudes and intentions when it comes to the issue of race in politics (Feldman and Huddy 2005; Weber et al. 2014). In studies where people are given the choice between a white and a black candidate, people who are higher in self-monitoring are consistently more likely to report that they would vote for the black candidate (Terkildsen 1993), even though deep down they may acknowledge they have no intention of doing so. This is not a function of high self-monitors being more racially tolerant (indeed, they are not), but rather people who engage in more self-monitoring are more likely to shift their behavior in order to make a positive impression on others.

This is a pivotal point. Higher self-monitoring does not mean that a person is more sensitive or more responsive to others, just as lower self-monitoring does not mean that a person is tone-deaf and impolite. Self-monitoring also does not affect a person's feelings about conflict. A person who is high in self-monitoring might relish confrontation, for example, while a low self-monitor might avoid situations that are likely to produce conflict (Snyder 1987). Self-monitoring simply affects the tendency to modify one's behavior. Those higher in self-monitoring are more likely to adjust their behaviors to make a better impression on others, while those lower in self-monitoring are less willing to misrepresent their true preferences for the sake of making a positive impression.[11]

It is not unusual to engage in this type of behavioral control. A faculty member who does not yet have tenure may engage in self-monitoring and suppress the urge to express her opinion at a faculty meeting, even when she strongly believes the senior faculty are about to make a very poor decision. Other instances of behavioral control may be more dramatic. The more a person self-monitors, the more likely he is to choose a physically attractive romantic partner and to avoid dating someone that does not meet a certain superficial standard (Snyder and Simpson 1984, Rowatt, Cunningham, and Druen 1998, Snyder et al. 1983). The need to make a positive impression can supersede personal preferences (Briggs et al. 1980, Snyder 1974, Snyder 1979, Zaccaro et al. 1991).

---

[11] We draw this point from personal communications with Mark Snyder.

In all of our examples, people adjust their behaviors because they have somehow arrived at the conclusion that taking some action will or will not create a positive impression. Something in their environment has suggested to them that a more socially desirable option is available and that behaving *in just this way* will make a better impression on others. In the following sections, we consider why people believe that being a partisan is socially undesirable.

2.2.2 The Role of Negative Information

To help explain what pushes people away from expressing their beliefs we turn to another beleaguered label that people are sometimes loathe to use: feminism.

In a recent poll, more than 80 percent of Americans reported that they believe that "men and women should be social, political, and economic equals." Despite this overwhelming support for gender equality, only 20 percent of those respondents would identify as a "feminist."[12] These survey results reinforce previous experimental studies that demonstrate disdain for the label. In one study, female college students were exposed to information that contained either positive or negative stereotypes of how feminists are perceived (Roy et al. 2007). The college students who were told that feminists tend to be viewed negatively began to avoid identifying with the group. Their views about gender equality did not change, but they came to believe that they would be judged negatively for identifying as feminists. "Women may be reluctant to self-identify as feminists," the researchers concluded, "Not because of their own views of feminists, but because they assume that others have negative views of feminists" (Roy et al. 2007, p. 148).

The feminism experiment offers a number of lessons, but one emerges as particularly critical for our purposes: people are less likely to openly express a group identity when they believe that associating with the group will be perceived negatively by others. This phenomenon is not unique to the case of feminism. Psychological evidence shows that when people have negative perceptions of activists involved in a particular political cause, they become reluctant to give any impressions that might suggest that they are members of the activist group. This result holds even for people who are highly supportive of the group's overall goals (Bashir et al. 2013). In the same way, when people perceive political parties in a negative light, we argue they are more likely to believe that associating with one of the two parties will make a poor impression on others.

We can consider two ways in which people can come to perceive parties in a negative light. First, individuals are likely to perceive parties negatively when they believe that partisanship as a whole is associated with negative traits. Such traits as inflexibility, closed-mindedness, a lack of ethics, a lack of intelligence,

---

[12] Swanson, Emily (April 16, 2013). "Poll: Few Identify As Feminists, But Most Believe in Equality of Sexes." *Huffington Post*. Results based on Huffington Post/YouGov poll conducted in April 2013 with 1,000 American adults.

and anger are all characteristics that individuals perceive to be particularly negative both politically and socially (Kinder et al. 1980; Rodríguez-Bailón et al. 2000; Hardy and Jamieson 2005; Oltmanns et al. 2005). In turn, as Americans come to associate parties with these types of characteristics (which, as we will discuss in Chapters 3 and 4, they do), then partisanship as a whole becomes enshrouded in a cloud of negativity. Despite individuals' true preferences, they come to believe that appearing partisan is socially and personally undesirable.

A second possibility is that the person's *own party* comes to appear as particularly undesirable. This may happen as a result of a scandal or a similarly negative political event that becomes intertwined with one party's image, rather than partisanship as a whole.[13] When people hear powerful negative information about their own party, they may respond by downgrading their opinion of the other party simply to convince themselves that their party – while beleaguered – is still superior (Groenendyk 2013). Yet despite this internal maintenance of support people may come to believe that outwardly expressing support for their party will not help them make a positive impression. On the other hand, people also do not want to express support for the opposing party, which may lead people to retreat from partisanship.

Overall, we predict that the belief that there are negative traits associated with partisanship in general will lead people in *both parties* to avoid identifying as partisans. Of course, there are certain cases where individuals from a particular party become increasingly likely to conceal their partisanship. Indeed, in Chapter 3 we analyze a gaffe by a Republican politician that seems to send Republicans into hiding. Nonetheless, while it is easy to find examples in which one party looks worse than the other, it is very difficult to find any examples in which either party looks all that good.

In recent years, parties have been portrayed by media less as principled representatives arguing eloquently for their beliefs and more as cranky children who do not want to share. We suggest that this type of coverage, which portrays the parties as stubborn and the disagreement between the parties as insurmountable, leads people to view partisanship as increasingly undesirable. Certainly, this type of media coverage is not entirely unwarranted. Public fights between the parties and occasions of political gridlock invite media to portray the parties as petulant children. At the same time, as we show and discuss in the next section, the media fixation with partisan disagreement has grown over the last thirty years, amplifying the existing tension between the parties.

2.2.3. You're Wrong, Mr. President!

Debate is part of any healthy electoral process, but sometimes debates between candidates devolve into unconstructive bickering, suggesting to the listener that

---

[13] Here we are talking about the type of scandal that not only affects the politician at the heart of the scandal but comes to envelope the party as a whole.

the parties do not simply disagree but that there is no room for them to *ever* come to an agreement. For example, consider the following exchange between President Barack Obama and Republican candidate Mitt Romney during their final debate of the 2012 campaign in Boca Raton, Florida:[14]

GOVERNOR ROMNEY: You're wrong. You're wrong, Mr. President.
PRESIDENT OBAMA: I – no, I am not wrong.
GOVERNOR ROMNEY: You're wrong.
PRESIDENT OBAMA: I am not wrong. And –
GOVERNOR ROMNEY: People can look it up, you're right.
PRESIDENT OBAMA: People will look it up.
GOVERNOR ROMNEY: Good.

The exchange between Obama and Romney is just one example of language that conveys anger and stubbornness. This tone of rhetoric is steadily gaining presence in political debates.[15] Analyzing presidential debates from 1996 to 2012, we see that an increasing percentage of the discussion is taken up with these types of interactions (Figure 2.1). A person who believes they are doing their civic duty by watching a presidential debate may instead be confronted with the idea that partisanship is not simply a debate about the best course for the country but rather insurmountable disagreement; partisanship means anger and inflexibility.

Given this exchange between Obama and Romney alone, it should come as no surprise that media coverage often portrays the differences between the two parties as profound and largely insurmountable. Looking beyond the debates, the parties give journalists plenty of material for stories about partisan disagreement: parties deliberately emphasize differences (Abramowitz 2010, Lee 2009), often refuse to compromise (Harbridge 2015), and engage in incivility (Mutz and Reeves 2005; Lee 2009).

Although the source material is certainly there, media coverage also amplifies the disagreement and makes it more salient. Tracking patterns of news coverage, Boydstun (2013) finds that there is "stickiness" to the way journalists and editors cover news topics. Once journalists begin covering a story from a particular angle, Boydstun (2013) shows, they tend to keep producing stories on the particular topic that fit the particular angle. Moreover, stories that display tension and conflict are often perceived as more newsworthy than stories that

---

[14] Transcript taken from *New York Times*, "Transcript of Third Presidential Debate" (October 22, 2012). http://www.nytimes.com/2012/10/22/us/politics/transcript-of-the-third-presidential-debate-in-boca-raton-fla.html. Note that other debate transcrips classify portions of this transcript as "crosstalk."

[15] Identifying unconstructive partisan language can be difficult in the apparatus of a political debate. Debates were coded through an analysis of tone, word choice, and figurative language that ultimately paired an individual candidate with the negative outcomes of a party, past events, or other similar criteria that produced no beneficial discourse for the debate. We offer more information on our approach to analyzing the debates in our online appendix to this chapter.

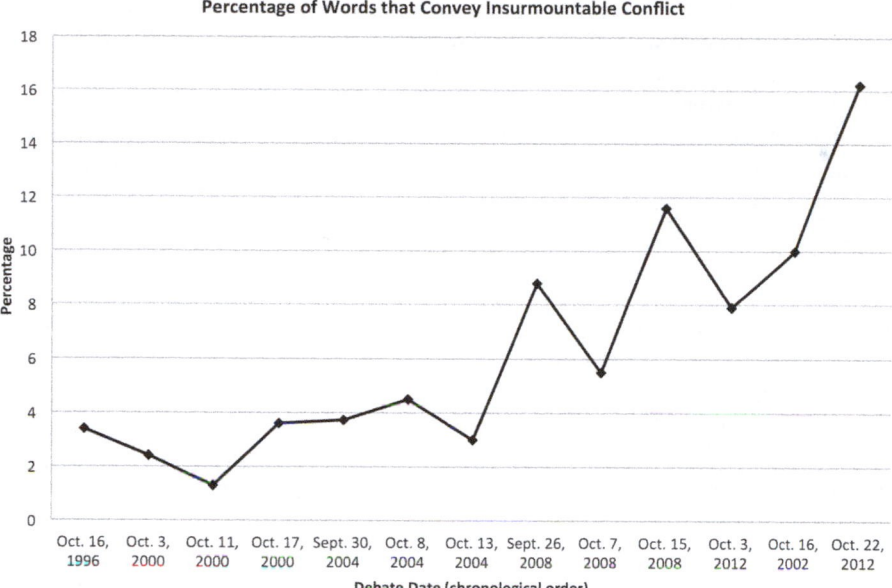

FIGURE 2.1. Rate of Partisan Disagreement in Presidential Debates.
Percentage calculated from the total number of words in a debate. The coding is discussed in section A2.1 of the appendix for this chapter.

are conflict-free (Gans 1979). This points to the idea that a media focus on partisan conflict is self-perpetuating. Across a wide range of political stories, journalists have a tendency to pinpoint and cover instances of partisan disagreement because these instances fit an existing narrative and are deemed particularly newsworthy. The parties may certainly deserve the negative coverage, but the media often can and do exacerbate the depth of partisan disagreement in America.

2.2.3.1 *Media Coverage of Partisans and Independents*
In a June 2014 *New York Times* piece headlined "Polarization is Dividing American Society, Not Just Politics," Nate Cohn argued, "partisan and ideological animosity is dividing American society."[16] This type of coverage of polarization has been growing steadily since about the 1990s. After analyzing *New York Times* coverage of Congress from 1980 to 2004, Levendusky (2009) concludes that "the data are unambiguous: the *Times* attention to Congressional polarization increases dramatically over time" (p. 33). Moreover, Levendusky distinguishes between articles that present polarization regarding a specific issue (for example, welfare) and articles that present polarization as a

---

[16] Cohn, Nate (June 12, 2014) "Polarization is Dividing American Society, Not Just Politics" *New York Times*. Appeard online in The Upshot blog.

general topic. While discussions of issue-specific polarization remain relatively constant (and even slightly decline) over the twenty-year period, the number of newspaper stories suggesting that the parties are divided across numerous issues increases dramatically (Levendusky 2009).

Levendusky's data stop in 2004, but we extended the analysis to 2012 and found that the number of stories about polarization continued to increase. This is not simply a function of the *Times* expanding and allowing more room for stories. If we track the percentage of *New York Times* stories that include polarization, we also see an increase from 2000 to 2012.

The increase in stories that mention polarization is not the only indicator of a shift in coverage that highlights disagreement. Boydstun (2013), for example, analyzes the content of front-page stories in *The New York Times* from 1996 to 2006. Throughout that time period, Boydstun's data show that 10 percent of political front-page stories that were *not* campaign-focused dealt with conflict either within or between the two parties. Moreover, 27 percent of all front-page that even tangentially considered campaign regulation or government ethics focused on partisan conflict.[17]

The percentage of the front page devoted to partisan conflict also increased over time. From 1996 to 2000, about 7 percent of all front-page political stories considered partisan conflict. After 2000, 15 percent of all political front-page stories focused on conflict. This increase is even greater when we use Boydstun's data to consider off-election years. In 1997 and 1999, 7.4 percent of political front-page stories covered partisan conflict. In 2003 and 2005, this number increased to 21.2 percent. And after 2000, about 35.5 percent of all front-page non-campaign focused political stories were devoted to partisan conflict, compared to about 21.5 percent pre-2000.

Just as media often denigrate partisanship, they simultaneously place being politically independent on a pedestal.[18] Even as scholars and some journalists have come to realize that independents are not model citizens, people who eschew partisanship are still often portrayed as ideologically moderate and politically pivotal. In an opinion piece published in the *Bangor Daily News*, for example, Joe Pickering, a Maine voter and member of the organization IndependentVoting.org wrote, "Independent voters are growing in numbers and influence because we care enough about the damage partisan politics is doing to our republic to sever ties to the parties and seek a new kind of process and real solutions."[19] Adding to the appeal of appearing above the fray,

[17] The 27 percent excludes explicit campaign stories. Overall, conflict stories make up 4.95 percent of stories in what Boydstun terms the "government and regulation" group. Comparatively, less than 1 percent of stories focused on lobbying reforms and 1.01 percent focused on special interests.

[18] To be sure, independents have their critics too and we will visit one such critic, Stanley Fish, in Chapter 5.

[19] Joe Pickering, Jr. (August 25, 2014). "Two-Party System Disempowers Voters: Independent Voters' Rise Will Bring Back Balance." *Bangor Daily News*.

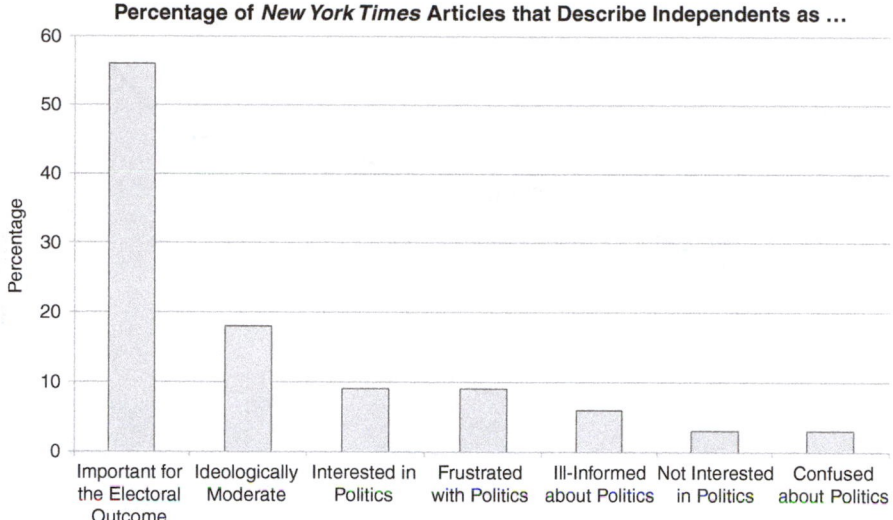

Percentage of *New York Times* Articles that Describe Independents as ...

FIGURE 2.2. Reporting on Independent Voters in *The New York Times*.
Percentage of stories from April 2013 to April 2014 on independents that contain this type of content. The coding is discussed in the section A2.2 of the appendix to Chapter 2.

independents also remain a coveted voting bloc, keeping politicians and pundits guessing until the eleventh hour. Just four days before the 2012 presidential election, CBS News ran the headline: "Will Independents Really Decide the Election?"[20]

This type of reverential coverage of independents is not merely anecdotal but is a strong pattern across news reports. To quantify the degree to which independents are described positively and negatively by news media, we conducted a focused content analysis of *The New York Times*'s coverage of "independent voters" from April 2013 to April 2014. Each article was coded for whether it explicitly described independents as ideologically moderate, interested or not interested in politics, confused or ill-informed about politics, frustrated with politics, and electorally important. Figure 2.2 displays these results.[21]

Over half of all articles explicitly referred to independents voters as important for the electoral outcome – for example, calling them "coveted" (*New York Times*, October 4, 2013). Approximately 10 percent of articles described independents as moderate, interested in politics, but also frustrated with politics – for example, by explaining that independent voters are "frustrated with

---

[20] Leigh Ann Caldwell (November 2, 2012). "Will Independents Really Decide the Election?" *CBS News*.

[21] Coding was done by a trained, independent coder who did not know the hypotheses being tested with the collected data.

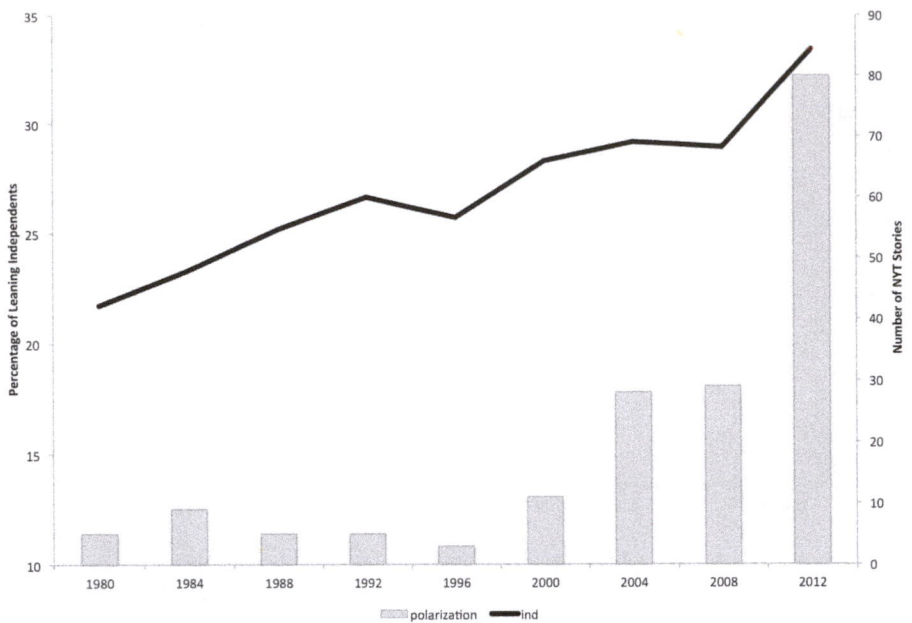

FIGURE 2.3. Percentage of Leaning Independents versus Coverage of Polarization. *Polarization refers to stories that mention polarization. Independents are respondents who identify as leaning independents in the ANES.*

Washington's inability to get things done" (*New York Times*, April 12, 2015). By contrast, few reports cast independents in a negative light. Less than 5 percent of articles, for example, described independents as politically uninterested or confused. The data confirm the same sense that many media observers share: while partisans are cast as combative, mainstream media depict independents as important (and often normatively useful) political actors.

2.2.3.2 *Putting Media Coverage and Partisanship Together*

If media portray partisans as bad and independents as good, it is no surprise that more and more people are going undercover. One indicator of partisan avoidance is the number of people who report that they are independent but then admit that they lean toward a particular party. To consider this point, we can plot the percentage of leaning independents by year alongside the average number of stories that mention polarization in *The New York Times* over those same years.

In Figure 2.3, the left axis is the percentage of leaning independents, while the right axis represents the number of stories in *The New York Times*. The line plots the percentage of leaning independents, while the bars represent the number of stories. The figure highlights a pattern: increases in the number of stories suggesting partisan disagreement run parallel to increases in the percentage of leaning independents.[22] In particular, the increase in leaning independents is especially pronounced after 2000, just as polarization and partisan disagreement stories grow.

The connection between independents and coverage of partisanship brings us back to the concept of self-monitoring. If high self-monitors amend their expressed preferences for romantic partners and consumer goods for the sake of making a good impression, then we expect that a concern with social desirability will influence their political statements. We expect, therefore, that people who engage in more self-monitoring should be more likely to hide their partisanship if they believe that expressing partisan preferences will cast them in a negative light. This means that both high and low self-monitors should agree that independence is seen as superior to partisanship, but only high self-monitors should change their behavior to make a more positive impression.

If confessing one's partisanship might make a poor impression on others, people who are lower in self-monitoring should nevertheless continue to truthfully report their partisan preferences. To repeat the words of psychologist Mark Snyder, low self-monitors "express it as they feel it" (Snyder 1974, p. 527). They will make the switch to "independent" only if they come to believe that this label better describes their political preferences.

2.2.4 Behavioral Consequences of Undercover Partisanship

Given the negative coverage of partisans, individuals hoping to make a good impression may come to believe it is wiser to present an independent image to the world, or at the very least to avoid a strong association with a party. One obvious way to eschew partisanship is to publicly identify as independent or describe one's partisan connection as significantly weaker than it is in actuality. But avoiding partisanship can take on many more consequential behavioral forms.

Avoiding partisanship extends well beyond the responses Americans give to pollsters. Partisanship can manifest itself in the way we behave on a day-to-day basis. Broadcasting one's preferred candidate on social media, wearing a button, displaying a yard sign, seeking out partisan information, and even discussing politics with friends are all political actions that may make it difficult to hide one's partisanship. When a person believes that partisanship does not make a positive impression, he or she may be hesitant to engage in these modes of civic participation.

We do *not* suggest that only people who already identify as independent will avoid these behaviors. Indeed, an individual might be concerned that public

---

[22] The percentage of leaning independents is from the American National Election Study (ANES). The number of stories about polarization and partisan divide was collected via the *New York Times* Chronicle application. We look only at presidential years because the ANES did not run studies in 2006 and 2010, so to retain consistency and rely on one source, we focus on presidential years.

displays of partisanship make a poor impression yet still be willing to admit his partisan preferences in an anonymous survey. But he may be much more hesitant to act in ways that make him appear partisan in front of his peers. This is what makes identifying as independent, to use our common refrain, the tip of the iceberg. The increasing number of Americans who identify as independent is just one indicator of a broader set of outcomes associated with a retreat from partisanship.

That we look beyond independent identification is an important break with previous work. Indeed, previous scholarship on partisanship has focused on whether people self-identify as independent when asked. By assuming that undercover partisanship is isolated only among people who report that they are leaning independents, scholars have neglected the important consequences of avoiding partisanship for civic participation and grassroots politics. This is a notable omission in scholarship since – as we already note in Chapter 1 and discuss in greater detail in Chapter 5 – parties increasingly rely on ordinary individuals to spread their message and serve as "salespeople" (Stimson 1993).

The rise of new technologies has only deepened candidate dependence on the spread of their messages via social media. According to data scientists at Facebook, gubernatorial and congressional candidates produced more than 150,000 Facebook posts between August and October 2014 (Messing et al. 2014). Their goal was to spread their campaign message. Indeed, the Facebook data team reports that these posts received about 20 million "likes," "shares" and comments (Messing et al. 2014). Of these 150,000 posts, many were about campaign events and many encouraged their supporters to "spread the word." While candidates have turned to social media, the parties have begun using various forms of grassroots political participation such as bumper stickers and lawn signs to create maps of supporters.[23]

Technology aside, scholars have long argued that simple human conversation is the most persuasive way for the party to transmit its message (Lazarsfeld et al. 1948), and the actions with the most political voice (Verba et al. 1995) are those that are the most overtly partisan. In other words, parties can only aggregate preferences if citizens are willing to express them. If people avoid partisanship, both parties and politics will suffer by consequence.

2.2.5 Summary of Theoretical Expectations

The preceding sections lead us to three expectations about when and why people deliberately avoid and even misreport their partisanship. The factors described in this chapter intersect to increase the chance that a person hides from partisanship, but for clarity of discussion we describe them as separate points in the following summary.

---

[23] Lois Beckett (January 18, 2013). "Four Graphs That Show How Democrats Predict Your Political Beliefs." *ProPublica*.

Our first theoretical expectation focuses on how exposure to particular information leads people away from partisanship: *The more people are exposed to information that portrays partisans in a negative light, the more likely they are to go undercover.*

Exacerbating this informational effect are people's individual characteristics, in this case, their willingness to change their behaviors to make that positive impression. This characteristic is termed "self-monitoring": *The higher people are in self-monitoring, the more likely they are to go undercover.*

When information and self-monitoring come together, we predict strong motivations to avoid partisanship. These motivations have broad political consequences. We predict that the joint effect of informational exposure and self-monitoring will lead to many forms of "going undercover," of which identifying as independent is just one indicator: *The motivation to avoid partisanship may lead people to go undercover, where going undercover can take on the form of identifying as independent and/or avoiding political actions that are openly partisan.*

The intersections of these three points will guide the remainder of the book.

2.3 WHY AMERICANS AVOID PARTISANSHIP AND WHY IT MATTERS

We began this chapter with the suggestion that political parties are like a movie people are too embarrassed to admit they like. People often want to make positive impressions on others. Once they determine that an opinion or action is unlikely to make such a positive impression, many people willingly and consciously suppress their preferences. When asked about their favorite movie people will answer with the title of an Academy Award winner or some other critically acclaimed film, rather than admitting that they love a movie about a tornado with flying sharks.[24] In much the same way, when asked about their partisanship, people will report that they are independent even when they have a clear preference for one of the two parties. Some people are more likely to do so than others, a distinction that reinforces the idea that when people go undercover it is to avoid making a negative impression on others.

Moreover, people base their perceptions of what others view as socially desirable on the information they receive. Information that suggests that being partisan makes a poor impression on others nudges people toward hiding their own partisanship. This view of partisan politics as something undesirable is one

---

[24] Note, this is not a hypothetical; this is the plot of the movie *Sharknado*. At the time of this writing, there have been two sequels to this movie (*Sharknado 2* and *Sharknado 3*). This example assumes that the social cues individuals have received suggest that it is more positive to like critically acclaimed moves. It is possible, of course, that some people have instead received social cues that it is preferable to report that you enjoyed movies widely acknowledged to be terrible, in which case our example would work in the opposite way.

that the American context readily provides. Accounting for these conditions helps us to clarify what leads people undercover and, in turn, the nature of independent identification itself.

We also suggested at the start of this chapter that the possibility of being like the movie that no one will admit to enjoying should worry American political parties. Some readers might argue that the fact that some people refuse to call themselves "Democrat" or "Republican" hardly signals partisan collapse. So long as these people vote for the party, their day-to-day aversion to politics is irrelevant. While this is a pragmatic perspective, our approach points in a different direction.

Usually when an individual completes a survey, he does not know his interviewer personally. If a survey is on the Internet, the respondent never even hears a real human voice ask the questions. If people misrepresent their partisanship even in these anonymous settings, then what are they doing when they are with friends and family and those whose opinions they value? If people are as concerned with making positive impressions on others as decades of psychological and sociological research suggest, then it is doubtful that the tendency to make a positive political impression is merely limited to a single partisanship question in an anonymous survey. Rather, self-identifying as independent, we argue, is merely one indication of a broader tendency to avoid partisanship.[25]

For all the people who are unwilling to tell an anonymous interviewer that they prefer Democrats or Republicans, there are even more people who are unwilling to tell their friends that they prefer a particular candidate, who are unwilling to take a political action that may seem partisan, and who are unwilling to give off the slightest impression that they may have a partisan political position. Maybe parties do not need to worry about the fact that people pick "independent" when asked a question on a survey, but they should worry that people are unwilling to take partisan actions.

We suggest that going undercover leads people to avoid partisan labels (such as identifying as a Democrat or Republican), avoid partisan activities (for example, wearing a campaign sticker), and even avoid partisans themselves (like friends and neighbors who openly affiliate with a party). This aversion to partisanship has profound consequences for everyday politics. As partisans go undercover, parties will no longer be able to count on grassroots campaigns, word-of-mouth efforts, and simple mobilization through social networks.

The possibility that fewer people are willing to display partisan stickers and signs limits the extent to which parties can recruit members, spread their

---

[25] Importantly, we want to distinguish between an unwillingness to take partisan actions and low level of engagement (Abramowitz 2010). Specifically, we are focusing on willingness to take actions that are outwardly partisan, rather than general willingness to participate in politics. Our argument rests on the idea that people who avoid partisanship will avoid outwardly partisan actions but may not be politically disengaged in other ways (indeed, we demonstrate these patterns in Chapter 6).

messages, and, yes, get the all-important votes. When people are unwilling to advertise their partisan interests and hesitate to encourage others to participate lest they seem too partisan, fewer people participate. At a time when elections are won or lost on the ground – be that ground a neighborhood or Facebook – parties depend on people being willing to advertise their membership. Indeed, as of the writing of this chapter, the most recent midterm elections were the most expensive in history (Wallack and Hudak 2014). Despite the "record shattering" amounts of money spent in the 2014 election, turnout hovered at around 36.4 percent (Wallack and Hudak 2014).[26] Parties, it seems, must spend record amounts of money to coax and cajole voters to act on their behalf. Perhaps the increasing numbers of people avoiding partisanship are not so inconsequential after all.

Avoiding partisanship matters for American democracy. If there is a group of true independents, people who are genuinely untethered to either party, then, theoretically, every new election these people could be recruited to help a candidate whose platform they found more convincing. People who are "undercover partisans" are different. Undercover partisans avoid partisanship not because they disagree with the parties ideologically or politically but because being a party member is embarrassing. It is these people who will stand in the way of parties' political efforts.

[26] The 36.4 percent is out of the voting eligible population. Notably, this is a midterm election so we would anticipate lower turnout, but this turnout is substantially lower than even midterm elections on average. *The Washington Post*, for example, reported that the 2014 midterm election had the lowest turnout since World War II (see Jose A. DelReal (November 10, 2014) "Voter Turnout in 2014 Was the Lowest Since WWII" *Washington Post*: Post Politics, online feature)

3

How Do You Like Me Now? The Desirability of Political Independence

> "But by and large, given the vast differences between the parties these days, independent voters are basically confused, clueless people ... "
> – Paul Krugman, economist and Nobel Laureate

Over the past half century, the American political parties have – by most measures – been moving further and further away from each other. Democratic politicians have become more liberal and Republicans have become more conservative (Abramowitz 2010; Layman et al. 2006; Levendusky 2009).[1] It is this growing contrast between our major parties that makes the ever-expanding percent of independent voters just so baffling to American political spectators, such as Nobel Prize–winning economist Paul Krugman. Independent voters, he concludes in the pages of *The New York Times*, must be nothing more than a set of "confused, clueless" people.[2]

Linda Killian falls on the other side of the spectrum. In 2012 Killian, a Washington journalist and political commentator, published a book with the following dedication: "For all the Independent and Swing voters who love this country and want to make it better."[3] The book is called *The Swing Vote: The Untapped Power of Independents* and it stands as a love letter to people who call themselves politically independent. Killian presents a series of extended conversations with independents across America. Incensed by the extreme levels of disagreement between the two parties, these people express serious misgivings about the American partisan system.

"I don't get why they can't work with each other," Scott Clinger, a forty-seven-year-old policeman from Ohio tells Killian (p. 11). The frustration is

---

[1] We are speaking specifically about polarization among elites, rather than polarization among the public. Polarization among the public remains a matter of debate (see Fiorina et al. 2005).
[2] Paul Krugman (July 12, 2011). "Psychodrama Queens." *New York Times Blogs*.
[3] Capitalization in the original dedication.

palpable: "*ridiculous* and *embarrassing* are two words frequently used by independent voters to describe many of our political leaders and their antics," writes Killian (p. 45).[4]

The key word is *embarrassing*. The very conditions that Krugman believes should have increased people's urgency to pick a side have instead pushed Killian's interviewees to distance themselves from parties. Clinger, the forty-seven-year-old policeman, calls the parties "crazy" (p. 11). A fifty-two-year-old small business owner tells Killian she thinks the types of partisan debates that lead to gridlock are "stupid" (p. 17). A thirty-one-year-old father of three describes partisan politics as a "big dog and pony show" (p. 12). Another independent tells Killian Americans are "tired" of partisan politics (p. 12).

Although at first glance their views seem incompatible, Krugman and Killian actually begin from the same starting point. They are both acutely aware of the gulf between America's two competing parties. Yet whereas Krugman believes it foolish to retreat from choosing a side, Killian believes it noble to opt out of partisan politics.

In this chapter, we begin to present evidence that avoiding partisanship in America is neither foolish nor noble. People do not call themselves "independent" because they are "confused" or "clueless." For at least some independents, we suggest, the decision to avoid partisan labels is a logical reflection of the political landscape around them. At the same time, avoiding partisanship does not make a person a fair-minded judge, willing to give each side its due consideration while trying to make the best choice for the country. Rather, the decision to identify as independent may stem from a more self-interested place: people believe that avoiding partisanship will make a better impression on others. As a result, Americans pick "independent" not because the label is reflective of their political perspective but because being independent is perceived as more socially desirable than partisanship.

3.1 PARTISANSHIP AS AN IDENTITY

The way that Americans associate with a political party is often compared with how they might associate with a religion. Green, Palmquist, and Schickler (2002) conceptualize partisanship as a social identity. They suggest that people determine their partisan identities by asking themselves: "What kinds of social groups come to mind as I think about Democrats, Republicans, and Independents? Which assemblage of groups (if any) best describes me?" (Green et al. 2002, p. 8). Once they settle on a party identity that feels right, Americans tend to stick with one party for life. Indeed, as Groenendyk (2013) shows, even when people start to develop negative views of their own party, they react by developing even more negative views of the opposing party, just to ensure that their own party remains the "lesser of the two evils" (Groenendyk 2013). But

---

[4] Italics in original.

what happens when individuals do not simply perceive one party in a negative way but rather associate negative traits with the *party system as a whole?* We argue that many Americans have come to believe that there is something socially undesirable about identifying with either of the two parties. The outcome is an increase in proclamations of political independence.

As Philip Zimbardo (2007) shows, human behavior is largely controlled by unwritten social rules and implicit norms. The perceived social desirability of certain actions guides people's behavior in meaningful ways: visitors at a library instinctively whisper quietly as a result of environmental norms (Aarts and Dijksterhuis 2003), guests at a hotel are more likely to reuse their towels after learning that most of their fellow guests do the same (Goldstein et al. 2008), and survey respondents tend to provide the responses that they believe most Americans would approve of (Holbrook and Krosnick 2010). These are the forces we described in Chapter 2: when people believe that there is something negative about partisanship, they become more likely to avoid partisanship. One such way of avoiding partisanship is by identifying as independent, a group they perceive to be more socially desirable.

In this chapter, we focus on avoiding partisanship by avoiding partisan labels, but we will show in later chapters that avoidance of partisanship can take on many forms. In this chapter we present three experiments that demonstrate the social appeal of political independence. We show that the label "independent" carries with it more social desirability than do the labels "Republican" and "Democrat." This desirability is persistent in the face of political debate. More importantly, we show that perceptions about the desirability of eschewing partisan labels affect how people describe their own partisanship to others.

We conclude this chapter by examining how a need to present a socially desirable image affects the way Americans reveal their partisanship during a time of partisan scandal. Relying on the 2012 case of Todd Akin, a politician who rose to prominence after discussing his opinions on rape, we see hints of what happens when a political misstep embarrasses an entire political party and the people who associate with it.

These results will set the foundation for the remaining chapters. To track the different ways in which people avoid partisanship, we must first establish the desirability of appearing independent. Once we establish that being independent is perceived as positive and desirable, we will turn to the way people perceive parties (Chapter 4) and, more importantly, how avoiding partisanship affects individuals' behaviors (Chapter 5).

3.2 SELECTING A PARTY TO MAKE AN IMPRESSION

People may characterize themselves as independents and avoid a strong association with partisanship because they believe that political independence makes a better impression on others. As we theorize in Chapter 2, informational and individual conditions affect whether people give in to this belief and change their behavior. Before we can consider how these different conditions intersect and lead people away from partisanship, we must begin with a simple test to establish that people do believe that being independent makes a better impression than does being a partisan.

In this first test we consider both people who report that they lean independent and people who report that they are "pure" independents. Although we distinguish between the two groups at certain points in this chapter – particularly when we rely on our most conservative test in the third study of this chapter – we believe that *both* groups are important to our argument. Our theoretical arguments rely on the idea that people can treat partisan categories as signals, and both the "leaning" and "pure" independent categories are signals of avoiding partisanship.

3.2.1 Making the Best Impression

We begin with a simple experiment designed to determine whether people believe certain opinions or actions are more socially desirable than others (Holbrook et al. 2003).[5] We recruited a national sample of 330 adults from all over the United States to participate in this study (Study 3.1). The participants were a diverse group, representing a variety of different ages, income levels, education levels, and, most importantly, political parties.[6]

We asked all of these people to answer a simple question about their partisan identity (generally speaking, are you a Democrat, a Republican, or an independent?), but we manipulated the instructions they received prior to being asked the question. Participants were randomly assigned to one of two groups. We asked people in the first group to answer the partisanship question as if their goal were to make the *best* possible impression on others. We asked people in the second group to select a partisan identification as if their goal were to make the *worst* possible impression on others.[7] If there is some consensus about which type of partisan identification makes a positive impression and which makes a negative impression, then we should see a difference between the responses provided by these two groups.

We present our first set of results in Figure 3.1, which displays the percentage of respondents who identified as leaning independents (on the left side of the figure), pure independents (in the middle of the figure), and strong partisans

---

[5] Holbrook et al. (2003) use this approach to showcase socially desirable responding to questions about racial issues.

[6] We include details about the demographics of the sample, as well as the recruitment process in Appendix A1 (see table A1.3 for demographics). The treatments and randomization checks are in the online appendix to Chapter 3.

[7] These instructions mean that a participant could select a partisan group that is not at all reflective of their actual partisan preferences. A participant who is a Democrat, for example, could select "Strong Republican," believing that this is the way to make the worst possible impression.

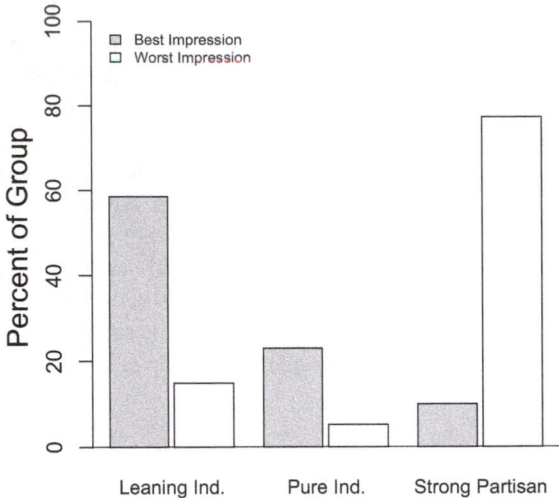

FIGURE 3.1. Percentage Identifying as Leaning Independent or Pure Independents, as only Pure Independents, and as Strong Partisans to Make the Best or Worst Impression. *Difference between groups significant at p < 0.01 for each of the categories.*

(on the right side of the figure).[8] We separate each category according to those who were asked to give the best impression, and those who were asked to give the worst impression.

Our results show clear and significant differences between those who were asked to select the party identification that gives others the best versus the worst impression. Among those who tried to make the best impression, 60 percent of respondents placed themselves into an independent category, while only 14 percent of those who were asked to make the worst impression did the same (p < 0.01). Even when we limit our analysis only to those who selected that they were "pure" independents and did not lean to either party, we still see significant differences between groups. Among those asked to make the best impression on others, 23 percent identify as pure independents, whereas only 5.1 percent do so when asked to make the worst impression (p < 0.01). In sum, when tasked with making a good impression, people are overwhelmingly likely to report that they are independent.

There is also a clear consensus among our participants that the best way to give off a bad impression is to be a strong partisan. Among those who were asked to make the best impression, only 10 percent identified as strong partisans. In contrast, among those asked to make the worst impression, 77 percent

---

[8] Full randomization checks, as well as checks that show that both groups were politically similar prior to treatment are included in the online appendix to this chapter.

report strong partisan attachments. This group difference is again not only statistically significant (p < 0.01) but also substantively large.[9]

These simple results reinforce our most basic assumption: people seem to agree that identifying as an independent makes a more positive impression on others than does being a partisan. Yet, in this first study we provided our participants with no additional political information, no reminders of why they might prefer one party over the other, and no examples of how the two parties differ. This is not, of course, how most Americans consider politics. When we hear candidates speak, when we watch political news, or when we engage in political discussions, our perceptions of parties can change and shift (Nicholson and Segura 2012).

One could expect that exposure to an actual political debate might reinvigorate Americans' allegiances and improve their perceptions of partisanship. Alternatively, conventional wisdom might suggest that hearing critiques from one party against the other might motivate our participants to cling closer to their own partisan identities (Groenendyk 2013; Taber and Lodge 2006). Our next step is to consider whether the desirability of independence can withstand exposure to a real political debate.

3.2.2 The Influence of Political Debate

Our first study suggests that Americans hold independents in the highest esteem. In contrast, identifying as a strong partisan is seen as an unappealing way to present oneself. Of course, in their day-to-day lives, people do not make judgments about the social benefits of a particular response without also considering the reality of the political landscape. That is, the way people describe their partisanship is often a reflection of how they view politics and parties. With this in mind, we turn to a second study in which we first expose our participants to a real exchange between politicians and then we ask them which partisan group makes either the best or the worst impression.

---

[9] As an additional robustness check we also examine the average strength of their reported partisanship. The standard party identification scale offers a seven-point response scale: strong Democrat, weak Democrat, leaning Democrat, pure independent, leaning Republican, weak Republican, and strong Republican. We can collapse these responses into a four-point scale, where 1 represents pure independents, 2 represents leaning independents, 3 represents weak partisans, and 4 represents strong partisans. Comparing this new strength scale, we find that participants who were asked to make the best impression responded, on average, with 2.27 – meaning they were relatively close to the "pure independent" end of the scale. Meanwhile, participants asked to make the worst impression answered with an average score of 3.58 – meaning these people were more likely to select strong partisan categories. Again, this is a strong, statistically significant difference between groups. In addition to the study presented here, we replicated this study on a sample of 104 adults recruited through an Internet convenience sample. We obtained nearly identical findings: individuals assigned to the positive group were overwhelmingly more likely to select independent categories than those assigned to the negative group. We discuss this in greater detail in the online appendix to this chapter.

3.2.2.1 *Informational Cues*

Americans hear about politics in a variety of ways: from families, friends, neighbors, colleagues, and, of course, media. These snippets of information can be direct, like when a neighbor knocks on your door to campaign for a local party, or much more subtle, like when we catch just a glimpse of the news as we flip through the television channels. In this study (Study 3.2) we presented 127 participants that were recruited over the web with a discussion of the partisan climate and actual coverage of a political event that prominently features partisan disagreement: a presidential debate.

Most Americans, at one time or another, have watched a presidential debate. The first televised election debate – a duel between John F. Kennedy and Richard Nixon – aired in 1960. Kennedy and Nixon would go on to have four more debates, with *over half* of all American households tuning in to each one. Debates officially became a landmark of American political campaigns in 1976. Since then, even the *least* watched debate to date (between Al Gore and George W. Bush in 2000) reached over a quarter of American households.

As we showed in Chapter 2, televised debates are increasingly riddled with rhetorical antagonism and conflict. This is precisely the type of political exchange that might cause Americans to associate partisanship with negative traits. As a result, if this study follows our predictions, then exposure to these debates should reinforce the idea that identifying as an independent will make a better impression on others than will identifying as a partisan.

In our study we first presented participants with information about the partisan climate in the U.S. and then turned the focus to a 2012 debate involving candidates with whom our study participants were likely already familiar: President Barack Obama and Governor Mitt Romney. Below is an excerpt of that debate (for the full text see web Appendix A3):

ROMNEY: In the last four years, you cut permits and licenses on federal land and federal waters in half.
OBAMA: Not true, Governor Romney.
ROMNEY: So how much did you cut (inaudible)?
OBAMA: Not true.
ROMNEY: How much did you cut them by, then?
OBAMA: Governor, we have actually produced more oil –
ROMNEY: No, no...

We wanted to ensure that our results were robust to different presentations of the debate, so we randomly assigned some our participants to see the debate in "cross-talk" form and some to see the debate as in more "traditional" form. The difference was that in the "cross-talk" condition the candidates interrupted each other, whereas in the "traditional" condition participants first saw a statement from Obama and then a statement from Romney. Both types of debate exposure lead to similar results, and we present the results of the "cross-talk" condition in the text, and the results of the "traditional" condition in the

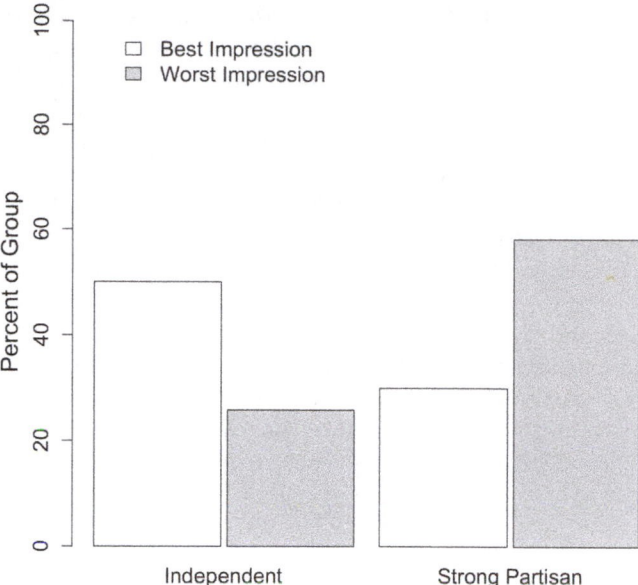

FIGURE 3.2. Influence of Presidential Debate on Using Partisanship to Make Impressions.
Group differences significant at p < 0.05 for independent, and p < 0.01 for strong partisan (one-tailed).

appendix.[10] After the participants read about the debate, we again randomly assigned each of them to one of two impression groups: some participants were asked to select the partisan group that makes the best impression, and others were asked to select the group that makes the worst impression.

3.2.2.2 *Study Results*

In Figure 3.2, we display the percentage of participants in each group who selected each of the partisan categories. Again the same clear pattern emerges: after reading about the partisan climate and a transcript of a dispute between the two major party candidates, individuals randomly assigned to give the *worst* impression were still more likely to identify as strong partisans.

While these results follow from the predictions we present in Chapter 2, this finding might initially seem contrary to what political scientists have previously argued. Scholars have long maintained that presidential debates convey an "image of democracy" to "citizens around the globe" (Kraus 2000, p. 2; also see Bishop et al. 1978), which "positively serve" the "political system at large" (Ranney 1979). Moreover, research suggests that exposure to open

---

[10] Results are shown in web Appendix A3. In this appendix we also discuss a version of this study that considers the effect of the debate without first giving participants information about the partisan climate. These results are again similar to those shown in the text.

disagreement between the two parties should lead individuals to shift *more closely* to their preferred party (Groenendyk 2013; Lodge and Taber 2013; Taber and Lodge 2006). Presidential debates are seen as opportunities for candidates to solidify support among their co-partisans. Debates, in fact, are believed to be so important for the electoral process that, when asked whether they have watched a presidential debate, respondents who did not actually watch the debates tend to lie on surveys and pretend that they have for the sake of appearing politically engaged (Prior 2012).[11]

What is driving this difference is that we are focusing on the *expression* of partisanship. In doing so, we are demonstrating something quite different from earlier assumptions about the effects of exposure to partisan debate. Debate may lead people to *inwardly* strengthen their partisan attachment, but *outwardly* they do not trust partisanship to make a good impression. In sum, even when we account for information exposure, our baseline expectation holds: people believe that independence makes a better impression than does partisanship.

3.3 PUTTING YOUR BEST FOOT FORWARD

We have shown through these first two experimental tests that people tend to view independence as more desirable, while believing that identifying as a strong partisan gives the worst impression. Exposure to partisan debate does not diminish these perceptions. Even after reading excerpts from a debate between two candidates (which previous literature suggests could strengthen partisan ties), individuals still believe that being a partisan is less desirable than being an independent. People may (privately) prefer one party to another, but they also have clear ideas about the way partisans from either side of the aisle are publicly perceived.

As we theorize in Chapter 2, however, perceptions of partisans only translate into behavior under specific informational and individual conditions. We have shown that exposure to debates contributes to people's desire to eschew partisanship. Our next step is to consider the role of information more systematically. In the next study, then, we directly consider whether the conditions we describe in Chapter 2 affect the way people describe themselves even without being deliberately prompted to make a positive impression.

3.3.1 Effect of Information on Independent Identification

We began this chapter by referring to partisanship as a social group. Much like race or ethnicity, partisanship is thought to be highly stable over time and resistant to change. While Americans might certainly hold stable political

---

[11] Thus, self-reported viewership of presidential debates is yet another example of social desirability bias.

preferences *in secret*, we argue that the way they express their partisanship is highly dependent on whether they believe partisanship makes a positive impression. In our next experiment, we begin to explore the conditions that lead Americans to shift away from revealing their partisanship.

3.3.1.1 *Information about Parties*

In previous studies we asked people to select which partisan identifications make the best or worst impressions on others. We now turn to a study in which participants have no such instructions (Study 3.3). Rather, in this study we simply observed the way people describe their own partisan identification, as well as their attachment to a party, under various political conditions. This allows us to consider which political conditions are most likely to drive a partisan undercover, as well as the types of people who are most likely to be susceptible to these conditions.

In most of the studies in this book, we present our participants with written excerpts that simulate the coverage they might come across if they follow political news. These brief media reports are an informational source that many Americans are realistically likely to be exposed to on a regular basis. In this particular experiment, we randomly assigned our participants to one of three news clippings. The first news clipping had absolutely nothing to do with politics. Instead, it described the annual American tradition of Groundhog Day. We called this group our "control" condition and it served as a baseline against which we could compare our other two groups. Participants assigned to the second group read a news clipping that highlighted the potential for bipartisanship – that is, for Democrats and Republicans to come together to work constructively. This clipping was deliberately designed to reflect America's more partisan-friendly political past, as well as prior academic beliefs in the importance of partisanship (e.g., APSA 1950).[12] We call this group the "partisan unity" group.

Participants who were randomly assigned to our third group read a news clipping about partisan disagreement. This clipping suggested that disagreement between Democrats and Republicans in Washington has become insurmountable. This clipping was designed to reflect modern media coverage of American politics and is similar to the types of stories one might read in mainstream publications.[13] We called this final group the "partisan disagreement" group. All clippings contained an equal number of words, and the partisan unity and partisan disagreement treatments were similar in their opening sentences.

---

[12] In 1950 the American Political Science Association (APSA) compiled a report about the state of partisanship. The report discussed the state of the parties but began with the assumption that parties and partisanship are important to American democracy.

[13] Indeed, this follows from a content analysis of *New York Times* articles about partisanship, conducted from a sample of more than 1,000 articles published over the past five years. This content analysis not only produced a rate of disagreement discussion (more than 30%) but also served as a model for our treatment.

We provide the text of each news clipping in full in Appendix A3, which also includes a discussion of the pre-tests conducted to validate these treatments.

Participants in this study ($N = 404$) are part of the YouGov panel. This panel includes millions of Americans, and the participants of our study were randomly selected from this entire panel.[14] This approach has several benefits, the first being that it produces a nationally representative sample of Americans. The second benefit of the panel is that we already know some information about the participants. Most importantly for us, each participant had already answered questions about his or her partisanship prior to participating in our study. We can use these additional data first to demonstrate that there are no differences in partisanship across our three groups before the start of the study (the full results of this test are in Appendix A3). We can attribute any observed differences at the end of the study to the types of information we offered to our participants. Second, this information allows for a more direct and rigorous test of our predictions. Since our argument rests on the idea that certain political conditions lead people to hide their partisanship, we can test whether our treatments affect those who identified as partisans prior to participating in the study.

3.3.1.2 *Self-Monitoring*
Our goal is to measure variation in partisanship. We also want to show that people gravitate away from partisan categories because they want to make a better impression on others. We can do so by directly measuring levels of self-monitoring. As we discussed in Chapter 2, self-monitoring is a key component of impression management and represents the extent to which a person is willing to change behaviors in order to make a more positive impression on others. Those who are higher in self-monitoring are more likely to bend their opinions and behaviors to make better impressions, while those lower in self-monitoring are less likely to do so.

Capturing an underlying individual trait is difficult, but psychologists have developed a series of questions designed specifically to measure self-monitoring (Snyder 1974). More recently, Berinsky and Lavine (2012) adapted these questions to political studies.[15] To capture self-monitoring in this study – and the studies that follow in the next chapters – we rely on the scale developed by Berinsky and Lavine (2012).[16]

---

[14] This study was part of a larger study that included 800 participants, who were all members of the YouGov survey panel. We include more information about this panel and about the participants, in particular its demographics and recruitment strategy, in Appendix A1 and Table A1.3. The participants were randomly assigned to take part in varying experimental tests; the remaining tests did not concern partisanship.

[15] The Berinsky and Lavine scale has been validated using data from the American National Election Study (ANES).

[16] We include the full set of questions, as well as a discussion about self-monitoring measures in the appendix.

3.3.1.3 Results

Although this study follows a simple, three-group design, it is a highly conservative test. Our study relies on a single exposure to political information to alter the way people express their partisan preferences. Moreover, our goal is to consider whether our treatment affects people who previously willingly identified as partisans. In our analyses, we focus on the overall weakening of partisan ties in response to our experimental treatment. We do so by comparing both the partisan disagreement and partisan unity groups to the control condition and examining whether these news clips affect high and low self-monitors differently. If people gravitate away from partisanship because they are trying to make the best impression on others, then we should observe the strongest effects among high self-monitors.

We consider partisan preferences in two ways. First, we measure partisan identification using the traditional seven-point partisan scale; this scale identifies degrees of partisanship (strong Democrat/Republican or weak Democrat/Republican) as well as degrees of independence (leaning of pure independent). Second, we follow more recent work on partisan ties (Huddy et al. 2015; Klar 2014b) and consider a different approach to capturing partisan identity. As Huddy et al. (2015) argue, the traditional seven-point partisanship scale does not always allow scholars to ascertain people's group connection to a party. Rather, Huddy et al. (2015) advocate for the use of questions that focus on the importance of a partisan identity to a person's social identity. Compared to the traditional seven-point partisanship scale, they argue, measures that focus on the importance of partisanship are better able to predict whether a person will take participatory actions on behalf of a party. Since the connection between partisanship and political behavior is important to us, we too consider a measure that focuses on the importance of partisanship to a person's identity. In turn, if exposure to partisan disagreement is leading people undercover, we should observe that people distance themselves from partisanship both in terms of their self-description and in terms of the reported importance of partisanship to their group identities.

We consider group differences using two self-monitoring groups created by splitting the scale at the median; those above the median on self-monitoring are high self-monitors, and those below the median can be considered low-self monitors. We also focus specifically on participants who did *not* self-identify as independent (but rather self-identified as Democrats or Republicans) when asked about their partisanship prior to taking part in our study.[17] For ease of discussion, we call these individuals "past partisans." We focus on these past partisans because we want to consider the process of going undercover, and

---

[17] This focus on people who did not identify as pure independents is what produces slightly higher rates of strong partisans in some groups. For example, across the whole sample, 40.1% of participants identify as strong partisans. Among people who did *not* identify as pure independents prior to our study the rate is 48% – in line with our control group.

focusing on people who previously offered a partisan identification is the best way to trace this process.

Since our analysis focuses on past partisans – people who were partisans pre-treatment – the first indicator of going undercover is a weakening of the connection to a party. Here we see that among past partisans exposure to partisan disagreement significantly decreases the extent to which people who are high in self-monitoring identify as strong partisans (Figure 3.3a, left set of bars). While 51.9 percent of high self-monitors identify as strong partisans in the control group, 35.2 percent identify as strong partisans after being exposed to the partisan disagreement treatment (difference significant at $p < 0.05$).[18] In contrast, while exposure to disagreement does slightly decrease the rate of strong partisanship among low self-monitors, this difference does not reach statistical significance, nor is the partisan disagreement group distinguishable from the partisan unity group. In sum, we already see evidence that exposure to disagreement leads to a push away from partisanship – a process most evident for those who are willing to change their behaviors to make a positive impression.

A decline in the rate of strong partisanship is not the only pattern. Among past partisans who are high in self-monitoring, exposure to partisan disagreement also increases the rate at which they now identify as leaning or pure independents. Most notably, we see a significant increase in the percentage of past partisans who now report that they are *pure* independents (Figure 3.3a, center set of bars). Although this effect is small, this is a very conservative test: prior to our treatment these participants identified as partisans. After exposure to disagreement these past partisans now report they are pure independents. Importantly, we observe no such results for participants who are low in self-monitoring (Figure 3.3b, center set of bars).

Although we observe patterns in identification, we can consider our participants' partisan preferences in another way. Certainly, partisan self-expression is about selecting a particular label when describing one's political preferences; however, partisan self-expression is also about a group connection to a party (Huddy et al. 2015; Klar 2014b). To consider this approach to partisan identity, we rely on the measure employed by Klar (2014b) and ask our participants: "How important is your political identity to you?" This question follows the initial seven-point partisan identification question and as a result cues our participants to focus on the *partisan* aspects of their political identities. Our participants placed themselves on a seven-point response scale where a score of "1" meant their identity as partisan was extremely unimportant and "7" meant it was extremely important.

Although this measure asks about personal importance, it is also a form of self-expression: describing oneself as someone for whom partisanship is important makes for a different impression than describing oneself as someone for whom partisanship is relatively unimportant. If exposure to partisan

---

[18] Results from a directional single-tailed test.

High Self-Monitors

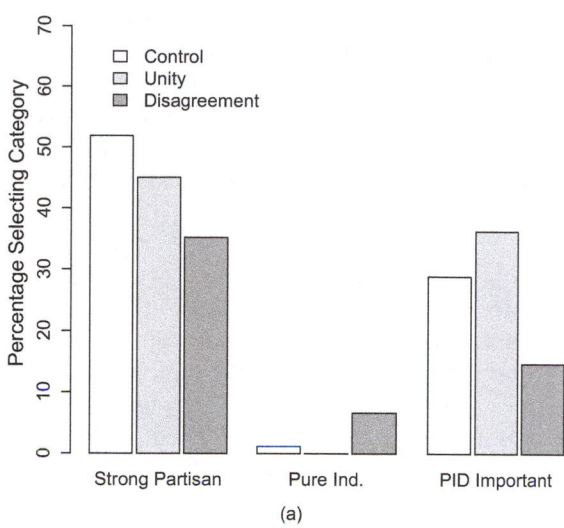

(a)

Low Self-Monitors

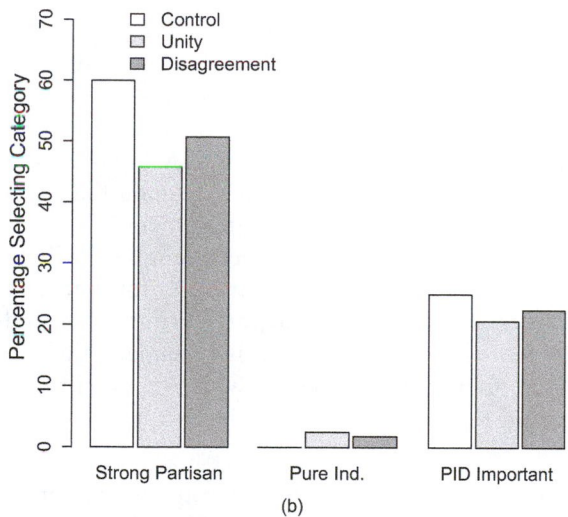

(b)

FIGURE 3.3. Identification and Partisan Importance by Condition and Self-Monitoring. *Group differences are significant for high self-monitors between the partisan disagreement and control groups at $p < 0.05$, one tailed, for strong partisanship. Differences among high-self monitors are significant for the pure independent measure at $p < 0.05$, one tailed, for the partisan disagreement condition and both other groups. Differences are significant at $p < 0.1$ for the importance of partisanship measure between the control group and the partisan disagreement group and significant at $p < 0.05$ for the partisan disagreement and partisan unity groups. There are no other significant group differences and no significant group differences in the low self-monitoring group.*

disagreement is leading partisans undercover, we should see changes in this type of self-description as well. This is an important measure for our broader argument. Klar (2014b), for example, demonstrates that it is the importance of one's political identity that drives engagement with politics (things like discussing politics and taking part in campaign activities). Similarly, Huddy et al. (2015) argue that it is the importance of partisanship to one's identity that leads people to take political action on behalf of a party. A decline in this group connection due to disagreement foreshadows the important behavioral implications of our theoretical arguments.

Again, we focus on individuals who identified as partisan prior to the start of our experiment. We see that in the control group, 28.9 percent of high self-monitors report that their partisan identity is "extremely important" to them. In contrast, after exposure to partisan disagreement, only 14.7 percent report that their partisan identity was important to them (Figure 3.3a, right set of bars). Notably, we even observe the same group difference if we limit our analysis to individuals who identified as partisans before *and* after treatment. Even those partisans who retained their partisan identifications were significantly less likely to report that these identifications were important to their identities. Again, we see no such changes among the low self-monitors. Among low self-monitors 25 percent note that their political identity is "extremely important" in the control condition, and 22 percent do so in the partisan disagreement condition (Figure 3.3b, right set of bars).[19]

In sum, even if we consider a different approach to measuring the way people associate with partisanship, we see that exposure to disagreement leads high self-monitors to shift the way they present their partisan identities. Not only do they disassociate from their party, but also they do so in ways that suggest a lower likelihood of political action on behalf of the party. Moreover, that we only observe these patterns among high self-monitors suggests that – as predicted – our results are due to efforts at impression management.

We want to be sure, however, that participants are becoming less willing to express their partisanship and are not simply becoming less interested in politics. Thus, we measure political interest across all three groups. We find that even as individuals become more likely to identify as independent, they do not express a declining interest in politics. Regardless of which news clip they read, all of our participants remain equally politically interested.[20]

---

[19] In the partisan unity group, 30.7% of high self-monitoring partisans report that their partisan identity was "extremely important" to them, while only 20.3% of low self-monitoring partisans report the same.

[20] Interested is measured on a 1–4 scale. The average rate of interest for high self-monitors is 1.66 in the control condition, 1.48 in the partisan unity condition, and 1.59 in the partisan disagreement condition. The average rate of interest for low self-monitors is 1.74 in the control group, 1.69 in the partisan unity condition and 1.69 in the partisan disagreement condition. There are no significant differences from control by group, nor are there significant difference-in-difference results for high and low self-monitors.

In these tests we dichotomize our self-monitoring measure to compare high and low self-monitors, but we can also use the full self-monitoring scale. To conduct one more check, we estimate a model that predicts the likelihood of identifying as a strong partisan using both our treatment and the full self-monitoring scale. The results of this estimation reinforce our findings (shown in full in Appendix A3). In sum, no matter which approach we take we find the same pattern: people who are higher in self-monitoring are more likely to identify as independent when they hear about partisan disagreement.

3.3.2 Information, Identification, and Issue Positioning

To this point, our three experiments lead to the same conclusion: people generally believe that avoiding partisanship makes for a better impression than does being partisan. They maintain this belief when exposed to political debates. When confronted with negative information about partisanship, as we show in the third study of the chapter, these beliefs make people who are high in self-monitoring more likely to report they are independent and that partisanship is not important to their identities. Before we continue with the remainder of this book, however, we must test whether the combination of information about partisan disagreement and self-monitoring leads people to change their issue positions. If Americans are masking their true partisan preferences under a cloak of independence, then their opinions about policies and political issues should not change.

To address this concern, we conducted a final study that in most ways replicates Study 3.3. The only difference in this final study is that it took place in two waves.[21] In wave 1, we asked our participants a set of questions about their partisanship and issue positions; in wave 2, we exposed the same set of participants to our three key treatments: control, partisan unity, and partisan disagreement. Following treatment in wave 2, we asked participants about their partisanship, and we asked them again about their positions on the same set of issues. Given that we will want to consider the behavior of high self-monitors – people who are highly sensitive to what is or is not socially desirable – we deliberately design our issue measurement scales to minimize any hint of social desirability. In total, we examine positions on six different issues: protection of the environment, health care, same-sex marriage, abortion, government provision of goods and services, and the use of taxes to fund government programs. We include details of these measures, as well as additional measures in Appendix A3.

When it comes to party identification, this two-wave study replicates the results of Study 3.3. Again, high self-monitors in the partisan disagreement condition are most likely to identify as independents. Next, we do something we could not do in Study 3.3: we compare issue positions pre-treatment

---

[21] The re-contact portion of the second wave began one week after wave 1 was completed.

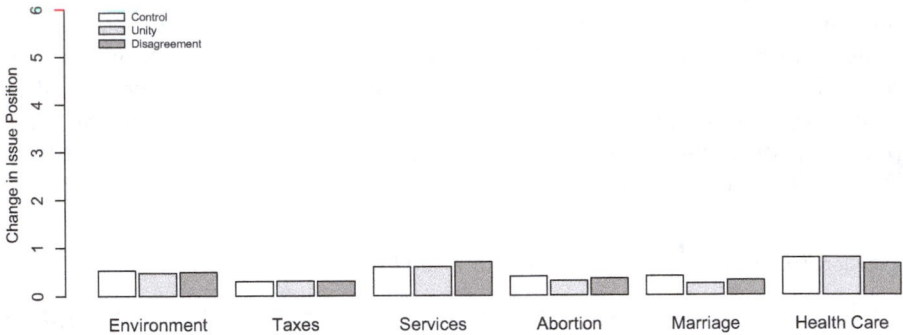

FIGURE 3.4. Changes in Issue Positions as a Function of Partisan Disagreement. *Group differences are not significant for any issues, in any conditions.*

(wave 1) and post-treatment (wave 2). Since we measure how people feel about the issues on a 1 to 7 scale, our comparison rests on the absolute value of the difference between the position in wave 1 and the position in wave 2. Under this measure, the greater the difference, the more the person moved on the issue; a score of 6, for example, would mean that a person moved from one end of the spectrum to the other, and a score of 0 means no change. This measure allows us to account for movement without making assumptions about the *direction* of this movement.

We see no movement in any of the issue positions we measure. Most importantly, we see no movement among those people who want to make the most positive impression, even when they are in the partisan disagreement condition. Even among high self-monitors, the relative distance between issue positions in wave 1 and wave 2 is no different in the partisan disagreement condition than it is in the control or partisan unity conditions (Figure 3.4). These results reinforce our previous findings: a desire to make a good impression, a willingness to change in order to do so, and negative information about partisanship come together to lead people to hide their partisan identities. These are shifts in expression of partisanship but not in ideology, as these very same conditions do not change how people view their positions on political issues.

3.3.3 Patterns of Partisan Avoidance

The series of experimental studies we present in this chapter suggests that the way Americans express their partisanship depends largely on social context. In our three studies, we not only consider the possibility that expressions of partisan identification are malleable (Nicholson and Segura 2012) but also rely on new approaches to measuring party allegiance. These studies are the first to track why, when, and how people go undercover and hide from their partisan identities. True party preference may very well remain stable, but expressions of partisanship depend very much on context.

Our first study posed a simple question: would people select a particular partisan identity if they were asked to make a positive impression versus a negative impression on others? We find that participants asked to make a positive impression are more likely to select the category "independent," while participants asked to make a negative impression are more likely to select a strong partisan category. We observe a similar pattern after altering information conditions by exposing participants to a political debate.

Our third study further clarifies the implications of the social desirability of political independence. Even when people aren't directly tasked with impressing others, hearing about partisan disagreement discourages them from identifying with a party. Moreover, the fact that we are most likely to observe this effect among people who are concerned about the way others perceive them (i.e., high self-monitors) is a clear signal that this phenomenon is due to impression management. Identifying as politically independent is more desirable, and so people call themselves independent because they want to make a positive impression. Moreover, as we show in the final two-wave replication of Study 3.3, even as people change how they report their partisanship, their issue positions remain constant. It's the self-presentation that changes, not the politics.

Of course, there is variability in the types of cues people receive about the parties and, in turn, variability in the extent to which they avoid partisanship. Yet, if we look at the electorate as a whole, we should find aggregate shifts in partisan identification when either party does something so embarrassing (to use Killian's [2012] term) that negative publicity is almost inescapable. We next leave the confines of our experimental settings to examine one such case in modern American politics.

3.4 TODD AKIN HAS THOUGHTS ON RAPE

If we had taken a poll of Americans on August 18, 2012, it is likely that the majority of poll respondents would not have been able to correctly identify who Todd Akin was. Given that numerous Americans cannot name their own congressperson, they would be unlikely to know the name of the representative from Missouri's second district.[22] Even though Akin had earned the Republican Party's nomination for U.S. Senate and was campaigning to unseat a high-profile incumbent, he was far from a nationally known figure.[23]

---

[22] In a study of 1,805 adults conducted by Pew in July 2014, approximately 48% were not able to identify the party of their representative. These 48% were about evenly split between people who reported the incorrect party (22%) and those who gave no responses, indicating that they did not know the answer (26%). Patterns from Pew report "GOP has Midterm Engagement Advantage," July 24, 2012. These patterns will appear different than Pew public data because the Pew report matched cases to zip codes; the public Pew data from the same study does not do so.

[23] Akin was running to unseat Claire McCaskill, a Democrat who had been embroiled in a scandal.

This changed on August 19, 2012 when Akin did an interview with a local St. Louis television station. Akin was asked about his position on abortion and, specifically, whether he thought abortion should be legal in cases of rape. Akin answered as follows:

First of all, from what I understand from doctors, that's really rare. If it's a legitimate rape, the female body has ways to try to shut that whole thing down. But let's assume that maybe that didn't work or something. I think there should be some punishment, but the punishment ought to be on the rapist and not attacking the child.

And suddenly Akin became famous.

In the five years that preceded his bid for the Senate, *The New York Times* had only mentioned Akin thirteen times and *The Washington Post* had mentioned him only twenty-three times.[24] In the single *month* after his interview, his media coverage tripled: *The New York Times* mentioned Akin a total of forty-seven times, and *The Washington Post* mentioned him seventy-four times. When Pew asked 1,010 Americans whether they had followed news about Akin's remarks, 47 percent reported that they had followed the incident either "very closely" or "fairly closely."

Akin's comments had profound implications for the entire Republican Party. *Washington Post* reporters who interviewed the Missouri delegation to the 2012 Republican National Convention in Tampa, Florida, found that a number of delegates "spoke openly about the shame [Akin] had brought the delegation." Delegation members told reporters that people were calling their local Republican Party offices and asking to have Akin signs removed from their lawns.[25] As Republicans scrambled to distance themselves from his candidacy, Democrats argued that Akin's comments were reflective of the Republican Party as a whole.[26]

Akin's comments served as a powerful shock to media coverage of partisan politics. Often, embarrassing gaffes by little-known politicians (such as Akin) get scant national coverage. In contrast, when high-profile politicians make missteps, preexisting opinions about these well-known politicians color

[24] LexisNexis search for term Todd Akin, from August 1, 2007 to August 1, 2012.
[25] Rosalind Helderman and Jason Horowitz (September 9, 2012). "With Senate at Stake, GOP Waits on Akin's Next Move, McCaskill Goes on Offense." *Washington Post*.
[26] For example, several days after Akin's comments, the House Democratic leader, Representative Nancy Pelosi, included the following in an e-mail to a *New York Times* reporter: "All you need to know is that the House Republicans were willing to shut down the government rather than fund Planned Parenthood. This is in keeping with their efforts – whether it's Congressman Akin or Chairman Ryan or others – to deny investments in critical women's health services, weaken the definition of rape, and take away access to preventive care like cervical and breast cancer screenings" in Jennifer Steinhauer (August 21, 2012). "Akin Controversy Stirs Up Abortion Issue in Campaign." *New York Times*. Above citation is to the online version of the article. A similar article appeared in the *New York Times* print edition on August 22, 2012 page A1 as "Ignoring Deadline to Quit, GOP Senate Candidate Defies His Party Leaders: Unexpected Twist in Election Campaigns."

the way people respond to their involvement in a scandal. Moreover, not all gaffes and scandals are linked with the gaffe-maker's party as a whole. Akin, however, offers a unique opportunity to evaluate what happens when a gaffe by an obscure politician envelopes the rest of the party.

Given that Akin's remarks occurred during an election year (2012), pollsters were conducting public opinion surveys at regular intervals. We can use these polls to track American partisanship before Akin's remarks and after the media feeding frenzy. In fact, we can even use surveys conducted by the same survey organization so as to control for the particular sampling technique that each polling outlet employs. This approach, of course, offers us a crude instrument. A campaign is a fast-paced environment and numerous factors may shift the way people express their political preferences to others. As a result, we cannot, and do not, unconditionally argue that the changes we observe were caused by Akin's remarks. Rather, given the attention Akin's comments received and the extent to which Akin's views became intertwined with those of the Republican Party as a whole, partisan shifts are at least suggestive. Any increases in self-identified independents (and, in particular, independents who lean Republican) following Akin's comments, would hint that Republican-ism became particularly unlikely to make a positive impression and Republicans headed for cover. This is one of the mechanisms we suggest in Chapter 2: one party is maligned and that party's members disproportionately go undercover.

We use data from Pew to track the percentage of independents before and after the Akin interview. First, we consider polls the week before the Akin interview and the week after. Second, we take polls conducted in the *two* weeks prior to Akin's remarks and in the two weeks after the media coverage of Akin reached a saturation point. We then use the average percentage of independents, rather than individual polls, to ensure that no single poll is an outlier.[27]

When we first compare the polls taken the week before and the week after Akin's comments, we see that on August 12, 2012 (one week before Akin's interview), 31 percent of the 1,002 Americans Pew interviewed identified as independents. One week and some 500 newspaper articles after Akin's interview, a poll completed on August 26, 2012 showed that 38 percent of the 1,010 people Pew interviewed identified as independent. The respondents in both studies were interviewed and recruited in the same exact way, yet a two-week period increased the number of independents by seven percentage points.[28]

---

[27] The pre-polls were conducted by Pew on July 29, August 5, and August 12. The post-polls were also conducted by Pew on August 26, September 2, and September 9 (listed dates are the end-dates of the polls). In between these polls there is a poll that occurs on August 19 – the day on which Akin gave his interview. As we cannot be certain that the poll concluded prior to the interview, we exclude this poll. We include all the details of the polls in the online appendix to this chapter.

[28] Moreover, this percentage of independents was about 5 points higher than the average rate of independents in polls conducted over the last five months.

Is this a meaningful increase or just a random fluctuation? As a baseline for comparison, we can consider the surveys Pew conducted around the same time in the summers prior to 2012 and the summers after 2012. From August 7 to August 21, 2011, the percentage of independents decreased by only 4 percentage points. Around the same time in 2010, the change was a single percentage point. We see a two percentage-point change during the same time period in 2009, and we see *no change* during a similar time in 2008. We find a four percentage-point change for a similar time period in 2014.[29] In short, the seven-point percentage increase in independents is unusual for this particular time period – even when we consider 2008, a year with a presidential campaign.[30]

We can consider these results in a different way by taking the average percentage of independents two weeks before and two weeks after Akin's comments. Doing so again shows an increase in the percentage of people who identify as independent. In short, even when we broaden the scope of consideration to account for the possibility that a single poll is an outlier, we see an increase in independents.

We can use these data to consider other types of changes. For example, are these independents reporting that they *lean* a certain way? We rely on the average measure and consider how many independents report that they lean toward the Republican Party prior to Akin's comments and the average percentage of leaning Republicans after Akin's comments. Of people who identify as independents two weeks prior to Akin's comments, on average 36.5 percent report that they lean Republican. In the two weeks after Akin's interview, on average 42 percent of independents identify as leaning Republicans – an increase of nearly 6 percentage points. During this same time, the percentage of independents who identify as leaning Democrats stays virtually the same, even decreasing very slightly by just about 2 percentage points. Notably, by the middle of October these patterns disappear.[31] Evidently, the increase in independents following Todd Akin's controversial comments was due to a growth in independents with Republican preferences. That is, Republicans (and not Democrats) decided to identify as independents.

Again, we do not mean to suggest that these results represent a direct causal connection between Akin's comments and partisanship patterns in

---

[29] There are no appropriately matching dates in 2013. The dates that do come closest to matching show a severe decrease in the percentage of independents from July to mid-August, though this difference could be due to different survey types and sampling procedures. If we shift our analysis to cover late August to mid-September in 2013, we see a small change – just 4 percentage points. The full set of surveys used in this result is presented in the online appendix to this chapter.

[30] Of course, this is within the confines of the time periods in our analysis. We are not suggesting that this change is unique on any other dimension.

[31] Again, we compare surveys conducted using similar polling structures. In late September and early October the percentage of independents fluctuates with no particular pattern, and the percentage of leaning Democrats and Republicans also shows no patterns.

America.[32] Certainly these are merely blunt comparisons based on surveys completed by a single polling company. Indeed, it is possible that a different set of polls, conducted by a different polling company, could show a different pattern. Yet, nevertheless, in the wake of Akin's comments, Democrats worked hard to send the message that Akin's thoughts on rape were reflective of Republicans as a whole. Akin's comments were – by his party's own admission – embarrassing for the Republican Party. The patterns we show with the Pew data suggest that party-wide scandals like this one can help to push at least some partisans undercover.

3.5 TAKING CUES

For some Americans the label "independent" may reflect a political position or an ideological stance. For others, as we show in this chapter, choosing to describe oneself as "independent" is a much broader form of self-expression. Choosing independent – rather than Democrat or Republican – is an effort to make a positive impression on others. In these cases, identifying as independent is a way to avoid partisan labels in the hope of impressing others. It is a decision that, as we suggested at the start of this chapter, is neither selfless nor noble but rather driven by self-interest.

The results we present in this chapter underscore two important ideas. First, our research underscores a growing body of work on the malleability of partisan images (e.g., Nicholson and Segura 2012). Even more importantly, however, we begin to suggest in this chapter that systematic motivations lead certain partisans undercover. Some of these motivations lie in people's own characteristics. Some people are more or less willing to misrepresent their preferences, and, as we will show later, behaviors to make better impressions on others. Other motivations are external. The more negative information about the parties that people receive, the more they wish to be viewed as independent. We do not need particularly egregious gaffes, like Todd Akin's comments about rape, to set this process in motion. Even subtle messages that highlight partisan disagreement or suggest that the parties are unlikely to unite can lead people to avoid partisanship and subsequently increase the desirability of independence. Akin's comments provide us with a particularly notable incident that drove Americans to mask their partisanship, but ordinary political media coverage of partisan debate (or even a conversation with a friend) is enough to drive Americans undercover.

---

[32] Indeed, it is possible that a different polling company – or even differently sampled surveys by Pew – could produce different patterns in independents. We rely on the fact that Pew is a reputable polling company and the fact that all our comparisons come from the same type of Pew study, thus controlling for fluctuations due to polling technique. Nonetheless, it is important to acknowledge that we cannot conclusively eliminate the alternative explanation of random polling flux.

In showing why and when identifying as independent is particularly desirable, we have already moved beyond much of the existing political science research on political independents. We now turn to even broader goals. Do the same motivations that propel people undercover actually have consequences that reach beyond partisan identification? Could these motivations affect the way people judge those who are honest about their partisan identities? In the next chapter we expand the scope of our analysis and consider the undesirability of partisanship.

4

Everybody Hates Partisans

"I don't like either political party. One should not belong to them – one should be an individual, standing in the middle. Anyone that belongs to a party stops thinking."

– Ray Bradbury, writer

By the end of this chapter the reader should reach one conclusion: people dislike partisans. One might even go as far as to say that people *hate* partisans. When the two parties debate and disagree, people start to view partisans in a negative way. They do not want to work with partisans, they do not want to live with partisans, and they think partisans are generally unattractive, incompetent, and unlikable.

This may not seem surprising given the results in Chapter 3. After all, we show that there is a prevailing belief that being independent is more socially beneficial than being a partisan and, more importantly, that people shift away from partisan labels to make a better impression on others. But the level of dislike for partisans that we demonstrate in this chapter *should* be surprising for a number of reasons.

First, the extent to which people dislike partisans is surprising given the importance that political scientists often place on political parties. Political parties are considered the backbone of the American democratic process, the sorting mechanism by which voters' preferences are translated into governmental outcomes (Aldrich 1995; Schattschneider 1942). In addition, partisans are often more likely to be politically active (Verba et al. 1995), and political participation is something that academics consider a good thing (Holbrook and Krosnick 2010). Partisan debate is widely considered an important component of any healthy democracy.

Second, a preference for one option need not translate to a dislike of the other alternative. A person, for example, may prefer Coca-Cola but have little ill will toward Pepsi and may even be willing to drink Pepsi if it were the only option available. Similarly, a person may believe that the label "independent" is a more socially beneficial signal but might also view partisanship as a moderately desirable (or at least relatively neutral) label. But, as we will demonstrate in this chapter, this is not the case.

We find little evidence of positivity toward partisanship, especially when views of partisanship are paired with news about partisan disagreement. Through a series of studies we see that the flip side of the social benefit of being independent is negativity toward partisanship. People do not report that being independent makes a better impression because being a partisan has an overall neutral effect on impression management. Rather, people report that being independent makes a better impression because they find partisans, in a word, loathsome.

4.1 ASSESSING PERCEPTIONS OF PARTISANS

It should come as no surprise to anyone who has lived through an American election that there is no love lost between many Democrats and Republicans. Although the dislike is often personal (Iyengar and Westwood 2014), it is rooted in the deep ideological differences between members of the two parties. We want to consider an even broader question: how do people feel about *partisans*? Forget, for a moment, about the actual party a person supports. Does simply supporting *any* party make a poor impression on others?

Scholars use a variety of techniques and measures to capture how Democrats and Republicans feel about each other. One popular measure asks people to rate Republicans and Democrats on a "thermometer" ranging from 0 to 100: the "warmer" you feel toward a party, the higher the thermometer score. Another popular measure asks people to list everything they like and everything they dislike about both parties (Konda and Sigelman 1987).

More recently, Iyengar, Sood, and Lelkes (2012) relied on measures designed to capture the *affective* components of how Democrats and Republicans feel about each other: questions that ask people how they would feel, for example, if someone close to them married a person of the opposing party. These types of questions show that people not only disagree with the opposing party but that Democrats have an intense affective dislike of Republicans just as Republicans have a great deal of negative affect for Democrats.

It is no surprise that people dislike members of the other party, but in this chapter we argue that some people may even dislike members of their *own* party who are strong partisans. We can start with a variation of the Iyengar et al. (2012) measures of affect. In our study, we consider how people would feel about having a new colleague at work who identifies as a partisan (Study 4.1). We tell a group of participants that the colleague is a partisan who likes to talk about politics and who had *voted for the same presidential candidate* as the participant. We then track how changes in political context affect people's willingness to work with this partisan colleague.

Much as we did in our earlier studies, we randomly assigned our participants (N = 156, demographics in Table A1.4) to read one of three news clippings: a news clipping about partisan unity, a news clipping about partisan disagreement, or a nonpolitical news clipping about Groundhog Day.[1] Among participants who only read about Groundhog Day, 23 percent reported that they would be unhappy with a politically inclined coworker. Similarly, among those who saw information about partisan unity, 25 percent reported that they would be unhappy with this new coworker.

In contrast, we find that participants who read about partisan disagreement were significantly more likely to report that they would be unhappy to work with a colleague who enjoyed discussing politics. Forty percent expressed discontent at the thought of working with this new politically inclined colleague – even though the hypothetical colleague *agrees* with them!

These results show that when people are reminded of partisan disagreement, they become uncomfortable with the idea of being around partisans – even like-minded partisans. Yet these results are a first step in our quest to understand how people feel about partisans. We are not just interested in people's reasoned arguments about how they view the political positions or even the political behavior of partisans. Rather, we are interested in their more visceral responses to partisans. We are interested in what motivates people to hide their partisanship *even when it may be in their best interests to become politically involved.*

To capture these types of responses we turn to an array of new, unique measures of partisan affect. These measures do not overtly mention politics but rather focus on the conditions under which people may encounter partisans in their daily lives. As a result, these measures will allow us to better capture the day-to-day effects of exposure to partisan disagreement.

4.2 IMAGINE ME AND YOU AS PARTISANS

The way someone feels about a political concept is inextricably linked to the way they visualize that concept. The type of image that comes to mind, for example, when a candidate speaks about a political issue has a profound effect on the way a person evaluates not only a candidate's position on the issue but also the candidate himself (Valentino et al. 2002). Moreover, as Petersen and Aarøe (2013) demonstrate, the vividness with which people visualize concepts fundamentally affects how they make political choices that relate to those concepts.

Research in psychology suggests that people store knowledge both verbally and visually (Paivio 1971; Prior 2014). Much of the work in political science

---

[1] These are the same treatments as those we use in Chapter 3, Study 3.3; the treatments are included in our online appendix for Chapter 3. The only difference is that the introduction to the treatment reflects the passage of time, now beginning with the statement, "With President Obama well into his second term…"

focuses on the way individuals store verbal descriptions of political concepts (see, for example, Price et al. 2002). In turn, scholars are generally less concerned with the way people visualize political topics, which Prior (2014) argues is a critical omission.

Of course, many (if not most) political groups and concepts can be visualized as any one of a vast array of images. Just consider, for a moment, the variety of images that come to mind when one hears the term "environmentalist." One can imagine a young person in an "I (heart) The Earth" t-shirt, an older man with long gray hair, a woman dressed in tie-dye hugging a tree, a pleasant college student, an unpleasant college student, a protestor with a sign, a man riding a bike, a conscientious environmental lawyer, and the list could easily continue. The visualized image is reflective of the way people feel about the political concept.[2] A person who visualizes a kindly old man planting a public garden likely feels very differently about environmentalists than does a person who, upon hearing the term, envisions young militants launching attacks on employees of an energy firm.[3]

So what do people visualize when they hear the term "partisanship"?

4.2.1 Capturing an Image

The idea that people may conjure an image when they hear the term "partisanship" seems simple, but actually capturing the image that comes to mind is more difficult. We could ask people to quickly write down the image they are thinking of, but this means that we are dependent on people's verbal descriptions as opposed to the visual component. Alternatively, we could ask people to draw the images that come to mind. This, of course, frees us from relying on their verbal descriptions but leaves us limited by people's artistic abilities. Measurement is difficult if people cannot effectively reproduce the image they see in their head.

We avoid both of these limitations by leveraging a key characteristic of the Internet: the ability to find hundreds of thousands of images within seconds.

To capture how people visualize partisanship we invited a group of 192 Internet-savvy adults to participate in a study (Study 4.2, demographics in Table A1.4). We asked participants to find an image online that best fits their perception of partisanship. After they located the image (or images), they simply gave

---

[2] The causal relationship between visualization and opinion can move in both directions. For example, as Valentino et al. (2002) show, the type of image can move opinion. In contrast, however, an opinion may be formed first and subsequently produce an image; this is the type of causal chain a model like Petersen and Aarøe's (2013) would suggest. What matters for us, however, is not the causal direction but the idea that visualization and feelings are linked, and that the visualization may often be more reflective of a person's feelings than the verbal description of these feelings.

[3] For example, see reporting by Patrick Sawer and Emily Gosden in *The Telegraph* ("Anti-Fracking Protest Turns Violent," May 4, 2014).

us the website address where we could find it.[4] This sample was deliberately made of adults who knew how to search for images, meaning that the results we obtained were not systematically limited by a lack of skill among certain participant groups.

Once we had a list of the online addresses the participants had provided, we retrieved all the images. Two independent coders who were unaware of the purpose of this study then coded each image for content. The coders considered various attributes of the images, focusing on such factors as whether the image depicted anger, suggested that disagreement was insurmountable, depicted fighting, or was just overall negative. In Table 4.1 we offer examples of different types of images and how those images were coded.[5] Using this approach we will track how information about the parties affects the way people visualize partisanship. Our new measure will allow us to capture these visualizations in an unprecedented way: *through actual images*.

We are interested in using these images to consider how people visualize parties generally as well as how different political contexts might affect the images people offered. After all, we argue that people are most likely to hide their partisanship when they receive information that suggests that there are negative traits associated with partisanship (Chapter 2). Certainly, a negative visualization of partisanship is a key indicator of our mechanism at work. In this case, prior to asking people to search for images, we randomly assigned our participants to read one of four news clippings. Participants either read a news clipping that suggested the parties could come together (partisan unity), a news clipping that suggested that the disagreements between party elites were insurmountable (elite partisan disagreement), a news clipping that suggested insurmountable disagreements between ordinary citizens (mass partisan disagreement), or a news clipping that was nonpolitical and instead discussed Groundhog Day (control).

Three of the news clippings (partisan unity, elite partisan disagreement, and control) follow the structure of the clipping we discussed in Chapter 3, but the fourth news clipping is a new addition. We include this fourth news clipping because in this particular experiment our goal is to consider how people visualize *partisanship* generally – not specifically among elites. If we only focus on elites, we run into the possibility of measuring how people feel about politicians and politics, rather than partisanship as a concept. By including a condition that focuses on partisan disagreement among ordinary Americans, we are better able to ensure the focus is on partisanship.

Absent from the analyses in this study – and in the remainder of the studies in this chapter – is self-monitoring. As we describe in Chapter 2, self-monitoring conditions individuals' willingness to *change their behaviors* in order to make

---

[4] We include the details of this sample in Appendix A1.

[5] In the online appendix to this chapter we include the full coding scheme for the images as well as a discussion of the coding instructions.

TABLE 4.1. *Sample Images and Codes for Study 4.2*

Coding	Images
Angry	
Fighting	
Negative	
Cheerful	

The images presented are sample images used to illustrate coding. In our dataset individuals provided a greater variety of images including photographs and editorial cartoons, which cannot be included here due to copyright issues.

a more positive impression on others. Indeed, as we theorize in Chapter 2, both high and low self-monitors may believe that there are negative traits associated with partisanship, but only high self-monitors would change their self-descriptions and behaviors because of these beliefs. For this reason in the previous chapter, we only relied on self-monitoring to analyze people's descriptions of their *own* partisanship. Following this logic, since the studies in this chapter focus on people reporting their perceptions of politics (rather than describing themselves or taking actions), we should not expect self-monitoring to condition our results. Indeed, key to the tests in this chapter is the idea that our effects can be traced across the whole sample. In the next chapter, when we consider how people mold and change their behaviors, we return to self-monitoring.

4.2.2 Visualizing the Party

In our first analysis, we compare images from participants in the control group to images from participants in each of the treatment groups. In particular, we focus on the attributes of these images. Does the image, for example, suggest that the parties are hopelessly divided? Does the image depict fighting? Is the image negative or is it cheerful?

Across all of these different attributes, we see statistically significant shifts toward negativity when people are reminded of partisan disagreement. Participants who read about partisan disagreement either at the elite or mass public levels were twice as likely to find an image that depicted anger as opposed to participants who read either the control news clipping or one about partisan unity (Figure 4.1a). They were similarly significantly more likely to produce an image that showed divisiveness (Figure 4.1b), one that portrayed fighting (Figure 4.1c), and one that was overall negative (Figure 4.1d). These images represent how participants visualize parties; reading about disagreement evidently leads people toward negative visualizations.

Across the entire sample, partisanship was generally associated with negative imagery. Reminders of political disagreement, however, strongly exacerbated this effect. And as disagreement led to more negative images, it also reduced the number of positive images. In the control condition, only 21.9 percent of participants found optimistic images to represent their visualization of partisanship – and this number shrinks significantly in the disagreement conditions. In fact, in the mass disagreement condition only 6.9 percent of images can be considered optimistic. In contrast, 28 percent of people in the unity condition found optimistic images.[6]

---

[6] We can use the available URLs to track that the majority of participants entered "partisan politics" as their search term in Google. This allows us to obtain and code the images that appear when one uses this term. This coding provides us with "base rates" of images of various types – i.e., the percentage of negative and fighting images available to an individual who enters "partisan politics" as a search term in Google. If our treatments have no effect and image selection is based only on the availability of images, then the percentages of images should follow this base rate. For example, the percentage of fighting images in each treatment should reflect the percentage of fighting images available to the participant who searched "partisan politics." This is not the case. Those in the control and unity conditions selected images that reflect negatively on partisanship at rates that are *below* the base rate of their availability. Meanwhile participants in the disagreement conditions selected negative images at rates above the base rate. It is important to note that because of constant shifts in the availability and prevalence of certain types of images on the web the base rates obtained are highly dependent on the time of search. A replication of this coding at a later date may – and most likely will – produce different base rates of partisan images.

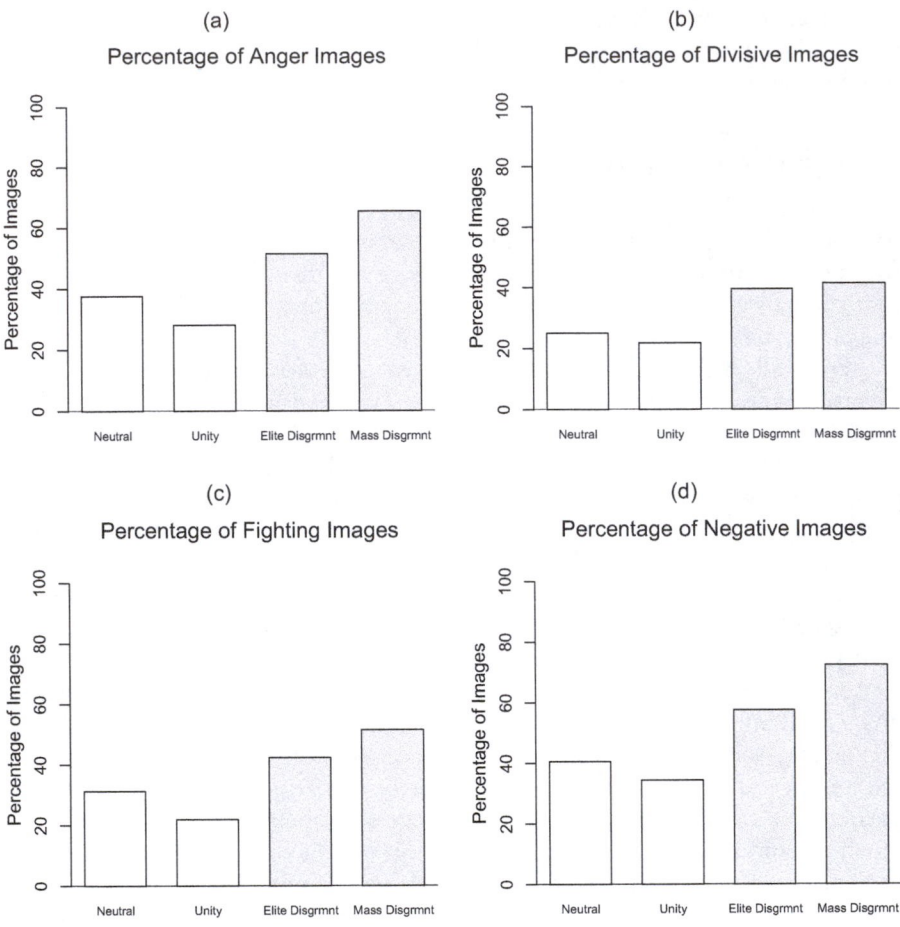

FIGURE 4.1. Chosen Image Types by Group.
For anger (a) the elite disagreement differs from the unity condition at $p < 0.1$; the mass disagreement differs from both the neutral and the unity conditions at $p < 0.05$. For divisiveness (b), the mass disagreement condition differs from the unity and neutral conditions at $p < 0.1$; the elite disagreement condition differs from unity at $p < 0.1$. For fighting (c) the mass disagreement condition differs at $p < 0.05$ from the neutral condition and at $p < 0.01$ from the unity condition; the elite disagreement condition differs at $p < 0.05$ from the unity condition. For negativity (d) the elite disagreement differs from the neutral condition at $p < 0.1$, and the mass disagreement differs from the neutral condition at $p < 0.05$; elite disagreement differs from unity at $p < 0.05$, and mass disagreement differs from unity at $p < 0.01$.

Remember that participants were instructed to choose an image that represents *partisanship* – not just Democrats or just Republicans. For decades, political scientists have predicted that reminders of partisan disagreement lead individuals to either cling to their own party or to blame the other party for inciting conflict (see, for example, Groenendyk 2013). Put another way, a Democrat may argue that Republicans are responsible for ruining partisanship, while Republicans may contend that it is Democrats who make partisan disagreement unbearable.

We suggest that partisan disagreement leads people away from partisanship *overall*. As testament to the point that our participants hold negative views of partisanship as a whole, we consider whether the images they selected depict only one party in a negative light or whether the selected images denigrate both parties. We find that exposure to partisan disagreement, regardless of type, significantly increases the number of images that cast *both* parties negatively. Among those assigned to the control condition, 28.1 percent retrieved images that suggest both parties provoke anger. Among individuals who were exposed to a treatment that describes elite partisan disagreement, 45.5 percent of images depict both parties as provoking anger. For those who read about disagreement among ordinary people, 55.2 percent of our participants found images that show that both the Democrats and the Republicans provoke anger.

In fact, even if one wanted to analyze those images that do vilify only one party (and not both), one could not do so: there are not nearly enough such images in our study to conduct any reasonable test. Fewer than 5 percent of all the images in our study show that only one party provokes anger. This small number of images is almost evenly split between images depicting Democrats as troublemakers and those that show Republicans in the negative role.

As an additional proxy, we consider the number of images that include President Barack Obama. As the leader of our country, he may be viewed as representative of the federal government. As the leader of the Democratic Party, he may be viewed as a symbol for that party alone. Again, not only do we see that few images overall include Obama (fewer than 10 percent across all conditions), but we also see no statistically significant group differences in the rate of these types of images.

In sum, in this study we see that when people hear about partisan disagreement, it clouds their perception of both parties, or more generally, *partisanship*. Moreover, given that we see similar results in both our elite disagreement and mass public disagreement conditions, we see little evidence that the images captured frustration with politics rather than frustration with partisanship.

When we remind individuals of partisan disagreement, they find images that speak to their anger and frustration with partisanship, rather than with a particular party. If, as psychologists suggest, the way people visualize a concept is reflective of the way people feel about this concept, then political parties certainly do not suffer from overwhelming levels of public adoration.

4.3 THESE ARE THE PEOPLE IN MY NEIGHBORHOOD

To this point, our results suggest that when reminded of partisan disagreement, Americans associate partisanship with anger, fighting, and general negativity.

But do these images affect the choices people make in their daily lives? Could these negative images shape how people perceive the world around them? In this next study we consider whether negative views of partisanship affect how people view ordinary suburban neighborhoods.

The possibility that partisanship affects where people want to live is controversial but certainly not new. In *The Big Sort* journalist Bill Bishop argues that Americans increasingly self-segregate according to partisanship – or, at least, based on cultural inclinations that are correlated with partisanship. Democrats, Bishop (2008) argues, choose to live and work with other Democrats, while Republicans do the same with their co-partisans. As a result of this residential segregation, as Bishop calls it, Americans spend time only with people who agree with them, and there is almost no opportunity for an exchange of ideas across party lines. Not everyone agrees with Bishop. Nall and Mummolo (2014), for example, argue that the type of geographic sorting Bishop proposes is virtually impossible given the economic and employment constraints that most people face. Practicalities aside, however, there is something simple to Bishop's argument that appeals to many political scientists: Americans are angry about partisan politics and, as a result, they shun members of the opposing party. Even if people cannot restructure their lives to move to Berkeley, California and be among other Democrats, or to Jacksonville, Florida to live among fellow Republicans, they, at the very least, *wish* they could do so. But this argument does not consider another possibility: perhaps people would most prefer to live with neighbors who have no political affiliations at all.

4.3.1 Comparing Neighborhoods

We consider how people's attitudes toward partisans influence their residential preferences through a study that relies on a nationally representative sample of 513 Americans. In this study (Study 4.3, demographics in Table A1.3), we asked a group of people to read one of two news stories about partisanship. The first was about the potential for partisan unity and the second was about the potential for partisan disagreement (full wording in the online appendix to this chapter).

After reading these stories, we provided each participant with two photographs. Both of the photographs showed a clear picture of a neighborhood, and both neighborhoods were similar in character. We asked our participants how much they would like to live in each of the two neighborhoods, and whether they would want to attend social events with the people who might live in each of the two neighborhoods.

Each neighborhood was a picturesque American suburb, with well-maintained houses lined along a series of well-manicured lawns and long sidewalks that stretched out into the distance. In fact, these pictures were deliberately selected based on the types of physical characteristics that lead people to evaluate neighborhoods most positively: trees, pleasant aesthetic, space between houses, and overall neatness and cleanliness (Hur et al. 2010; Sirgy and Cornwell 2002).

We also wanted to make sure that nothing about the neighborhoods would affect people's judgments and potentially muddy our results. We did not want our comparisons clouded, for example, by a person's preference for Arizona weather over Minnesota weather. Therefore, our participants were not told where the neighborhoods were located (they were simply identified as Neighborhood A and Neighborhood B), and the photographs deliberately contained no defining features that would situate the neighborhoods in a particular geographic region. Indeed, the neighborhoods could have been located in any pleasant American suburb.[7]

In fact, both of these neighborhoods were perceived to be great places to live. In a separate pre-test conducted prior to our main study, we asked a different group of 90 adults how much they would want to live in these neighborhoods and whether they believed these were good neighborhoods. On a scale of 1 to 10, where 10 meant that a person would very much want to live there, people gave one neighborhood an average score of 8.0 and the second neighborhood an average score of 7.8 (not a statistically distinguishable difference). When asked to rate neighborhood quality on the same scale, these same participants gave the first neighborhood an average score of 7.9 and the second neighborhood an average score of 8.0.

On the surface, these were two equally desirable neighborhoods – that is, until we manipulated the photographs. We left one photograph untouched, but we digitally altered the second photo to create several different versions. For ease of discussion, we will call the untouched photograph of the neighborhood the *baseline neighborhood*. All participants saw a baseline neighborhood photograph that was completely identical in every way.

We altered the photograph of the second neighborhood that we showed our participants to create different conditions that we call (1) sign-free, (2) political signs, and (3) nonpolitical signs. Participants assigned to the sign-free version of the neighborhood saw the photograph of the second neighborhood in its original form – without any signs on any of the lawns.

Participants randomly assigned to the second condition (political signs) saw a photograph of the same neighborhood, except it had been digitally manipulated so as to include political yard signs on two of the visible lawns. The political signs did not mention a specific party and they advertised last names that were not associated with any high-profile political candidates. A person looking at the photo could only see that that there were some politically active individuals on the block, but they would not be able to determine which party these individuals supported.

Participants assigned to the final condition (nonpolitical signs), saw a photograph of the very same neighborhood digitally manipulated to include

---

[7] Furthermore, to avoid any additional confounds, we randomized which neighborhood was referred to as Neighborhood A and which was referred to as Neighborhood B.

TABLE 4.2. *Conditions for Neighborhood Study*

Group 1	Group 2	Group 3
Text: Unity	*Text:* Unity	*Text:* Unity
Image 1: Baseline neighborhood with no yard sign	*Image 1:* Baseline neighborhood with political yard sign	*Image 1:* Baseline neighborhood with nonpolitical yard sign
Image 2: Second neighborhood with no yard sign	*Image 2:* Second neighborhood with political yard sign	*Image 2:* Second neighborhood with nonpolitical yard sign
Group 4	Group 5	Group 6
Text: Disagreement	*Text:* Disagreement	*Text:* Disagreement
Image 1: Baseline neighborhood with no yard sign	*Image 1:* Baseline neighborhood with political yard sign	*Image 1:* Baseline neighborhood with nonpolitical yard sign
Image 2: Second neighborhood with no yard sign	*Image 2:* Second neighborhood with political yard sign	Image 2: Second neighborhood with nonpolitical yard sign

nonpolitical yard signs on visible lawns. The signs were for a graduation party. Manipulating the neighborhood to include a nonpolitical sign allows us to ensure that our results are not simply due to the fact that the presence of any yard signs leads people to lower their evaluations of neighborhoods.[8]

Our two types of political articles and three versions of the neighborhood photo (sign-free, political signs, and nonpolitical signs) leave us with six different experimental groups. We show these different groups in Table 4.2. The structure of the study was such that people first read the political article, and then later on in the survey they saw the neighborhoods and evaluated them.

After seeing the photos, our participants rated the quality of both neighborhoods on a 1 to 10 scale (where a score of 10 indicates the highest quality), they considered how willing they would be to live in each of the neighborhoods, and they told us whether they would rather attend a social event with the residents of the baseline neighborhood or the residents of the second, manipulated neighborhood.

4.3.2 Where Do You Want to Live?

We first track how people evaluate the quality of the two neighborhoods using the 1 to 10 quality scale. Because people rated the quality of these neighborhoods on the same screen, we can compare our baseline neighborhood to the

---

[8] The specific nonpolitical sign we showed was a sign promoting a graduation party, rather than a yard sale, so as to not give any indication of potential economic conditions in a neighborhood.

TABLE 4.3. *Neighborhood Quality Ratings by Information and Sign Type*

	No Signs	Political Signs	Nonpolitical Signs
Partisan Unity	−0.19	−0.68	−0.52
Partisan Disagreement	−0.24	−1.44	−0.20
Difference between Political Info. Groups	0.05	0.76**	−0.32

** $p < 0.05$, Ratings are based on the difference score described in the text.

second neighborhood using a difference score. We obtain this difference by subtracting the ratings our participants gave to the baseline neighborhood from the ratings they gave to the second neighborhood. So, for example, if a participant rated the second neighborhood at a 6 on the quality scale and rated the baseline neighborhood at an 8, the difference score would be −2. If a participant rated the second neighborhood at an 8 on the quality scale and rated the baseline neighborhood at a 6, the difference score would be +2. As a result, positive values on the difference score mean that the participant perceives the second neighborhood more positively, while negative values mean that the participant prefers the baseline neighborhood.

We use this difference score to consider both the presence of signs in the second neighborhood as well as the type of article a person read prior to seeing the photographs. First, we see that the type of article has no effect on people when they evaluate two neighborhoods without signs, and it has very little effect when people evaluate neighborhoods in which one has no sign and the other has a nonpolitical sign (Table 4.3).

Next, we see that regardless of article content, the presence of a political sign lowers the attractiveness of the second neighborhood relative to the baseline. Notably, we see the largest difference in perceived neighborhood quality among people who read the article about partisan disagreement. When people compare the baseline neighborhood to a second neighborhood with political signs, they significantly downgrade the quality of the second neighborhood. In short, while people do not seem to believe that a lawn sign inherently devalues the neighborhood, they do seem to perceive that a *political* lawn sign makes a neighborhood less attractive.

Hand-in-hand with quality ratings, political information also affects people's willingness to live in a neighborhood with political signs. Here we calculate the percentage of people who reported that they "very much" want to live in a neighborhood. Among people who read about partisan unity, the presence or absence of signs in a neighborhood had little effect on the extent to which they preferred the baseline neighborhood to the second neighborhood. The number of people who wanted to live in the baseline neighborhood does increase by about 3 percentage points when the second neighborhood has a political sign, but this change is not significant. In short, participants who read about partisan

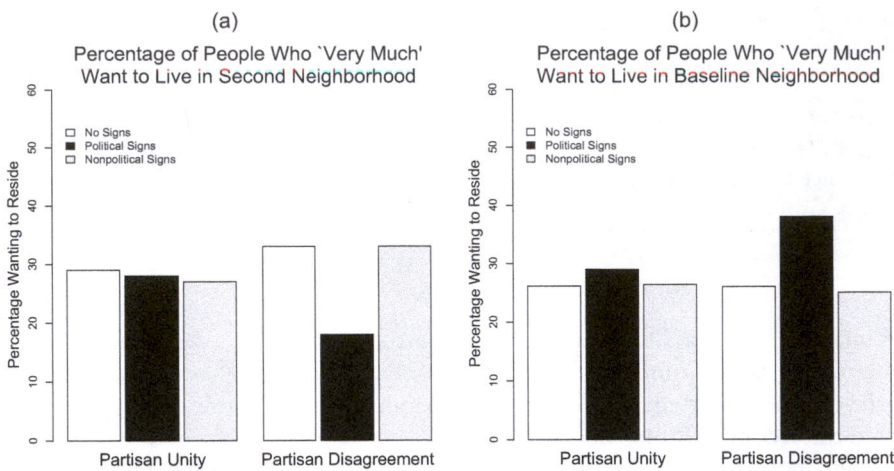

FIGURE 4.2. Treatment and Willingness to Live in Neighborhood.
This is the percentage of people who report that they "very much" want to live in the particular neighborhood. Differences are never significant by sign type for participants in the partisan unity conditions. In the partisan disagreement conditions, the ratings for the "partisan signs" neighborhood are significantly different from the ratings for the other neighborhoods at $p < 0.05$.

unity seemed relatively unconcerned about the extent to which their neighbors might be partisans (Figure 4.2a and 4.2b).

This was not so for those participants who had read about partisan disagreement. Although people are equally likely to report that they would "very much" want to live in the second neighborhood when it had no signs at all or had a nonpolitical yard sign, we see that people become significantly *less* likely to report that they would want to live in this neighborhood when it includes a home with a political sign. In fact, the addition of political yard signs produces an almost 15 percentage point decrease in the number of people who would "very much" want to live in the neighborhood.

These first two tests are about the physical qualities of the neighborhoods, but what about the people who live in these neighborhoods? We next investigate the extent to which the presence of political signs changes how our participants feel about neighborhood residents. The political signs should merely suggest that the residents of these neighborhoods were fulfilling their civic duty and taking part in the political process – something that we, in fact, encourage people to do. Our results point to the opposing effect: negative views of partisanship cast these signs of civic duty in a negative light.

With one final test, we asked our participants if they would rather attend a social event with residents of the baseline neighborhood or with residents of the second neighborhood. Now, this may be a difficult question. Our participants know nothing about the residents of these two neighborhoods. The photographs were chosen precisely because they betray almost no personal touches – no tricycles on the sidewalks, no basketball hoops, no lawn ornaments, and no cars. Indeed, the only people who see anything resembling a human touch are those assigned to conditions where the neighborhood has signs.

We first turn to the unity condition, where we see that people are generally ambivalent about the two neighborhoods. When the second neighborhood has no political signs, participants would rather spend time with residents of this second neighborhood than with those from the baseline neighborhood. Notably, when the second neighborhood *has* political signs, participants in the unity condition do lean toward the baseline neighborhood: 58 percent report that they would rather attend a social event with residents from the baseline neighborhood.

Participants who read about partisan disagreement also prefer the second neighborhood with no signs to the baseline neighborhood. When the second neighborhood has nonpolitical signs, 67 percent of participants in the disagreement condition report that they would rather spend time with residents from that second neighborhood. This is reasonable, given that the signs in the second neighborhood are for a graduation party – a fun social event.

The pattern changes when people who read about partisan disagreement compare the baseline neighborhood to a second neighborhood with political signs. In this case, only 37.5 percent of people report that they would be willing to attend a social event with people from the second neighborhood. This is a statistically significant decrease in preference from both the no-sign and the nonpolitical sign conditions. The combination of partisan disagreement and political signs leads our participants to overwhelmingly prefer the residents of the baseline neighborhood.[9,10]

We observe virtually identical patterns of results *across all partisan groups*. When Democrats read about partisan disagreement and then see a neighborhood with a political sign, only 33.3 percent want to attend a social event with residents from this neighborhood. Among self-identified Republicans this number is 38.5 percent. In contrast, more than 60 percent of both Democrats and Republicans want to spend time with residents of the second neighborhood when the signs in the neighborhood are not political.

When people are reminded of partisan disagreement, they grow weary of partisans. They not only want to avoid working with partisans; they even

[9] We see the inclusion of the political sign decrease preferences for the second neighborhood in the unity condition as well, though the lowest percentage of individuals prefer the second neighborhood when the political sign is combined with partisan disagreement. Nonetheless, the fact that the sheer inclusion of a political sign leads to a decline in preferences for the neighborhood is meaningful.

[10] We also consider preferences for neighborhoods by estimating a model that includes controls for individual demographics. The model leads to the same results as the test we present in this section, and we include the results of the model in the online appendix to Chapter 4.

visualize partisans through negative images. But the weariness does not end there. While scholars can continue to debate whether Democrats and Republicans prefer to cluster together geographically, we find that Americans may be more interested in avoiding both of the two political groups whenever possible. This is especially likely to be true when people hear about partisan disagreement, something that is difficult to avoid these days.

4.4 HEY, GOOD-LOOKING

The information about partisan disagreement that we provide in our previous two studies is subtle. We do not offer any normative arguments about the role of partisan disagreement in politics. The stories we present to people do not suggest that partisans are unpleasant. We do not suggest that partisans scream or yell or that they are in any way combative. In fact, we offer people relatively little information about partisan disagreement. We simply tell people that it exists. Yet, when people hear about partisan disagreement, they visualize partisanship negatively and are less enthusiastic about living in the same neighborhood as people who may be active partisans.

These results show a dislike of partisanship, but they do not track evaluations of *partisans*. Perhaps people are so cavalier in their negative perceptions of partisanship because our studies have removed the human element of being a member of a party. Maybe people would be more hesitant to express their discontent if we put a human face on partisanship. Our next step is, quite literally, to do just that.

4.4.1 This Is What a Partisan Looks Like

The standards by which we evaluate one another are strongly dictated by social norms. This becomes painfully evident when we flip through old photo albums and see the clothes and hairstyles that our parents or grandparents proudly sported decades ago. What were they thinking? Who would ever wear that? As norms of fashion evolve, so do our preferences. Similarly, one notices dramatic changes in standards of beauty while strolling through an art gallery. The body shapes and sizes that we consider to be attractive change drastically over time, resulting in ever-evolving expectations for what our actors and models should look like (Strahan et al. 2006). In short, the manner in which we evaluate the physical attractiveness of others is highly dependent on social norms of beauty.

In the final study of this chapter we leverage the social context of beauty and consider whether social norms extend to the way that Americans evaluate the *physical attractiveness* of people who they believe to be partisans and those who they believe to be independents. Of course, beauty is highly subjective. While in our previous study we could create a baseline using a neighborhood with no signs, it is more difficult to create a beauty baseline. We deal with this inherent subjectivity in our next study by showing participants images of faces that were specifically developed by a computer algorithm to possess objective levels of attractiveness.

The faces we use in our next study (Study 4.4) were developed using computer software FaceGen 3.1 by psychologists Nikolaas Oosterhof and Alexander Todorov (2009).[11] Using a computer algorithm, Oosterhof and Todorov created a database of faces that have validated ratings on scales such as attractiveness, competence, trustworthiness, and likability. This typology contains particular faces that are, for example, consistently perceived as highly likable and others that are consistently perceived as highly unlikable. Since we have measures of the general levels of attractiveness, competence, likability, and trustworthiness associated with these faces, we can track how additional information about the faces may change the way people judge them.

We assigned the 163 participants (demographics of sample in Table A1.4) of this next study to one of two groups: some participants read a mere mention of partisanship (the control group), while others read an article about partisan disagreement. We then asked our participants to rate and rank the attractiveness, likability, competence, and trustworthiness of people we identified as partisans and others we identified as political independents. Since we have a baseline of how these faces rank on all these categories, we can track the conditions that lead people to either overrate or underrate the appeal of these faces.

4.4.2 Who Is Attractive and Likable?

In our first test, we presented people with faces from the Oosterhof and Todorov typology. All of the faces fell at the median level of attractiveness, likability, competence, and trustworthiness. Along with the faces, we informed our study participants whether the face belonged to a Democrat, a Republican, or a political independent. The fact that there is nothing exceptional about these faces will allow us to isolate whether the (arbitrary) partisan labels we assigned to these people matter in how our participants view them. Later, we will also consider whether the specific partisan label matters.

To measure how people evaluated these faces we first asked people to rate the faces on each key characteristic.[12] We rely on the same scales that Oosterhof and Todorov use, where 1 means that a face is low on that attribute and 9 means that it is high. These faces had all been previously shown to be at the median on the scales so we can expect very few ratings at either extreme point. For ease of

---

[11] We include more information about the faces in the online appendix to this chapter. All faces come from a database provided by Alexander Todorov and the Social Perception Lab.

[12] Although people rated Democrats and Republicans separately, we merge the measure to obtain an overall partisan score in the first analysis. In the second analysis, we will consider how people rate faces of their own party. We compare the percentage of people who placed the face in the lowest third of the attractiveness, trustworthiness, competence, and likability measures.

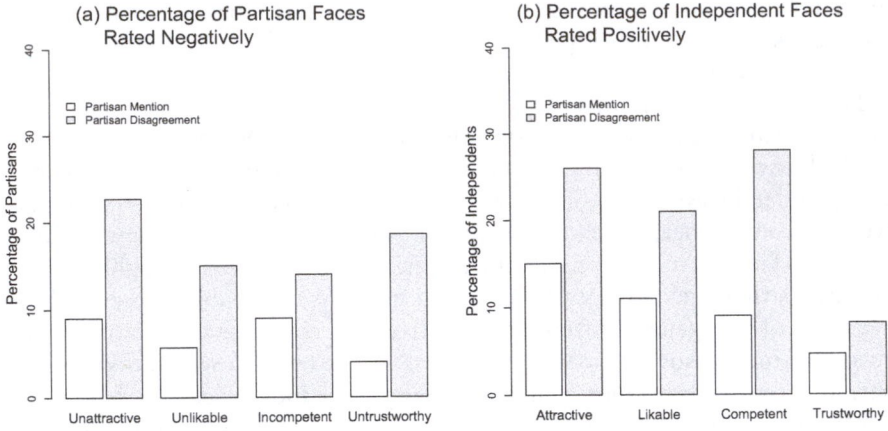

FIGURE 4.3. Ratings of Partisan and Independent Faces.
This is the percentage of people who placed either the partisans into the two lowest categories of ratings on each attribute or the independents into the two highest ratings on each attribute. Differences are significant at p < 0.05 for ratings of partisan faces on attractiveness, likability, and trustworthiness and they are significant at p < 0.1 for competence. Differences are significant at p < 0.05 for independent faces for attractiveness, likability, and competence; ratings do not reach significance for independent faces on trustworthiness.

discussion we present our results as the percentages of people who rate a given face in the lowest or highest three points of the scale. If our participants are rating the faces in accordance with the Oosterhof and Todorov scores, these percentages should be quite low, as most should rate them somewhere in the middle.

When we consider how our participants rate the faces of people they believe to be partisans, we see that 10 percent of participants in the control condition reported that the partisan face they saw was unattractive. This low percentage is to be expected, given that this face is at the median level of attractiveness. These evaluations change for individuals who were asked to judge the same face after reading about partisan disagreement. Among these participants, 22 percent judged *the very same face* to be highly unattractive. The very same average-looking partisan became uglier simply because people were reminded that the two parties disagree.

We see similar, statistically significant patterns for the remaining characteristics: likability, trustworthiness, and competence (Figure 4.3). While 4 percent of participants in the neutral condition judge the partisan face to be untrustworthy, nearly 20 percent of people believe that the very same face is untrustworthy in the partisan disagreement condition (Figure 4.3a). Again, these faces are at the median on all characteristics, yet simply reading that the parties disagree leads people to judge them distinctly more negatively. In this case, however, this negativity means that participants actually come to believe that these faces belong to worse people.

These results are not restricted to those participants who identified themselves as independent at the very beginning of the study. Even among people who themselves identify as Democrats and Republicans, information about partisan disagreement increases the number of participants who assign negative ratings to partisan faces. In the control condition, only 2 percent of all partisan participants rated our partisan face as unlikable. In contrast, 18 percent of partisan participants in the treatment group reported that the very same partisan face was highly unlikable. None of our partisan participants rated the partisan face as untrustworthy in the control condition, but approximately 25 percent rated the very same face as untrustworthy after hearing about partisan disagreement. That is to say, even Democrats and Republicans find partisans to be unattractive.

We next turn to attractiveness ratings of the faces we labeled as independent. Recall that the faces we use in this study were computer generated by FaceGen and have all been shown to be equivalent on attractiveness, likability, trustworthiness, and competence. Yet, nonetheless, we find that *all* of our participants rated independents as significantly *more* likable and attractive after reading about partisan disagreement. For example, 4 percent of participants in the control group rated the independent face as highly competent, but 28 percent of those in the treatment group rated the same face as highly competent. We see the smallest effect on trustworthiness ratings, but we should note that the number of independents viewed as trustworthy still *increases* after respondents read the article about partisan disagreement (Figure 4.3b). Again, this is not a function of self-proclaimed independent participants over-rating the attractiveness of the independent face. Among people who reported that they are partisans, we still see similar increases in positivity toward the independent. Only 7 percent of partisans report that the independent face is highly competent in the control condition. This number jumps to 20 percent among those who read about partisan disagreement.

When people were reminded of partisan disagreement they rated faces that were similar in every way as more attractive, more competent, more trustworthy, and more likable simply because these faces belonged to an independent. This is a notable result given that we rely on faces that are computer-generated and similar on each of these dimensions. Indeed, the fact that so few people place these faces at the extreme ends of the scale in the control condition speaks to the fact that there is nothing exceptional about them. Yet, a combination of the partisan label and partisan disagreement leads people to either underrate or overrate the attractiveness of faces designed to be average. In particular, people systematically underrate the attractiveness of partisans. Even when we put a human face on it, people seem to have little patience for partisanship.

We also considered how partisanship affects one's perceived attractiveness in another way. Using a database of faces, we selected five: two faces were computer designed to be high on attractiveness, two were low on attractiveness, and one was at the median. We then asked our respondents to categorize the faces: which faces did they think looked like partisans and which looked like independents? More importantly, did exposure to partisan disagreement affect how individuals categorized these faces?

Our results show that reading about partisan disagreement decreased the percentage of people who classify the two most attractive faces as attractive and partisan by about 25 percentage points (a statistically significant difference). The faces were identical across conditions, but simply reading about partisan disagreement led participants to believe that partisans could not possibly be this attractive.

We see a nearly identical pattern when we present our participants with five faces that the FaceGen algorithm generated on trustworthiness. Of these five faces, two were rated high in perceived trustworthiness, two were low, and one was at the median. Partisan disagreement decreased the tendency to categorize the faces highest in trustworthiness as partisan by about 28 percentage points. When the context is partisan disagreement, the majority of people believe the most trustworthy faces belong to independents.

As a final step we address an alternative explanation of our findings. Since we combine Democrats and Republicans to form our partisan faces, it is possible that the lower ratings stem from the fact that people assign low scores to members of the opposing party but assign consistently high ratings to faces from their own party. To address this idea, we ask a simple question: do people even judge members of their *own parties* more negatively than independents?

Here we focus on people who were willing to report a partisan identity. When reminded of partisan disagreement, 30 percent of partisans judge members of their own party to be unattractive; but only 20 percent say that independents are unattractive. Similarly, 30 percent of partisans say that faces labeled with their own party appear unlikable, but only 15 percent say that faces labeled as independents are unlikable. Thirty-five percent of partisans view co-partisan faces as incompetent and untrustworthy; only 25 percent view independents as incompetent, and 20 percent view independents as untrustworthy.

This is not to argue that when faced with partisan disagreement all participants begin to downgrade their parties. Certainly, there are some strong partisans who behave as previous literature would suggest and appear to deliberately cling closer to their party when reminded of partisan disagreement. Rather, we want to suggest that for many people, partisan disagreement diminishes partisanship, and leads them to perceive independents more positively.

These results could be reason for optimism for those seeking to meet new people. If you want to be seen as more attractive or more likable, you need not change a single thing about your appearance. Rather, you can wait until the two parties are locked in a particularly public battle (to make sure the media have spread the disagreement cue far and wide) and subsequently identify yourself as an independent. In contrast, if your goal is to block unwanted attention, then tell people you're a partisan.

Of course, political parties themselves are also seeking to "meet new people," so to speak. For parties, however, our results are a reason for pessimism. The more the parties engage in debate – which is, essentially, what the two parties must do on a nearly daily basis in the American political context – the more they turn people away. This effect is so strong that identifying as a political partisan can decrease the degree to which Americans find a person physically attractive. Telling people that a perfect stranger is a partisan leads them to believe that stranger is untrustworthy, unlikable, incompetent, and ugly.

4.5 DIRTY ROTTEN SCOUNDRELS

We began this chapter with a quote by famed American novelist Ray Bradbury. "I don't like either political party," he says, "Anyone that belongs to a party stops thinking." Bradbury's distrust of "majority-held" views was a theme that ran through his writing following the Cold War – disdain for the popular political credo was highlighted in such work as *Fahrenheit 451* and *The Martian Chronicles* (Hoskinson 2001, p. 127). Indeed, Bradbury's half-century-old work is highlighted by the "theme of distrust for the majority-endorsed view" (Hoskinson 2001 p. 128).

In contemporary times, this same distrust is increasingly evident in the way Americans view both parties that dominate the political landscape. Political scientists John R. Hibbing and Elizabeth Theiss-Morse (2002) have argued that close to half of all Americans believe that government would be better run by unelected independent experts, rather than parties or politicians. They refer to this model of governance as "stealth democracy"; one in which individuals need to be as disengaged from democratic politics as possible. Our findings support the disdain for partisan politics that Hibbing and Theiss-Morse put forth. Moreover, we show that this distrust extends to all partisans, and, as we will explain, this has deep-seeded attitudinal and behavioral consequences. In the first half of our book, we present support for our key hypothesis: political independence is socially desirable. Yet the desirability of independence is made even more powerful by the undesirability of partisanship. Regardless of whether you distrust partisans for philosophical reasons, like Bradbury, or you simply want to make a positive impression, being a partisan is a net negative.

Scholars before us focused on evidence of a growing social distance between Democrats and Republicans. We turn our attention to an additional – and potentially even more troubling – pattern in politics. Identifying with any party is highly off-putting to the American public. Americans do not want to spend time with partisans; they do not want to live near them; they think of them as negative and angry; and they find them personally unlikable and untrustworthy. Moreover, people are more likely to respond this way when they are reminded of partisan disagreement – a tendency that is as natural for parties as breathing is for people.

If partisans are ugly, what does this mean for *politics*? In the next chapters, we zero in on how the patterns we observe in this and the previous chapter affect political participation. Up until this point, our dependent variables have focused on individuals' *perceptions* of independents and of partisans. Next our focus turns to political behavior, and because self-monitoring is critical to connecting people's perceptions of partisanship to their actions, we again return to self-monitoring. In Chapter 5, we introduce a series of behavioral measures that allow us to investigate how people's feelings about independents and partisans are reshaping the way they engage with American representative democracy.

5

Partisanship and Political Participation

"Save America, Vote Independent"

– bumper sticker

One pundit who does not share the media's fascination with – and some might say glorification of – independents is *New York Times* columnist and noted curmudgeon Stanley Fish. In a 2008 column entitled "Against Independent Voters," Fish produced a 1,131-word battle cry in support of the American political party.[1] "What do independent voters do?" Fish asked, "Well, most of all, they talk about the virtue of being an independent voter." Fish indicted the independent for providing a lot of sanctimonious talk with no meaningful action. Far from working to promote a better political outcome, according to Fish, independents merely obsess over the ways in which they are above the fray. "I can't stand the partisan atmosphere that has infected our politics," Fish's fictitious independent laments.

Fish's argument, facetious as it may be, does raise an important question: what *do* independents do? Political scientists have long suggested that, at the very least, independents cast votes, largely for the same party, election after election – that is, independents who vote Democratic usually do so consistently and independents who vote Republican can be counted on to continue to vote for Republicans. It is this pattern that leads many researchers to conclude that independents are largely politically inconsequential (see, for example, Keith et al. 1992). We suggest that this focus on the ballot box not only is narrow but also has limited our understanding of why people hide their partisan identities and what undercover partisans mean for American politics.

In this chapter, we challenge existing evaluations of how undercover partisans participate in politics by shifting the question: What *don't* independents

[1] Stanley Fish (January 20, 2008). "Against Independent Voters." *New York Times*.

do? We already know that, for one, these people do not immediately tell researchers which party they support. More importantly, however, they may also be hesitant to share this information with their family members, friends, coworkers, and neighbors. This latter point is distinctly more consequential because politics is inherently social.

Midway through the twentieth century, Paul Lazarsfeld and his colleagues at Columbia University highlighted a crucial factor in how individuals form preferences during a political campaign: "the two-step flow of communication" (Lazarsfeld et al. 1948), by which political information travels from elites to voters and then outward to their friends and family. This influential concept effectively did away with "the image of the audience as a mass of disconnected individuals hooked up to the media but not to each other" (Katz 1957) and recognized the crucial role that political discussions among ordinary voters play in spreading ideas and persuading Americans to engage in politics. The very foundation of grassroots party politics depends on the two-step flow of communication: people sharing their partisan preferences and diffusing partisan messages across vast social networks. In what follows, we uncover a crack in this foundation. Motivated by a need to make a positive impression in the face of partisan disagreement, people shy away from undertaking social political actions that outwardly display their partisan preferences.

5.1 THE MYSTERIOUS DISAPPEARANCE OF PARTISAN BUMPER STICKERS

In 1996 James Banning, a professor of education, decided to examine the types of bumper stickers that college students and staff placed on their cars. Banning was not interested in politics – his goal was to categorize the cultures and subcultures present on the campus of what he described as a "large university…in the Rocky Mountain region with a student population in the range of 20,000 to 25,000" (Banning 1996, p. 30).[2] Banning viewed bumper stickers as "cultural artifacts," noting that they allowed people to express themselves and share an unspoken bond with others.

Over several weeks, Banning and his team of researchers engaged in an ethnographic study. The researchers would routinely visit campus parking lots, noting the numbers of cars with bumper stickers and writing down the messages of the bumper stickers verbatim. Banning found that the practice of displaying stickers was fairly widespread – about 1,800 cars (approximately half of all the cars on campus) had some type of sticker.

Banning noticed several bumper sticker trends. First, many of the stickers displayed what he called "pride in the local institution" – for example, stickers

---

[2] Although Banning never states so in his article, at the time of the article's publication he was a professor at Colorado State University – a location that can easily be described as a "large university campus" in the "Rocky Mountain region."

bearing the driver's alma mater or employer. Banning also found a number of bumper stickers displaying the driver's affiliation to a particular group or organization. Many of the drivers, he noted, displayed their commitment to "outdoor adventure," a trend Banning believed to be a function of the university's geographic location.

Yet within this vibrant bumper sticker culture, Banning noticed a surprising omission. Despite the fact that Banning conducted his ethnography during an election year, he saw comparatively few stickers devoted to political candidates or parties. While Banning was not a political scientist nor was his study conducted for political purposes, the absence of political stickers was difficult to ignore. Banning concluded that the absence of partisan stickers signified "apathy toward the political processes associated with government" (p. 14), but his data suggest something even more unusual. Among the some 1,800 cars with bumper stickers, Banning saw numerous displays of the drivers' commitment to various political *causes*: Save the Environment! Animal Rights! World Peace! Keep Abortion Legal! In fact, he noted that the different types of bumper stickers suggested that, "differences in opinion are being held on important issues." The sheer prevalence of these types of bumper stickers led Banning to conclude that, "these might be the issues that would attract and involve students in important debates." What he found, then, is not an absence of *political* stickers but rather an absence of stickers clearly displaying *partisanship*.

In this chapter we investigate why people are unwilling to display their partisanship even when they are perfectly willing to display their opinions on issues. But first, we must explain what makes actions like displaying bumper stickers so important for politics. To begin, we will place the simple bumper sticker into the broader context of political engagement.

5.2 SOCIAL POLITICAL ACTION

Americans communicate with government through their political actions. At the very least, a representative democracy depends on its citizens to turn out and vote. An even more healthy representative democracy depends on citizens taking numerous other participatory actions. Verba, Schlozman, and Brady (1995) note that there is a "wide range of activities beyond the vote," activities that have an indirect effect on elections but nonetheless play a potentially more important role in shifting political outcomes. Among these are *social* political actions.

Social political actions send direct messages not only to politicians but more importantly, to other voters. As a result, these actions can have powerful effects on the preferences of others. Research on social networks, for example, has uncovered the power of simple political discussions among peers (Ahn et al. 2013; Jackman and Sniderman 2006, Lupia and McCubbins 1998; Rolfe 2012; Ryan 2013; Sinclair 2012). Similarly, scholars have also suggested that actions such as displaying political yard signs, pins, and, yes, even bumper stickers carry a good deal of political weight (Makse and Sokhey 2014; Huckfeldt and Sprague 1992, 1995; Laband et al. 2009). Over the past several years these social political actions have increasingly moved online. As we discuss in Chapter 2, social media platforms such as Facebook and Twitter make it remarkably simple to share political preferences with huge groups of people. People can use these platforms not only to discuss their political opinions with others but also to display virtual "signs" and "stickers" signifying their political preferences (Fowler and Hagar 2013).

Speaking across disciplines, political scientists are of the same mind as Banning: these types of social signifiers, be they bumper stickers, Twitter messages, or campaign buttons, are crucial forms of expression and carry an important social weight. Political operatives agree that candidates depend on ordinary people making their political preferences accessible to their friends, family, neighbors, and just about anyone else they might meet. This reliance on social political actions is often called the "ground game" (Monson 2004), and, as both political scientists and politicians have argued, it can be pivotal for political outcomes. Focusing on field offices as evidence of ground game, Masket (2009) suggests that Obama's ground game efforts played a key role in securing several key counties for the Democrats (see also Darr and Levendusky 2014).[3] In election coverage in *The New York Times*, Ohio Governor Ted Strickland (who lost his bid for reelection) explains: "In a close race that's going to be decided by a handful of points, I think the ground game can absolutely make the difference."[4] In fact, *The New York Times* credited President Barack Obama's 2012 victory to the social political actions of his supporters. According to reports, Obama's campaign invested hundreds of millions of dollars in its "ground game" with the intent of motivating volunteers to reach out to their personal contacts (Enos and Hersh 2015).

Certainly parties would like to receive votes and donations, but they also depend on an army of citizens engaging in the "ground game" through various types of social political actions. Both the Democratic National Committee (DNC) and the Republican National Committee (RNC) encourage people to share their messages via Facebook and Twitter. A section of the DNC webpage, for example, is specifically devoted to brief articles and sound-bites that people can share with their social networks using a single click of the mouse.[5] Not to be out-done, the GOP webpage encouraged individuals to participate in

---

[3] Although, as John Sides argues in the political science blog The Monkey Cage, the effects of these field offices gave Obama fewer votes than his actual margin of victory. See post "How Much Did the 2012 Air War and Ground Game Matter?" (May 8, 2013), www.monkeycage.org.

[4] Jackie Calmes (June 26, 2012). "Obama Campaign Banks on High-Tech Ground Game to Reach Votes." *New York Times*.

[5] This section encourages people to become "Factivists," as of September 2015 the section contained the following message: "With the tools you'll get here, you'll be able to push back against Republican misinformation and defend our Democratic brand." (factivists.dnc.org/about)

"Victory 365" – a program that encouraged party members to "grow our party and win elections" by taking part in ground game activities.

The parties stress ground game for good reason: through large field experiments, personal citizen-to-citizen communication has been shown to have a powerful effect on political choices and actions (Green and Gerber 2008). Recent research suggests that other types of citizen messaging matter as well. Parties train their candidates to distribute campaign signs to willing citizens (Panagopoulos 2009) and carefully plan where these signs might be most effective (Faucheux 2003; Shaw 2004; Shea and Burton 2006). Parties, as Makse and Sokhey (2014) write, depend on the "organic diffusion" of various symbols of support. In turn, research shows that taking part in these social activities actually boosts other types of participation (McClendon 2014; Settle et al. forthcoming).

Adding to their importance is the relative "cheapness" of these actions. While contributing to a Political Action Committee (PAC) or volunteering with a campaign may limit participation by requiring investments of money or time, these more social acts are virtually free on both dimensions. To the extent that Verba et al. (1995) worry about "participation distortion" – or the idea that only some people have the resources to participate in politics – these social forms of participation are inherently equalizing.

Two critical conditions underlie these types of political actions. The first condition is a greater outward display of partisanship than more "traditional" or, as Huckfeldt and Sprague (1995) describe them, "individual" forms of participation. If a person wants to hide his political preferences, he can ensure that his vote or campaign donation remains anonymous. A person's friends and family will only learn that she sent a letter to a politician if she willingly shares the information herself. Not so with more social forms of participation. Discussing politics with others stands to make one's political affiliations crystal clear. Similarly, a sign, button, sticker, or Facebook status displays the person's political opinion to anyone within a certain social radius.

The second condition is that these social political actions are most effective if they include a clear indication of the individual's political leanings. It is certainly possible to advocate for an issue without invoking a party or to take a position without realizing that it is the position of a party. Yet, often advocating for an issue involves selecting a particular side, which can lead others to make inferences about the speaker's partisan leanings. Furthermore, people are at their most persuasive when they are clear about their political preferences (Huckfeldt et al. 2004). Otherwise, the persuasive effect of social actions weakens considerably.

In this chapter we will focus on these types of social political actions. As we argue in Chapter 2, when partisans go undercover, there are two factors at play. The first is a willingness to shift one's behavior in order to make the most positive impression possible on others – a factor that, as we have shown, can be weaker or stronger depending on the person. The second is the information about partisanship that people receive. The information most likely to shift one's behavior toward going undercover, we suggest, is that which reminds people of partisan bickering and partisan disagreement. As we show in Chapter 3, these forces make identifying as an independent seem more socially beneficial. Moreover, as we show in Chapter 4, partisan disagreement leaves individuals repulsed (even in a physical sense) by partisanship. Yet expressions of partisanship are much broader than picking a certain partisan category or reporting that you dislike another person. Rather, social political actions offer the strongest expressions of partisanship and play the most critical role in grassroots politics. In this chapter we will show what happens when the social value of being independent and the social stigma of partisanship collide while political action is on the line.

Over the course of three unique studies, we will track different social political actions: displays of partisan preferences in a social network, displays of partisan stickers and signs, partisan discussion, and visits to partisan websites. Because these are actions that require a clear display of partisanship, they will allow us the most direct means of observing the consequences of going undercover. Moreover, the studies that follow are unlike many previous experiments that simply ask people what action they might take in a hypothetical scenario. In these studies we will watch people take *real* political actions. We will see what people choose to reveal and what they choose to conceal on social media profile pages. We will take to the streets to see when people display and when they hide partisan stickers. In all studies we analyze our data using both simple group comparisons as well as more complicated selection models.[6] In the end we will offer a sobering conclusion: the same forces that lead individuals to go undercover when answering a simple question about their partisanship also lead them away from meaningful social political actions.

5.3 YOU ARE YOUR SOCIAL MEDIA PROFILE

In October of 2012, the social media website Facebook announced that it had reached a record that had previously seemed unfathomable: 1 *billion* active users. While Facebook is by far the leading social media website, Twitter – a website that allows users to share thoughts and ideas in 140 characters or fewer – currently boasts 271 million active users. These types of websites, argues Cornell University communication professor Jeff Hancock, stand to "affect almost all facets of human life," and are a means of "seeing how influential some people can be."[7]

According to a 2013 survey conducted by the Pew Research Center, 72 percent of all Americans use social networking sites like Facebook and Twitter.

---

[6] All selection models are in the online appendix to this chapter.
[7] October 5, 2012. "Facebook and Twitter Are Rewriting the World We've Always Lived In" *Science Daily*. Cornell University Release.

While the diversity of Facebook and Twitter participants is growing, the greatest concentration of social network users falls between the ages of 18 and 29. Among this particular demographic group, 83 percent participate in online social networks. What's more, Pew and the American Life Project report that 40 percent of social network users engage in political activity while on these websites. "The platform is more than social," wrote *The Atlantic*'s Rebecca Rosen of Facebook, "it's political."[8] Indeed, people use social media not only to obtain news about political campaigns but to share their political views with others, as well as to mobilize and persuade their peers (Smith and Rainie 2008; Zhang et al. 2010, p. 75).

Facebook and Twitter politics are, in many ways, contagious. People are more likely to take political actions if their "friends" on social networks post about their own political activities (Bond et al. 2012). Politicians have come to depend on this contagion effect. In 2012, for example, Facebook staffers even advised political candidates to post most content between the hours of 9 and 10 AM on a weekday – the time when Facebook users were most likely to check their newsfeeds and share posts with their friends.[9] Social media has become a critical tool in American politics – one that most politicians can no longer do without.

The political power of social media lies in the willingness of its members to express their opinions. When Facebook users state their partisan preference or announce the candidate they like best, they are making their political ideas known to at least their own network but also potentially to the world. Indeed, when a power Facebook user writes a post, he has the power to reach nearly 150,000 other people via the network.[10] If politics make individuals reticent to express their partisan preferences, then these tools will become less effective. To investigate the degree to which negative political coverage pushes partisans undercover on social media, we recruited a group of individuals – social media veterans – to participate in a new social networking website (Study 5.1). Then, we simply observed how changes in political context affected the types of information these people were willing to share with their "friends."

5.3.1 Creating a Social Network

The lifecycle of a social networking website begins when people decide to join the network and create their own profiles. Social media profiles form the

---

[8] Rebecca Rosen (February 3, 2012). "The Most Surprising Thing About How People Use Facebook." *The Atlantic*.

[9] Facebook Politics and Government Team (August 1, 2012). "Less than 100 Days until Election, Facebook Offers Tips for Campaigns." *Facebook.com*.

[10] This takes account of average numbers of "friends" and "friends of friends" and assumes that the user does not hide his content from friends of friends. Based on Pew 2012 Facebook use report.

identities that participants wish to convey to their networked connections. Regardless of how mundane one's day-to-day life might actually be, his social media profile might nonetheless portray a globetrotting foodie, a popular socialite, or a political activist. Psychologist Craig Malkin has researched the creation of social media profiles and noted, during an interview with National Public Radio, that "when people go on to Facebook they're often crafting a persona – they're portraying themselves at their happiest. They're often choosing events that feel best to them and they're leaving out other things." This phenomenon is, of course, not unique to social media. Psychologist Steven Cooper adds that "when deciding what shirt we're going to put on, or jacket, or dress, whether we're going to wear makeup, all these things, we're always cultivating postures." Cooper agrees, though, that social media takes this type of behavior to a whole new level. With over 1 billion people employing social media around the globe, Cooper says, the opportunity to "cover up and cultivate [our] images and personas" has "broadened."[11]

Our goal in this study is to examine how political conditions affect the way individuals present themselves to others on social media. We thus must begin our study *before* an individual has already created her social media identity. This provided a challenge: we needed to construct a brand new social network that individuals had not already joined. We programmed this network in the fall of 2013 and shortly thereafter invited a group of people to join (Study 5.1).

The invitees were limited to adults aged 18 to 23 so as to increase the likelihood that they already had prior experience with social media websites (sample demographics in Table A1.5). The invitees were all students at the same university, which reinforced to them that they would be forming a network of acquaintances, not simply strangers. The majority of Facebook users over the age of 18 have more than 100 "friends" in their network. People, however, only have limited levels of time and attention for social interactions and as a result maintain smaller circles of close friends (between five and eight people) within these much larger networks (Saramäki et al. 2014). We can expect a similar pattern among our invitees. Most of them had a smaller circle of closer friends within the university, a slightly larger circle of acquaintances, and a more vague attachment to the remainder of their classmates.[12]

Each participant received an email invitation to join a new social network that would allow them to discuss "current events" with their networked connections. Each email invitation was identical, with one notable exception. We randomly assigned the participants into one of two groups. We sent each group

[11] Andrea Shea (February 20, 2013). "Facebook Envy: How the Social Network Affects Our Self-Esteem." WBUR.org (NPR affiliate, Boston, MA).

[12] Since we deliberately invited these particular people based on their virtual network experience and their real network connections, our invitees are not necessarily representative of the American public. They are, however, representative of the types of people who are the most avid social media users. We include a more detailed description of our social network sample in the samples appendix.

a different article to serve as an example of something that might be discussed on the network. Some invitees saw an article that discussed partisan unity, while the rest saw an article that discussed partisan disagreement.

After reading the invitation and the example article, our participants determined whether they wanted to join the social network. If they were interested in joining, they were directed to a webpage that allowed them to complete their "profile page." Knowing that others would see the information they shared, participants could customize their profiles according to their preferences, sharing as little or as much as they wanted. Regardless of whether subjects chose to join the network (and complete the profile) or not, every invitee was asked to complete a separate survey.

5.3.2 Who Makes Politics Public?

As we explained in Chapter 2, partisans go "undercover" because they believe there is something negative about partisan politics and they want to make the best impression possible by disassociating themselves from it. In our study, we exposed participants to partisan negativity by mentioning partisan disagreement in the example article included in their invitation. Then, in our survey, we measured their concern about making a positive impression and the willingness to change behavior to do so through the *self-monitoring* scale. As the reader will recall, high self-monitors are more likely to adjust their expressed attitudes and behaviors to accommodate social norms, while low self-monitors, in contrast, are more willing to express their true beliefs regardless of the social consequences.[13]

Another important note here is that our study has two steps: joining the network and providing information. It is, of course, possible that the two steps are not independent – people who join the network may be different from those who do not, which may in turn affect the information they share. As a result, we analyze our data in two ways. In the text we present simple group-level comparisons at both stages and in the web appendix we present a model that directly accounts for the possible selection effects in this study. Importantly, both results lead to the same conclusions about the relationship between self-monitoring, exposure to disagreement, and the willingness to express partisanship.

We see that the article has no effect on the chance that a low self-monitor will join the social network. High self-monitors, however, are more susceptible to our manipulation. When high self-monitors read an article about partisan

---

[13] The measure creates a scale that can be split down the middle, with those in the upper range categorized as high self-monitors and remaining half categorized as low self-monitors. It is notable that these are not unusual types of people; most people can be classified as either high or low self-monitors. In fact, both types of people are prevalent enough to affect aggregate political outcomes on issues that are susceptible to social desirability, such as racial policies (Weber et al. 2014). Scale is shown in the online appendix to this chapter.

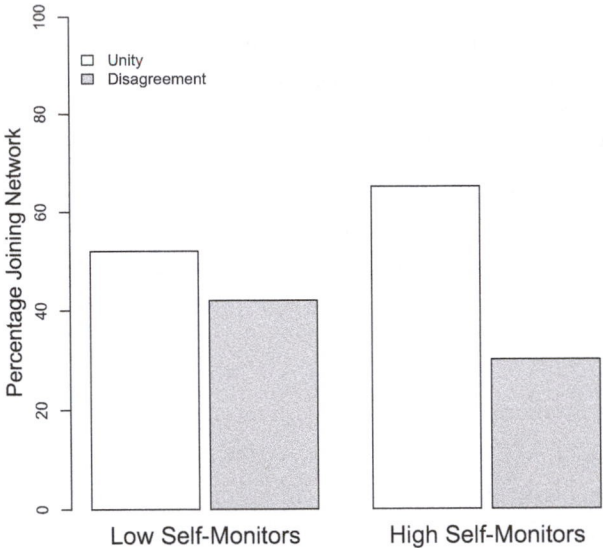

FIGURE 5.1. Effect of Disagreement Invitation on Joining Social Network.
This is the percentage of individuals by group who want to join the social network. High self-monitoring individuals who received the disagreement invitation are significantly less likely to join the network than other groups (p < 0.05).

disagreement they become significantly less willing to join the network. The need to make a positive impression intersects with information about partisan disagreement, and people subsequently amend their social political actions.

For those who *did* agree to join the social network, we still see an important distinction between high and low self-monitors. For those who care to make a good impression (i.e., high self-monitors), exposure to partisan disagreement changes the type of personal information they are willing to share.

All participants had the option to reveal two pieces of political information about themselves on their profile pages: their partisanship and their candidate preference in the recent presidential election. Participants were free to choose whether they would reveal this information to their connections or conceal it. In Figure 5.2a, we display the percentage of high and low self-monitors who chose to conceal their partisanship, and in Figure 5.2b we display the percentage of high and low self-monitors who chose to conceal their candidate preference.

For low self-monitors (left side of Figure 5.2a), the likelihood of concealing partisanship was not affected by reading about partisan unity (illustrated in the white bars) nor by reading about partisan disagreement (illustrated in the gray bars). Regardless of the article they read, slightly less than 40 percent of low self-monitors decided to conceal their partisanship from their profile page. For high self-monitors (right side of Figure 5.2a), the article they read had a large effect on their behavior. For those who read the partisan unity article,

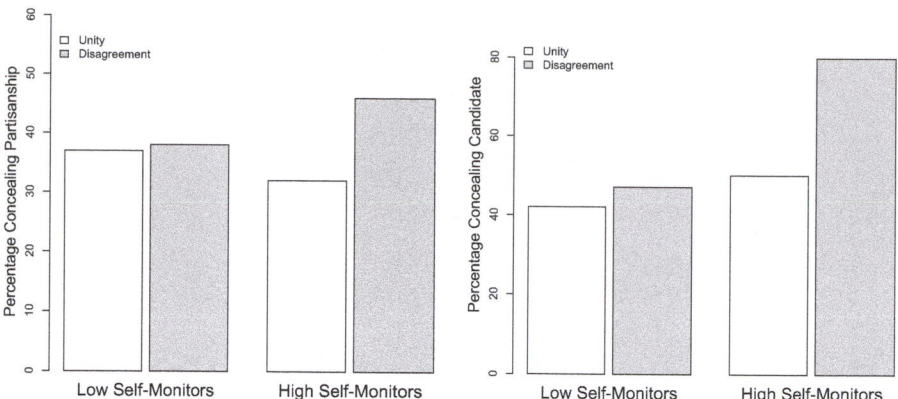

FIGURE 5.2. Effect of Disagreement Invitation on Mentions of Partisanship and Candidates Figure 5.2a: Concealing Partisanship Figure 5.2b: Concealing Candidates.
The results display the percentage of network members concealing their partisan identities. The difference between high-self monitors in the disagreement groups and the remaining groups is statistically significant at $p < 0.05$ for candidates, $p < 0.1$ for partisanship.

approximately 30 percent concealed their partisanship from public view. For those who read the partisan disagreement article, nearly 50 percent decided not to include their partisanship.

We see a similar pattern when we look at the decision to reveal candidate preference. Low self-monitors were unaffected by the invitation when deciding whether or not to reveal their preferred political candidate (left side of Figure 5.2b). Regardless of invitation type, only about 40 percent conceal their preference from their contacts.

For high self-monitors, on the other hand, the article to which they were exposed had an even stronger effect on their willingness to reveal this highly partisan piece of information. Concerned with the impressions they might make on others, about half of high self-monitors who read about partisan unity hid their candidate preference; while roughly 80 percent of high self-monitors who read about partisan disagreement requested that their candidate preference not be included on their profile page.

If these participants were reticent to display their political preferences, it was *not* due to the fact that they lacked political opinions. As we learned through a separate survey with our participants, the participants held clear preferences among candidates and among policy positions in general. Receiving an invitation that mentioned partisan disagreement did not change their political positions – it simply changed their willingness to display these publicly.

Moreover, the article that the participants read affected only the types of *partisan* information that they were willing to reveal in their profiles. When we examine other aspects of their profile pages, it is clear that the partisan cue had

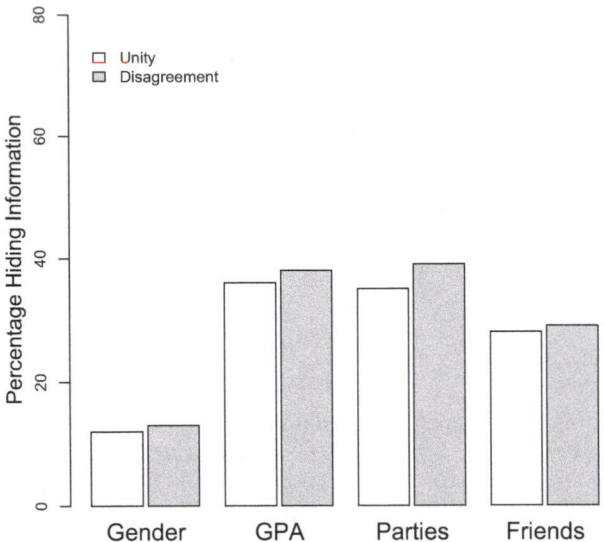

FIGURE 5.3. Effect of Disagreement Invitation on Nonpolitical Information. *This is the percentage of high self-monitors who opted to conceal nonpolitical infor-mation about themselves. None of the differences between the groups that received the unity and disagreement information reach statistical significance.*

no effect on people's willingness (or unwillingness) to reveal any other type of information. High self-monitors who received the partisan disagreement invi-tation and those who received the partisan unity invitation were equally likely to display their gender, their grade point average (GPA), the number of close friends they have, and the frequency with which they attend parties (Figure 5.3). Concerns about making a positive impression produced a profoundly political effect. Reinforcing this result, we also estimate a multivariate model that relies on a two-stage approach, estimating the chance of displaying information con-ditional on joining the network in the first place (results in the online appendix to this chapter).[14]

In sum, we find that when individuals who are willing to change their behavior to make the most positive impression on others (those higher in

---

[14] This particular study involves a two-stage process: first, people choose to join the network, and, second, they customize their profiles. We also estimate a multivariate model that first predicts whether a person joins the network and second predicts the type of information a person dis-played *conditional on the likelihood of joining in the first place.* Although the most direct way to observe experimental results is to simply compare group rates, this multivariate approach helps us to eliminate any potential alternative explanations. This more complicated estimation technique leads us to exactly the same place: a need to make a positive impression and partisan disagreement encouraged people to hide their partisan preferences from their social networks. We include the full results of our estimation process in the online appendix to this chapter (Tables A5.1, A5.2).

self-monitoring) encounter information about partisan disagreement, they avoid behaving in such a way that might betray them as partisans.[15] Political parties depend on the "organic diffusion" of their ideas across individuals (Makse and Sokhey 2014). In attempts to diffuse support throughout networks, parties and candidates have increasingly turned to social media. Our study raises a cautionary note: people's need to make a positive impression will trump their allegiance to their party. Individuals who possess political preferences and the platform to express them may nonetheless abstain. Parties must also convince the public that revealing these preferences is socially beneficial.

5.4 PARTISAN STICKERS REVISITED

The online social network is a relatively modern form of political participation. Though it has been gaining ground over the last decade, it has not traditionally been defined as a form of civic engagement. While a large and growing segment of people incorporate the Internet into political discussions and debates, there nonetheless remains a variety of more conventional ways to get involved in the political arena. We therefore return to one of the most classic expressions of partisanship, which we mentioned earlier in this chapter: stickers.

In 1979, well before James Banning tracked the number of cars with bumper stickers and proclaimed the student body to be politically apathetic, political scientists Paul Beck and Kent Jennings noted in the discipline's flagship journal, *The American Political Science Review*, that displaying campaign stickers and buttons was a crucial component of political behavior. "These behaviors," Beck and Jennings wrote, "are directed towards influencing elections, central institutions of conventional democratic politics" (1979, p. 740).

In the four decades since Beck and Jennings made their claim, stickers and buttons have not lost their influence. Writing about social political communication, Huckfeldt and Sprague (1995) note that yard signs and bumper stickers inform passersby of the prevailing political beliefs in a neighborhood. As a result, the authors define buttons and stickers as a highly social – and socially important – type of political participation. Taking this a step further, Keeter et al. (2002) connect the display of stickers and buttons to the overall health of civic engagement in America.

Stickers and buttons, though older and more conventional, are effectively similar to partisan displays on social media websites. These behaviors are inherently public; there is no point in having a political sticker or button if it is not displayed.[16] Given the very social nature of displaying these political signs, we

---

[15] This is of course just one sample. We replicate this study with a second sample (N=111) of different participants at a private Midwestern university (results included in the online appendix to this chapter).

[16] Of course, some people do collect political buttons and other campaign memorabilia. In this case, however, the collections are more a way of tracking history than supporting a particular party or candidate.

expect that the forces that lead individuals to avoid making political statements on social media websites should also diminish their willingness to participate in one of the oldest forms of political participation.

5.4.1 Please Take a Sticker

If parties, politicians, and candidates want to disseminate a message through stickers, buttons, and signs, they face two hurdles. First, a targeted person must *take* one of these items. Second, a person must actually *display* the item. It is not enough for a person to simply be interested in a sticker or button and it is not enough for them to report that they might be "highly likely" to display such an item. The political effectiveness of these forms of civic participation depends on the extent to which other people see them, and other people can only see them when they are prominently displayed.

If our goal is to track this highly social form of political participation, we cannot simply ask people if they are *interested* in displaying a sticker or button. Rather, we have to create opportunities for them to first take a real political sticker and we subsequently have to observe whether they display this sticker. With this goal in mind, we conducted a study on the streets of Tucson, Arizona. In this study we relied on a research team not only to watch people pick from various types of political stickers but also to check if people publicly displayed these stickers after the study was completed.

Over the course of two months, our research team randomly approached 645 people in Tucson to take a simple survey. Though the state is known for its conservative bent, the 526,116[17] residents of Tucson are a highly diverse group. The city is located at the intersection of three congressional districts, each of which is divided almost equally in half between Democrats and Republicans.[18] About 47 percent of residents are non-Hispanic whites, 41 percent identify as Hispanic or Latino, and 5 percent are African-American. The city has a median family income of $37,344 – somewhat below the national average. The fact that the city is home to two prominent organizations that each employ nearly 12,000 people means that on an average day one may find numerous people who have commuted into the city from surrounding areas. This further diversified the types of people our research team could encounter.

In conducting this type of recruitment, we follow the model set up by Brader (2006), who similarly invited Massachusetts residents to participate in a study. Our participants were approached as they went about their day-to-day lives and were simply asked for five minutes of their time. Our research team was deliberately instructed to vary the locations and times of recruitment: they recruited on weekdays and weekends. As a result, we obtained a sample of participants that

---

[17] This number is based on 2013 Census estimates.

[18] In 2014, the Democratic candidate won District 1 with 52.61% of the vote, the Republican candidate won District 2 with 50.04% of the vote, and the Democratic candidate won District 3 with 55.75% of the vote.

Democratic Sticker	Republican Sticker	Nonpartisan Sticker

FIGURE 5.4. Sticker Selection Available to Participants.
All stickers were printed by the same company and were the same size.

was largely reflective of Arizona as a state. We include more details about our sample of participants and the ways in which they reflect the U.S. population in the Appendix A1, Table A1.5.

These people were randomly presented with one of two versions of a survey. The first version began with the following sentence: "The 2016 Presidential Election is almost 3 years away." The second version began with the following sentence: "The 2016 Presidential Election is almost 3 years away, but both the Democrats and the Republicans have already started to launch aggressive attacks against one another." The second version was, of course, the partisan disagreement version. It was designed to suggest to our participants that there are negative traits associated with partisanship. We then asked participants a series of questions including those that allowed us to measure their self-monitoring.

Participants' responses to our survey questions provided only the first phase of our data collection. We were much more interested in what happened next. At the end of the survey, the participants were told: "As a very small token of our thanks, please take a sticker!" Participants were offered one of three sticker types: a sticker featuring the Democratic Party's donkey logo, a sticker featuring the Republican Party's elephant logo, and a sticker featuring a bald eagle (Figure 5.4). The bald eagle was selected for its resemblance to the actual bird, rather than for an overtly patriotic appearance (for example, it did not include the colors red, white and blue). This was done deliberately to hint at "Americana" without making the image highly patriotic as there is research to suggest a connection between overtly patriotic images and Republican positions (Carter et al. 2011, though see Klein et al. 2014, which suggests that the connection between patriotic objects and Republican attitudes may be highly conditional and does not replicate more generally).

All three stickers were equal in size and equally vivid, having all been obtained from the same company. As each participant walked away, members of our research team noted which sticker the participant had chosen and what the participant did with his or her new sticker. Members of our research team were not aware of the specific conditions to which our participants were assigned.[19]

5.4.2. Who Displays Stickers and Who Goes Undercover?

As we predicted in Chapter 2 and as we saw in our social network experiment at the beginning of this chapter, two forces discourage people from taking actions that may betray their political preferences. The first is exposure to partisan disagreement – information that suggests to people that there are negative traits associated with being a partisan. The second is a focus on willingness to change behavior to make the most positive impression on others. Concerned with how others may judge them, people flee undercover when confronted with a reminder that partisanship involves bickering and disagreement. Given our theoretical predictions and these earlier findings, we expect similar results when it comes to partisan stickers. We expect that when people who worry about making positive impressions and are willing to change their behaviors to do so (whom we call "high self-monitors") hear about partisan disagreement, they will become less likely to select a partisan sticker. Even if they *do* select a partisan sticker, we expect that they will be less likely to *display* their sticker publicly. We will contrast these people to low self-monitors – people who are unwilling to change their behaviors for the sake of making a better impression.

We consider the results of our study in stages. First we consider who selected a partisan sticker, and then we consider whether that sticker was displayed. As this is again a two-stage process, we conduct an additional check on our results by estimating a multivariate model that relies on a two-stage approach to estimate the display of stickers conditional on having chosen one in the first place. We include these multivariate results in the online appendix to this chapter (Table A5.4). Though we present simpler analyses in text, the results of our two-stage approach lead to the same conclusions.

When we consider who selected a partisan sticker, the first thing we see is that reminding low self-monitors of partisan disagreement had virtually no effect on their behavior: about half of the low self-monitors who were told of partisan disagreement selected a partisan sticker and about half of low self-monitors who were *not* told of partisan disagreement selected a partisan sticker at the end of the brief survey.[20] This is, of course, to be expected. Unwilling to adjust their

---

[19] In total, there were forty-seven different research assistants; each research assistant was assigned a random set of treatments. Although the research assistants knew the overall purpose of the project, they were not aware of how the experimental conditions mapped on to the general project, nor were they aware of the conditions to which people were assigned.

[20] Of low self-monitors who received the disagreement message 55% took a partisan sticker; of low self-monitors who did not receive the disagreement message 57% took a partisan sticker.

attitudes and behaviors, low self-monitors simply selected the type of sticker they liked best.

This was not so for high self-monitors. Confronted with partisan disagreement and driven by a need to make a positive impression, high self-monitors avoided the partisan stickers, instead choosing the politically neutral eagle sticker. Reminding high self-monitors of partisan disagreement reduced the number of people taking a partisan sticker by nearly 20 percentage points. In the treatment group, where respondents were reminded of partisan disagreement, only 40 percent of high self-monitors selected a partisan sticker. We can compare this with 60 percent of high self-monitors in the control group (who were *not* reminded of partisan disagreement). Again, much like in the social network study, our high self-monitors became the group least likely to take a social political action.

What is important to note here is that the reminder of partisan disagreement in our survey was subtle: a single phrase included in the survey instructions. After reading this set of instructions, individuals answered a series of questions – a number of which were not actually political. It is striking that a single, subtle phrase at the start of the study resulted in a substantial reluctance to choose a sticker affiliated with a major political party.

Of course, taking a sticker is largely meaningless if one does not actually display it. After all, as scholars suggest, the power of these social political actions is in their public nature. To restate Huckfeldt and Sprague (1995), political signs are only useful insofar as others see them. As a result we cannot simply conclude our analysis with the fact that someone took a certain type of sticker; we must ask a follow-up question: What did people *do* with their token stickers? Does reminding certain participants of partisan disagreement make them less willing to publicly display the partisan stickers they did take?

While our survey monitors could not follow the participants home, they could observe what people did with the stickers very shortly after receiving them.[21] After each participant selected a sticker, our survey monitors noted whether the sticker was displayed where other people might see it (for example if it was placed on the participant's clothing, bag, cell phone, or laptop) or whether the sticker was tucked away from the eyes of others. We use this information to consider what people who took partisan stickers did with their newly acquired potential for political communication.

We first see that, again, low self-monitors who were reminded of partisan disagreement were equally likely to display their partisan stickers as those low self-monitors who were not reminded of it. In contrast, reminders of partisan disagreement affected high self-monitors much differently. Driven by a need to make a positive impression, the few high self-monitors who initially selected

---

[21] People took stickers along with the backing paper, meaning that they could choose whether to remove the backing paper and actually apply the sticker or to keep the sticker on the backing paper.

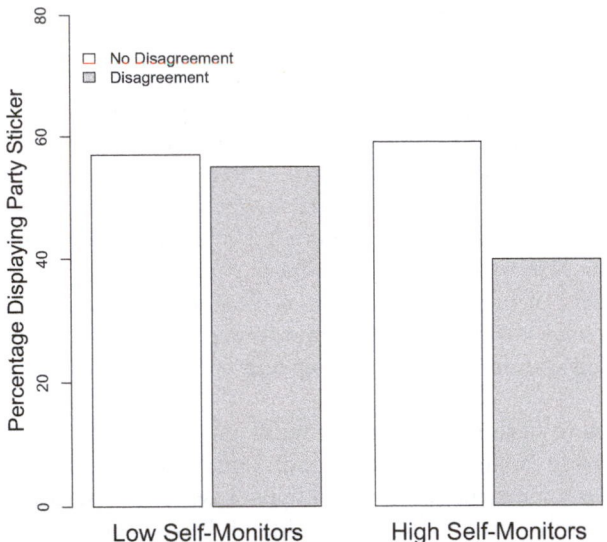

FIGURE 5.5. Effect of Disagreement Message on Partisan Sticker Display.
The bars represent the percentage of individuals who selected partisan stickers openly displaying these stickers. There is a statistically significant difference between high self-monitors who receive the partisan disagreement message and the remaining groups (p < 0.05).

partisan stickers were even less likely to display them. Instead these people opted to literally place their partisanship under cover (Figure 5.5).

5.5 CAN I TALK TO YOU ABOUT POLITICS?

To this point we have shown that the stigma of partisanship and a need to make a positive impression on others leads individuals to avoid outward partisan displays on their social media profiles and to avoid other partisan signifiers. Now we turn to one of the most powerful and least costly forms of social political action: face-to-face discussions about politics with other people.

It is difficult to overstate the importance of face-to-face expressions of partisanship for the success of electoral campaigns. Political scientists who partner with campaigns to study the effect of mobilization efforts repeatedly demonstrate that knocking on doors to personally vouch for a candidate is the most powerful strategy for encouraging citizens to get out and vote on Election Day (see Gerber and Green 2000; Green and Gerber 2008; Green et al. 2003). Sinclair et al. (2013) further show that certain door knockers are more convincing than others. When individuals are contacted by people from their own neighborhood they are even more likely to turn out to support a party.

These *personal* expressions of partisanship – telling your neighbor that you support a certain candidate and explaining why – are crucial for the success of a campaign. Indeed, President Obama's 2008 victory has been widely credited to a focus on word-of-mouth advertising. According to *The Economist*, Obama and his campaign created "a huge network of volunteers, recruited and coordinated in large part online, to proselytize on his behalf ... [trying] to contact as many potential supporters as possible in person."[22] When Vice President Joe Biden visited Florida during the 2012 campaign, he "urged volunteers to canvass their neighborhoods," calling it "the thing that matters most."[23] Biden pled, "You're not just asking 'vote for us' – you're vouching for us. ... The hardest thing for a man or woman to do is to say 'I vouch for you." Reflecting on John McCain's loss in 2008, Rich Beeson, national political director for the Romney campaign, echoed Biden's sentiment: "We learned from a lot of research and testing that volunteer door knocking is the purest form of voter contact."

Both political science scholars and political campaign professionals agree that interpersonal contact with partisan supporters is a key factor in mobilizing support. Yet critical to the political power of person-to-person political communication are the *types* of people engaged in contact. Of course, the most extreme, most ideological, and most "enthusiastic" members of each party are consistently willing to publicly display their partisanship and to travel far and wide to sing the praises of their party. Yet research suggests that person-to-person communication is most effective when the person vouching for the party is a friend or neighbor. As Enos and Hersh (2015) write, "local neighborhood canvassers have much bigger effects on voters than out-of-area canvassers (Middleton and Green 2008; Sinclair 2012; Sinclair et al. 2013), and ... canvassers demographically or socioeconomically similar to voters are particularly effective" (p. 17). The best "salespeople" for a party, it seems, are people who come closest to resembling the "customers."

Taken together this means that the consequences of undercover partisanship can be especially sharp if undercover partisanship shrinks the pool of people willing to be public about their support of the party. As more and more people go undercover, the group willing to "vouch" for a party may become limited to extremist, pure ideologues and party zealots. Ironically, Enos and Hersh (2015) show, these types of people – though willing and "enthusiastic" messengers – are substantially less effective at mobilizing the public on behalf of a party or a candidate. In short, the possibility that undercover partisanship leaves people less likely to publicly show their support of the parties can have sharp political consequences.

5.5.1 Fostering Discussion

To investigate whether Americans are less willing to convey their outward partisan preferences in the face of disagreement, we launched into a third study. For this study, we relied on a nationally representative sample of 400 American

---

[22] April 14, 2012. "Growing the Grassroots." *The Economist*.
[23] Trip Gabriel (October 21, 2012). "Campaign Boils Down to Door-to-Door Voter Drives." *New York Times*.

adults (demographics in Table A1.3).[24] In this study people would be asked to answer a brief selection of survey questions regarding things like economic inequality and the frequency with which they attend church. Nestled within these questions was a brief discussion of current politics. Some participants received information about partisan disagreement, some received information about partisan unity, and some read a nonpolitical discussion of Groundhog Day (full text of these treatments in Appendix A2). This information was both brief and, again, subtle.

At the end of the survey (after they had read either the political information or the information about Groundhog Day) we measured people's willingness to engage in relatively accessible yet critical modes of participation: encouraging their friends to side with a particular party (Scheufele 2002; Verba et al. 1995) and obtaining additional political information (Brader et al. 2008). Of course, it would be quite simple for our participants to simply *tell us* in a survey that they would be willing to obtain more information despite being unlikely to take either type of action in the real world (Vavreck 2007, Krupnikov and Levine 2010). What we wanted to see, however, was if people were willing to *actually* take these actions (Fowler 2006, Fowler and Kam 2007, Brader et al. 2008). To do so, we observe the extent to which participants are willing to visit an overtly partisan website and are also willing to provide their real email addresses to a partisan site's mailing list. This allows us to track whether people are truly interested in obtaining partisan information and, by extension, their broader commitment to the party.

5.5.2. Who Is Willing to Participate?

We begin our investigation by relying on two measures: the first asks people whether they would be willing to persuade others to vote for a certain party and the second asks them if they would be willing to sign up for a clearly partisan website. These are both actions that require that a person be proudly, obviously partisan. Indeed, this discussion question was deliberately designed to raise partisan cues. Moreover, these two behaviors are linked: as we discussed earlier in this chapter, parties depend on people to first sign up to receive messages from the party website and then spread these message to their friends. Following our theoretical conclusions and previous results, we again focus on two factors: the type of partisan information a person received and the extent to which a person is concerned with the way others view him (i.e., his level of self-monitoring). In the analysis that follows, we are interested in people who are *unwilling* to either persuade or to sign up for a partisan website.

The key comparison in these analyses is the difference between high and low self-monitors (final column of Table 5.1) in the disagreement condition and in

---

[24] Recruitment details for this sample are in Appendix A1 and the online appendix to this chapter. Sample is identical to one used in Study 3.4.

TABLE 5.1. *Effect of Partisan Disagreement on Political Action*

	High Self-Monitoring		Low Self-Monitoring		Difference Between High and Low Self-Monitors	
Change from control group	Disagreement	Unity	Disagreement	Unity	Disagreement	Unity
Unwillingness to Persude or receive more information (%, revealed measure)	+7.4	+1.9	−7.7	+4.2	14.7**	2.3
Unwillingness to Persude or receive more information, partisans only (%, revealed measure)	+13.0	+1.1	−15.3	+0.1	−28.4***	−1.0
Abstaining from action because action "too public" (%)	+16.6**	+5.2	+2.0	+2.3	−14.6**	−1.9

*Values are percentage point changes from the control. *p < 0.01, **p < 0.05, ***p < 0.01 (two tailed).*

the unity condition. When it comes to taking partisan actions, we see significant and large differences between high and low self-monitors in the disagreement condition (Table 5.1). High self-monitors in the disagreement conditions are significantly less willing to persuade others to support a particular candidate or to sign up for a partisan website than are low self-monitors in the disagreement condition. In contrast, there is little difference between high and low self-monitors in the unity condition. Moreover, these patterns are equally as strong when we consider individuals who identify as partisans: even high self-monitors who are willing to identify with a party are less willing to be public about it. This directly reflects the mechanisms underlying our effects: confronted with negativity and concerned about the way others view them, people go under-cover.

We take our analyses a step further by asking participants who do not take action *why* they do not wish to do so. Respondents were offered a variety of response options, including that the action is too much of a public display of politics. As we demonstrate in Table 5.1, not only do we see different responses to this question across condition, but we also see a significant difference between high and low self-monitors. High self-monitors in the disagreement condition are significantly more likely than low self-monitors in the same condition to report that they would avoid action because it is public. We see no such differences in the unity condition.

Finally, we also consider whether these results reflect an aversion to partisanship specifically or an aversion to politics as a whole. We distinguish between these two possibilities through a deliberate twist in our study. While our participants were invited to visit a partisan website, they were also asked about their interest in clearly political but not *partisan* information. This allows for a comparison. To visit a partisan website (and join its mailing list) means that a person must identify the party she prefers. Interest in general political information, on the other hand, does not require that a person identify any specific partisan preferences. If our effect is due to a withdrawal from *partisanship*, then we should see no changes in general *political* interest. This is indeed the case. The high self-monitors who avoided partisan websites after receiving information about partisan disagreement are no less interested in politics than is anyone else in our study. In short, these people are not apathetic; they are just reluctant to display their partisanship.[25]

For people who care about the impressions they make on others, exposure to partisan disagreement leaves them significantly less likely to take on social political actions. Encouraging your friends to support the party that best represents your preferences plays a crucial role in helping that party achieve electoral victory. Despite this, Americans, traumatized by partisan bickering and verbal assaults lobbed across the aisle, come to believe that displaying partisanship is social suicide. A better bet is to feign neutrality – even if one has clear partisan preferences. To be sure, this recusal from political activity is one that carries great consequence for American political parties.

5.6 SECRET ADMIRERS

We opened the chapter with a simple question from Stanley Fish: "What do independent voters do?" Emboldened by the anonymity of the ballot box, these undercover partisans may still cast their votes for their secretly preferred parties. The fact that independents still vote should be cold comfort for parties. Rather, parties should be much more concerned about what these people *do not* do; parties should be growing increasingly uneasy about the social actions these undercover partisans do *not* take.

To consider why this is the case, imagine two musical bands; for ease of discussion, let's call one *The Partisans* and the other *The Independents*. Imagine that both bands start out with a modestly successful album and a modestly

---

[25] The difference-in-difference analysis reveals that there is a non-significant difference between high and low self-monitors in the disagreement condition.

large fan base and occupy equivalent points on the spectrum of musical fame. Now imagine that musical critics generally dislike *The Partisans*; they believe their music is derivative and they imply that people who like *The Partisans* are musically unsophisticated. This sets the bands down two different paths.

As a result of the music critics, some proportion of *The Partisans'* fan base grows embarrassed to admit in public that they listen to the band. While they may continue to purchase their albums, they are too embarrassed to post videos of *The Partisans'* songs to Facebook. While they may buy a ticket to the band's next concert, they are unlikely to invite their friends along. They will not call radio stations to request its songs, and they will certainly not recommend *The Partisans* to people who haven't heard of the band before. They will offer no public evidence of the fact that they like this band. This, in turn, means that *The Partisans'* fan base atrophies. Sure, it can count on people to covertly purchase its albums, but it cannot count on these people to broaden its base. Its fans are too embarrassed to admit they are fans, and *The Partisans* will never be able to grow more successful.

Now imagine that the music critics are kinder to *The Independents*. As a result, fans of this band proudly display their musical preferences. They not only buy the album and attend concerts, but they fill Facebook newsfeeds with clips of the bands' songs, they wear the official band shirt, they urge their friends to listen to the new album and to join them at the concert. *The Independents'* fan base grows through sheer word-of-mouth efforts. Sure, people may never persuade fans of *The Partisans* to become fans of *The Independents*, but social displays of enthusiasm do persuade those who were lukewarm about the band's music to give it another chance. Despite a similar start, *The Independents* grow more and more successful, selling more and more albums in the process.

We can apply a similar logic to politics. Of course, any party values votes and donations, but the long-term success of a political party also depends on the breadth of grassroots mobilization. In 2008 and 2012, Barack Obama's campaign engaged in extensive person-to-person communication efforts to promote the candidate's message (Enos and Hersh 2015). Yet while on the aggregate this communication was often successful at mobilizing individuals to act in support of the candidate, there is evidence to suggest that at least some of the citizen "salespeople" attempting to promote Obama were not as successful as they should have been (Bailey et al. 2014). Enos and Hersh (2015) reason that this lack of success is due to the characteristics of these "salespeople" – these were not ordinary partisans but rather ideological, zealous activists.

This brings us back to an earlier argument. No matter how many partisans go undercover, there will always remain some people who are willing to promote the party. The question, however, is not whether *anyone* is willing to promote the party but rather if the people who remain willing to promote are effective at doing so. Undercover partisanship, we suggest, leaves parties with a shallow pool of public supporters. Once parties cannot count on ordinary people to be *publicly* supportive, their future electoral success grows precarious.

As we discussed throughout this chapter, it is social political actions – actions through which people publicly proclaim their partisan affiliation – that often set into motion other types of participation. Posting partisan Facebook messages, proudly displaying stickers and signs, and discussing politics with others all produce some of the strongest forms of political mobilization. Scholars often focus on mobilization by party organizations and political elites (Rosenstone and Hansen 1993), but field studies of real campaigns show that ordinary voters are most likely to act when they are encouraged to do so by other ordinary voters. Even more broadly, social political actions tell other people which parties people like them support (Huckfeldt and Sprague 1995). Going undercover by eschewing these social political actions, then, sends a different message: "there is no party for me."

6

Undercover Partisans in America

"I don't really label myself as Republican or Democrat."
— Barbara P. Bush, daughter of President George W. Bush

We may not have a true monarchy, but since 1900 three families have been often thought of as American multigenerational political royalty: the Roosevelts, the Kennedys, and the Bushes. The Roosevelt family famously has both a Republican branch and a Democratic branch. The Kennedy family and the Bush family, on the other hand, are "single party" families: Kennedys are Democrats, and Bushes are Republicans.

Yet when *People* magazine asked the youngest generation of the Bush family — twin sisters Barbara Bush and Jenna Bush Hager — about their political affiliation, their answer proved unexpected. "I don't really label myself as Republican or Democrat," said Barbara. Jenna agreed, "We're both very independent thinkers." Barbara and Jenna are the daughters of Republican President George W. Bush, granddaughters of Republican President George H. W. Bush, great granddaughters of Republican Senator Prescott Bush. The Republican Party, some might argue, is in their blood. Yet, when asked about it publicly, even the Bush twins shy away from partisanship, preferring to convey an independent image.[1]

Throughout this book, we have argued that this reluctance is not necessarily due to sincere political ambivalence. Are the Bush twins truly undecided? Do they really have no preference for the party that their great-grandfather represented as senator, their grandfather represented as president, their father

---

[1] Cheryl Chumley (September 5, 2014). "Bush Daughters Decline Republican Label: We Are Both Very Independent." *Washington Times*. See also Sandra Westfall (May 17, 2010). "The Bush Twins on Their Own" *People* 73(19), p. 114.

represented as president, and their uncle represented as governor?[2] Perhaps.[3] But it is also possible that the Bush twins use the term "independent" to carefully manage the impressions others form of them. Like many other Americans, they might believe that refusing to identify with a party helps them to promote a positive image.

Across a variety of studies, we show that as people try to make positive impressions, they become more likely to move away from parties. The label independent is just one indicator of eschewing partisanship; shifting away from parties may also take the form of avoiding political actions that could betray one's partisan preferences. In this chapter we address one remaining question that is often leveled against experimental research: can we observe this pattern outside of the "laboratory"?

6.1. EXPERIMENTAL POLITICS

The studies we present in the previous three chapters of this book are part of a growing movement in the study of politics: the use of experiments. Once the purview of psychologists, chemists, and physicists, over the last two decades political scientists have turned to experiments in order to answer critical questions about the way individuals relate to politics (Druckman et al. 2011). The benefit of experimental research rests in its ability to isolate a causal relationship: What causes the outcome that we observe (Druckman et al. 2011)?

An important consideration when pursuing experimental research is the extent to which the patterns we observe in experiments can be replicated across different "persons, settings, treatments and outcomes" (Shadish et al. 2001, p. 83) – a concept referred to as *external validity* (McDermott 2011). We ensure that our experiments are externally valid by relying on different and diverse groups of participants, different experimental stimuli, and different measures of our dependent variables and even by varying the setting in which people participate in our studies. Our goal is to produce experimental findings that illustrate Americans' motivation for avoiding partisanship. In this chapter, we further broaden the scope of analysis and turn to national survey data to test whether our findings are reflective of contemporary American politics.

6.2. MEASURING MASS POLITICAL PREFERENCES

In Chapter 2 we discussed *The American Voter*, a book based on the first large-scale political surveys of Americans' political preferences. These surveys, which

---

[2] In addition, Jenna Bush Hager's father-in-law is former Virginia Republican Party Chairman John Hager, and her husband, Henry Hager, served as an aide to Karl Rove.

[3] In 2011, for example, Barbara Bush was a vocal supporter of same-sex marriage and even worked with the Human Rights Campaign, an organization that advocates for LGBT causes, to produce a video urging New York to adopt same-sex marriage.

began in 1948, were so beneficial for understanding what Americans think about politics that they became an election-time tradition and, in 1977, were formally established as the American National Election Studies (ANES).

Each election year, the ANES rely on a wide-ranging set of questions and employ a large, nationally representative sample that has long been considered the "gold standard" of sampling. Moreover, the ANES are often conducted as a panel so that researchers can measure the way the same group of individuals feel about politics at two different points in time – for example, during a presidential election and during a midterm election.[4] One additional characteristic of the ANES is particularly valuable for our purposes. In 2006 the survey included a measure of self-monitoring to identify the extent to which people's opinions and behaviors are a function of their concern with making a positive impression on others.[5] We theorize that people who are most likely to avoid partisanship are those who are most concerned with making a positive impression on others, so the 2006 ANES study gives us a unique opportunity to test our theory on a national sample of Americans. Using these data, we can analyze the degree to which concerns about making a positive impression (self-monitoring) influence reported attitudes and actions.

6.2.1 Capturing Mechanisms with Survey Data

Our goal is to demonstrate that people avoid partisanship when two key conditions collide. First, people avoid partisanship because they want to make a positive impression on others. We capture this motivation through self-monitoring – a measure that accounts for the extent to which a person wants to make a positive impression on others and is willing to change his behavior to do so. Given the fortuitous inclusion of self-monitoring questions in the 2006 ANES, we can measure this key mechanism using an approach similar to the one we used in the experimental studies we discussed in previous chapters.

Second, people avoid partisanship when they believe that being partisan portrays a negative image. This second condition depends on the informational context. In 2006, political coverage created a context that cast partisanship

---

[4] Most commonly, however, the ANES interviews occur before and after a single election.

[5] In the 2006 ANES, respondents were randomly assigned to two versions of the self-monitoring scale. Version one relied on the traditional psychological approach to self-monitoring (true/false questions) and version two relied on similar questions but with a five-point response option scale. Berinsky and Lavine (2012) argue that the five-point version was a stronger predictor of social desirability in various situations, but both versions similarly point to a general tendency to make positive impressions. In the analyses in this chapter we use the true/false scale. Nonetheless, given that in this particular case there are respondents who are randomly assigned to one of the two versions, we are able to replicate the main results of this chapter with both types of scales. We include this information in the online appendix to this chapter. Moreover, in the online appendix we also highlight cases where the two measures *do not* lead to similar results. We present these dissimilarities so that the reader may form a full impression of the findings.

in a particularly negative light. Ethics scandals had swept through Congress (Hendry et al. 2008), and President George W. Bush's popularity was in decline (Jacobson 2009). That same year *The New York Times* published numerous articles about negative campaigning, polarization and fighting in Congress.[6] Meanwhile, as Carmines et al. (2008) demonstrate, the candidates running for office in 2006 received negative coverage on television. At the time of the 2006 ANES, for example, nearly 40 percent of NBC's political coverage painted the Republican candidates in a negative light, and none painted the candidates in a purely positive light (Carmines et al. 2008, p. 26). Although NBC was somewhat more kind to the Democratic candidates, the positive stories that network produced were outnumbered by the negative ones. Overall the political context in 2006 equated partisanship with negativity.

Since it is difficult to pinpoint exactly what information people may have picked up prior to answering their survey questions, we hold the informational context constant and consider how individual differences might affect the way that people respond to the same informational context. In their study of how party conventions and debates affect political choices, Hillygus and Jackman (2003), for example, cannot specify whether people watched the full convention or whether they watched the post-debate coverage. Rather, their analysis relies on theoretical expectations about the way certain types of people should respond to media coverage of debates (Hillygus and Jackman 2003). Similarly, Druckman (2004) cannot account for the type of news people actually followed during the 2000 Senate campaign in Minnesota. Instead, Druckman (2004) considers the types of issues present during the entire campaign. Like Hillygus and Jackman (2003), he relies on his theoretical argument that attentive voters will respond differently to these issues and then shows that these attentive voters behaved quite differently from those who were inattentive.

In our case, we expect that when people believe that there are negative traits associated with partisanship, they are more likely to avoid behaviors that might identify them as partisans. Importantly, we argue that people who are higher in self-monitoring are *especially* sensitive to these contextual factors. As we show in our previous chapters, we see the strongest evidence of behavioral change when people who are higher in self-monitoring are exposed to information about partisan disagreement.

Given that the 2006 informational context is generally negative toward the parties, we expect that respondents who are higher in self-monitoring will be less likely to engage in behaviors that may display one's partisanship.[7] We can

---

6 We use a word count approach to calculate the total number of articles in *The New York Times* that included the words "polarization," "negative advertising," "partisan fighting," or "partisan bickering." This approach is similar to the approach described in the online appendix to Chapter 2.

7 In our experiments we randomly assign the informational context. It is, of course, likely that our experimental participants have already gathered a great deal of information from the general media environment suggesting that there are negative traits associated with partisanship.

also consider an additional check on our approach. People who pay more attention to the news should be even more aware of the broader political context of disagreement (Zaller 1992). As a result, people who are higher in political awareness *and* higher in self-monitoring should be particularly likely to avoid partisan behaviors. After all, these are the people who know the most about political conditions and who are most sensitive to information suggesting that there are negative traits associated with partisanship.[8]

6.2.2 Varieties of Partisan Avoidance

Existing research often focuses on the simple act of reporting that one is independent (when one is actually partisan). In contrast, our work broadens the way in which people avoid partisanship. As we theorize (Chapter 2) and show (Chapter 5), identifying as independent is certainly one way to avoid partisanship, but it is not the only, nor is it the most consequential, manner of going undercover. Even someone who refers to him or herself as a "Democrat" or a "Republican" when taking an anonymous survey could nonetheless be motivated to avoid public behaviors that broadcast this partisan identity to the world.

For these reasons, we do not limit ourselves to examining only those respondents who report that they are independents. Indeed, what distinguishes our work from decades of previous research is that we broaden our measures to consider a range of consequential ways in which people avoid partisanship. In addition to the way people describe themselves, we consider how people describe their political networks. Moreover, we also analyze whether self-monitoring decreases the frequency with which individuals engage in a series of self-reported participatory behaviors such as attempting to convince others to support a candidate and willingness to discuss politics. Following our experimental results, we expect that as people care more about making a positive impression on others, they are less likely to engage in behaviors that betray their true partisan identities.

6.2.3 Searching for Patterns in a Survey World

Many different factors influence the degree to which Americans are willing to publicly identify themselves as partisans. As a result, even if we observe that people higher in self-monitoring are more likely to avoid partisan behaviors,

---

Following Druckman and Leeper (2012) this effect should only attenuate our results, since our informational treatment reflects the real world. We address this point of pre-treatment bias in the online appendix to Chapter 3.

[8] Importantly, there is no reason to believe that a relationship exists between awareness and self-monitoring. In fact, a model that predicts political knowledge by self-monitoring does not produce statistically significant results.

this relationship may be due to something else. In other words, just because two things occur simultaneously does not imply that one caused the other. To reduce the possibility that some other factor is responsible for the outcomes we are measuring, we depend on a set of control variables in our analyses that scholars often use to explain the outcomes we are studying.

For example, we control for a set of traditional demographic variables: gender, race, education, income, age (Rosenstone and Hansen 1993; Campbell et al. 1960), and marital status (Beck and Jennings 1975) – all of which can determine the degree to which Americans participate in politics. We also control for a set of additional variables that affect how people relate to politics: the extent to which they are interested in politics (Rosenstone and Hansen 1993), the number of years people have spent living in their community (Rosenstone and Hansen 1993), and the degree to which they believe government responds to people like them (Craig et al. 1990).[9] We also control for factors that influence a person's relationship with the political process such as whether they have been contacted by a political organization and encouraged to participate (Rosenstone and Hansen 1993) and the competitiveness of the election in a given state (Franklin 2004).

In the analyses we present in this chapter, we estimate a series of statistical models and then present our findings in illustrated figures. Each figure shows the likelihood of representing oneself in a particular way or taking a particular action if one is a low self-monitor and the chance of taking the same action if one is a high self-monitor.[10] In order to discuss our results, we provide descriptions of the estimation techniques we use. We present some estimation details in this chapter, but we save the more technical details of our model estimates for the online appendix to this chapter. Also in Appendix A6 we include a wide variety of robustness checks, including alternative specifications of our models and alternative measures for self-monitoring (our key independent variable).[11]

6.3. ABANDONING PARTISANSHIP

6.3.1. Picking "Independent"

People who want to make a good impression on others are more likely to avoid partisanship. When information suggests that there are negative traits associated with partisanship, those people who are higher in self-monitoring are even more likely to go undercover and hide partisan attachments. In our first

---

[9] In addition to this base of controls, we also account for factors that are particular to the political outcome at hand and we discuss these additional controls when we present the results from our specific models.

[10] In all of the figures the remaining control variables are kept constant at their means.

[11] In this online appendix we also highlight the limitations of our findings.

model we consider just one type of partisan avoidance and track whether high self-monitors are more likely to self-identify as independent than are low self-monitors. We follow previous work on independents (Keith et al. 1992) and treat our dependent variable as a three-point measure: the respondent identifies as a partisan (coded as 0), a leaning independent (coded as 1), or a pure independent (coded as 2).[12]

Since our outcome variable is three categories, we estimate a multinomial logit model. This model allows us to estimate the chance that a respondent placed himself into one of our three categories, controlling for a variety of possible factors that could have influenced his choice. We use our model estimates to consider whether being higher in self-monitoring increases the chance that a person reports that they are independent and decreases the chance that they pick a partisan label. In our analyses, we present the substantive change in hiding partisanship because of increases in self-monitoring; here we present the Z-score and p-value associated with this shift to show whether the effect of self-monitoring is statistically significant. When informative, we present the coefficient values as β_{SM}. Finally we also graphically present the chance that a high self-monitor and a low self-monitor avoid partisanship.

Turning to our first set of results (full model estimates shown in Table A6.2 of the online Appendix), we see that even small increases in self-monitoring significantly increase the chance that a person will report that he or she is a leaning independent, rather than a partisan (Z-score = 2.18, p-value = 0.029). We can take these results a step further by analyzing whether people at the higher end of our self-monitoring scale are more or less likely to identify as partisan than those at the lower end of our scale.[13] This comparison reveals that the chance of identifying as a partisan decreases significantly for those who are highest in self-monitoring (Figure 6.1a).

If people who are politically aware generally pay more attention to political coverage (Zaller 1992), then high self-monitors who are politically aware should be particularly likely to shy away from partisanship. To consider this possibility we estimate the very same model, except this time we account for the relationship between self-monitoring and political awareness through an interaction. We measure political awareness through an index of political knowledge following Zaller (1992).

---

[12] Our controls come from the 2004 ANES, as per the ANES recommendation. Our outcome measure of partisanship comes from the 2006 ANES. We use a multinomial logit to estimate our model. Given our estimation approach, we are cognizant that a certain sample size is necessary. As Long (1997) and Hosmer and Lemeshow (2000) note, the lowest suggested threshold of multinomial logit estimation is a ratio of one parameter per ten valid cases. Nonetheless, both suggest that the best threshold is one parameter per fifteen to twenty cases. Our model is deliberately specified to meet this threshold.

[13] Although we use the full self-monitoring scale in our model, to obtain the substantive effects we focus on the lowest and highest ends of the scale for ease of interpretation.

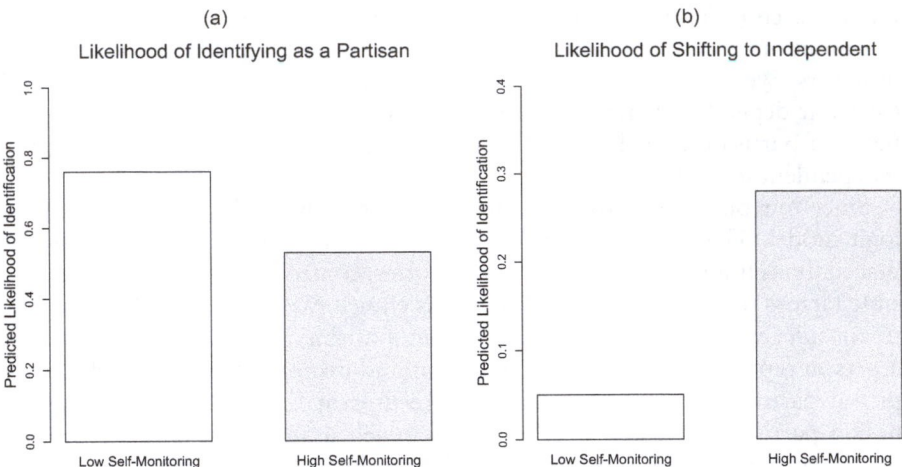

(a)
Likelihood of Identifying as a Partisan

(b)
Likelihood of Shifting to Independent

FIGURE 6.1. Effect of Self-Monitoring on Identifying as a Partisan or as an Independent
Figure 6.1a Figure 6.1b.
Differences between high and low self-monitors significant at $p < 0.05$ for Figure 6.1a, and $p < 0.1$ for Figure 6.1b. Estimates obtained when all other control variables set at means. All models included in the chapter appendix.

We find that the people *least* likely to identify as partisans are people who are high in self-monitoring and also have the highest levels of political knowledge. As Zaller (1992) argues, individuals who are high in political knowledge are highly aware of the political context. We find that even small increases in self-monitoring produce significant decreases in the likelihood that a politically aware self-monitor will identify as a partisan ($Z = 1.83$, $p = 0.068$).[14]

In sum, people who are high in self-monitoring – that is, those most willing to shift their behaviors to make a better impression – are most likely to avoid partisanship. Moreover, as people become more aware of the broader political context, those who are higher in self-monitoring are significantly less likely to report that they are partisans.

6.3.2. Partisan or Independent?

So far our analysis of survey data reproduces the patterns we find in our experiments. We can now conduct an even more stringent test. Because we have survey responses from the same respondents in 2004 and 2006, we can find out whether some people identified as a partisan in 2004 but then changed to an independent in 2006. If the desire to make a better impression discourages partisan identification, then our self-monitoring measure should predict who changes their reported partisanship over time.

---

[14] Robustness checks for these results are included in Tables A6.3, A6.4, and A6.5 of the online appendix to this chapter.

We again rely on our familiar model but this time our outcome variable distinguishes between people who shifted from partisan to independent (1) and those who retained the same identification from 2004 to 2006 (0). Given what we know about the stability of partisanship (Green et al. 2002), it comes as no surprise that the percentage of people who change their partisan affiliation is quite low – less than 10 percent. Nonetheless some shifts did occur and we want to know whether self-monitoring can help to explain this pattern. Our dependent variable is binary (1 = switched to independent, 0 = did not switch), so we estimate our results using a probit model, which is best suited to a binary variable with unequal distributions of outcomes.

First, we see that self-monitoring has a positive effect on the chance that an individual will switch from identifying as a partisan in 2004 to identifying as an independent in 2006 (β_{SM} = 0.46, p-value = 0.009, full model estimates included in Table A6.6 of the online appendix to this chapter).[15] In fact, an increase in the self-monitoring measure produces a significant increase in the likelihood of this change in self-reported partisanship (Z-score = 2.30, p-value = 0.021). Moving from lowest to highest self-monitoring increases the chance of moving from a partisan to an independent by more than 20 percentage points (Figure 6.1b).

Despite these shifts in partisan identification, we find that issue preferences remain stable. When we consider, for example, how people felt about abortion in 2004 and 2006, we see very little correlation between a change in abortion preference and a shift toward identifying as politically independent.[16] This pattern suggests that this newly found independence is more of a rhetorical rather than a truly ideological shift.

The results we have shown thus far reinforce the findings that emerged from our experiments. People who care about the way they are perceived by others are increasingly likely to opt for the label "independent." Even when we account for numerous other factors that often contribute to a person's decision

---

[15] The 2006 ANES relies on two different measures of the partisanship question. One question starts with "As of today" the other with "Generally speaking" We use only the "Generally speaking" measure for this test to match the exact partisanship question asked in 2004 and ensure that differences are not due to a change in question structure.

[16] We rely on the abortion question asked in 2006 that best matches a question asked in 2004. These two questions (detailed in the online appendix to this chapter) do have some differences in the response option wording but generally have the same structure, and the differences are slight. We use correlation so as not to propose a causal structure onto the relationship between changes in abortion attitudes from 2004 to 2006 and shifts toward independence. The actual correlation is 0.07, which is considered very low by methods that create correlation thresholds (Cohen 1988). We also use changes in the abortion position – rather than moderation – as independence does not necessarily mean greater moderation (Klar 2014c). Given that abortion is not the most ideal measure of ideological positions, we also measure church attendance as increases or decreases in church attendance can change overall political positioning (Campbell 2004). We find no evidence that these people changed their level of church attendance between 2004 and 2006.

to self-describe as a political independent, a person's concern about the way he is perceived by others still exerts an important influence.

A skeptic might have some remaining questions. Is it possible that people who are high in self-monitoring are simply more likely to change from survey to survey? Perhaps in their quest to make the most positive impression on others, people who are high in self-monitoring act like social chameleons. Perhaps high self-monitors are simply more likely to alter the way they describe themselves *in general*.

Fortunately, our data can show us if this is the case. To consider the skeptic's alternative explanation we rely on the very same model we used to analyze the chance of shifting from partisan to independent between 2004 and 2006, but now we analyze three additional possibilities: the possibility of shifting from independent in 2004 to partisan in 2006, the possibility of switching parties between 2004 and 2006, and the possibility of changing one's position on abortion from 2004 to 2006. If high self-monitors just tend to change their answers from one survey to the next, we should observe that self-monitoring increases the chance of changing in at least one of these cases.

The results, however, point in a different direction (full model estimates in Table A6.6 of online appendix to this chapter; full substantive estimates in Table A6.7 of the same appendix). The more a person self-monitors, the *less* likely this person is to shift his or her identification from independent in 2004 to partisan in 2006 ($\beta_{SM} = -0.40$, $p = 0.056$). Further, differences in self-monitoring do not predict whether people changed parties in general ($\beta_{SM} = -0.04$, $p = 0.846$), nor do they predict a different position on abortion ($\beta_{SM} = -0.08$, $p = 0.581$). Moreover, when we look at substantive effects on these outcomes for both high and low self-monitors, we see largely overlapping confidence intervals, meaning that high and low self-monitors do not behave differently when it comes to these types of political shifts. In short, we see little evidence that high self-monitors are simply people who are more likely to change. Rather, a desire to make the most positive impression on others predicts one very particular tendency: a shift from describing yourself as a partisan to describing yourself as independent.

6.3.3 A Bad Year for Republicans

Overall, issue positions do not appear to switch, and independents tend not to become partisans. The only shift we see over time is from partisan to independent. Our data provide a few clues as to why this might be the case. First, we point to the partisan composition of people who switched from identifying as partisan in 2004 to identifying as independent in 2006: 65 percent of them had started off as Republicans in 2004. We can also look to the differences between the 2004 and 2006 campaign. In 2004, incumbent President George W. Bush, a Republican, won reelection; that same year the Republicans gained majorities in both the House and Senate. In 2006, however, the Republican luster had begun to fade. The 2006 election saw the Republican Party embroiled in a series of scandals that were widely covered by media (Carmines et al. 2008) and were powerful enough to cost the party voter support (Hendry et al. 2008). Even more importantly, Hendry et al. (2008) show evidence that, scandals aside, simply having the label "Republican" was an "electoral liability" in 2006.

If people's willingness to identify as a partisan hinges on their belief that being a partisan makes for a positive impression, then we can begin to understand why in 2006 people would shy away from a scandal-ridden party whose president's approval ratings had plummeted (Jacobson 2009). Our data offer us additional evidence that in 2006 Republicans were hiding under the comfortable cover of "independent." People who switched from partisan in 2004 to independent in 2006 rated the Republicans significantly higher than did people who had identified as independent all along.[17] Moreover, directly estimating the relationship between self-monitoring and political awareness further reinforces this point. For people who are high in self-monitoring, an increase in political awareness increases the likelihood of shifting from partisan in 2004 to independent in 2006 by 0.21 (Z-score = 2.49, p-value = 0.013). The more aware people were of the political context the more they were concerned about making a positive impression and the less likely they were to reveal their partisanship.

Between 2004 and 2006 we saw a particular tendency for Republicans to go undercover, but overall this phenomenon crosses party lines. Indeed, in our experimental analyses, we see no partisan differences in the way people respond to news about partisan disagreement. Democrats are just as likely as Republicans to go undercover. As we argue in Chapter 2, at any given point people may hear negative information about either their own party or partisanship in general and this information leads them to avoid making their partisanship public. What we see in the case of 2004 to 2006 is a single period in time when the Republican Party was disproportionately more troubled than the Democratic Party, and consequently media coverage focused on emphasizing not only the negative traits of partisanship but also the negative traits of a *particular* party. Indeed, recent research suggests that avoiding the party is as much a Republican tendency as it is a Democratic one. Focusing on 2008 data, Smidt (2014) finds that after a divisive presidential debate, members of *both* parties were equally likely to retreat from partisanship and hide behind the label "independent" (Figure 6.2).

Of course, selecting the independent category on surveys is just one mode of eschewing partisan preferences. In some ways selecting "independent" rather

---

[17] We use both a difference of means t-test and the Wilcoxon Rank-Sum non-parametric test. The t-test suggests that people who shifted to independent in 2006 have significantly higher mean ratings of the Republican Party (a nearly 10-point difference on the 0 to 100 thermometer scale, p-value=0.0006). The non-parametric test suggests that scale for those who remained independent 2004 to 2006 is significantly different than the distribution for those who shifted from partisan in 2004 to independent in 2006 (p-value=0.0014).

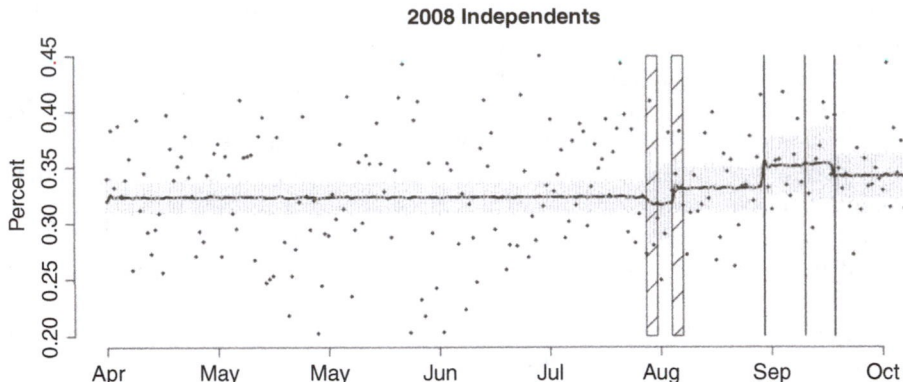

FIGURE 6.2. Shifts toward Independent Label Pre– and Post–2008 Debate. *Figure is from Smidt (2014), originally published in* Public Opinion Quarterly. *Lines represent presidential debates.*

than Democrat or Republican is the *least* politically consequential way of hiding one's partisanship. Our next step is to use our survey data to consider more politically consequential ways in which people avoid partisanship.

6.4 SOME OF MY BEST FRIENDS ARE INDEPENDENT

We next consider how people describe their friends and, more importantly, their political confidants. If it is undesirable to identify oneself as a partisan, then describing one's social network as partisan could also betray a partisan connection. Does the allure of political independence extend to the way we categorize our political discussants?

The 2006 ANES survey asked respondents to divulge much more information about their political habits than do most national surveys. As we already discussed, questions that measure self-monitoring allow us to consider the psychological mechanism underlying the phenomena we describe in our book. A second set of questions asked participants to name the people they are most likely to talk to – a way of describing the most central part of a respondent's social network. For this particular question, ANES randomly assigned respondents to one of two question types, called "network generators." One generator asked people to describe the people they talk to about "things that are important to [them]." The second generator asked people to list who they talk to about "government and politics." For ease of discussion, we call these two different generators "nonpolitical generator" and "political generator."

After being instructed to either think of their nonpolitical discussants or their political discussants, respondents listed the first discussion partner that came to mind and then described the partisanship of this person. Using these questions

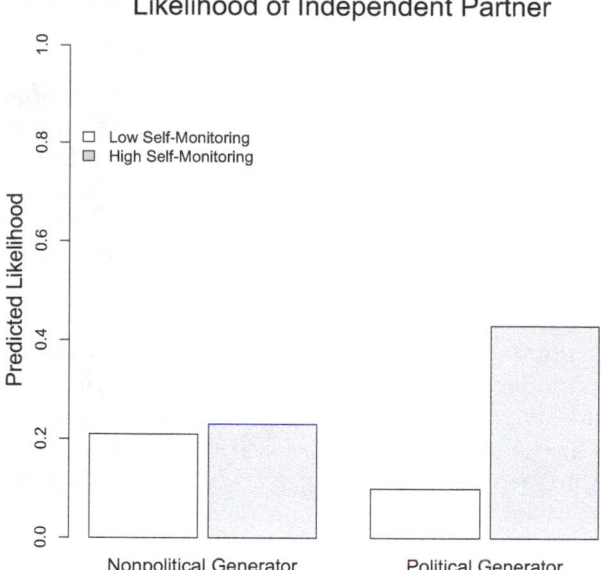

FIGURE 6.3. Likelihood of Reporting an Independent Discussion Partner. *Differences between high and low self-monitors are significant at p < 0.05 in the political condition.*

we can find out whether high self-monitors are more likely to describe their *political* discussion partners as independent, as opposed to their nonpolitical discussion partners. If one were truly attempting to hide their partisanship, then describing one's political discussion partners as independent, rather than partisan, would help to craft that image.

We again begin with our familiar base model. We then analyze how self-monitoring affects the way respondents describe their political or nonpolitical discussion partners. We continue to account for our baseline series of controls, and in this particular model we also introduce an important new control variable: Does the respondent describe *him or herself* as an independent? Controlling for whether the respondent is an independent allows us to show us that the results are driven by self-monitoring and that this is just one more indication of people avoiding partisanship. In addition, we also control for a person's general tendency to talk about politics.

We first see that self-monitoring has only a very small effect on the way people describe their *nonpolitical* discussion partners (effect = 0.01, p-value = 0.821, full model estimates in Table A6.8 of the Appendix A6, full substantive estimate in Table A6.9 of the same appendix). When it comes to nonpolitical discussions, individuals who are high and low in self-monitoring are nearly equally likely to report that their main confidant is independent (Figure 6.3). In fact, both high and low self-monitors are more likely to describe the person with whom they engage in nonpolitical discussion as a partisan, rather than as an independent.

In contrast, we see entirely different results when respondents describe their *political* discussion partners. In this case, even small increases in self-monitoring produce a significant increase in the chance of describing one's political conversation partner as an independent (effect = 0.10, p-value = 0.012). In fact, almost half of high self-monitors describe their primary political discussion partner as an independent (Figure 6.3). In contrast, low self-monitors are equally unlikely to report that their main discussion partner is an independent when they consider political discussions as when they consider nonpolitical discussions.[18]

The fact that high self-monitors are more likely to report that they discuss *politics* with independents could reflect one of two phenomena. First, it is possible that high self-monitors are going undercover when they are speaking to survey interviewers. If they are reticent to identify themselves as a partisan, they may be similarly unwilling to mention that their main political confidant is a partisan. After all, this sort of admission may unmask their true party preference. The second possibility is a much broader indication of how people hide their partisanship in their day-to-day lives. Perhaps high self-monitors are so focused on making a positive impression that they truly do restrict political discussion to those who similarly identify as independent. Taken together, our first two sets of results suggest that an interest in making a positive impression pushes people toward hiding their partisanship. We see this tendency not only in the way people describe their own partisan identification but also in the way they describe their friends.

6.5 POLITICAL ACTION

Parties need help. While they certainly need votes, voting is the least of what the parties are after. Both the Democrats and the Republicans depend on supportive citizens to openly persuade others to support them as well – be it through political discussion or through more direct attempts at persuasion. Scholars

---

[18] To consider the alternative explanation that this is simply about the respondent being independent him or herself, we estimate whether identifying as an independent has a different effect on how people describe political discussants as opposed to nonpolitical discussants. Focusing again on the substantive results, we see that independents behave virtually identically regardless of whether they receive the political or the nonpolitical generators. In the nonpolitical condition they have about a 30% chance of reporting that their main confidant is also independent. In the political condition they have about a 32% chance of reporting an independent confidant – neither a substantively nor a statistically significant difference. The effect of being independent is evidently different from that of self-monitoring. When asked about political conversation, high self-monitors are more likely to report that their main discussion partner is independent. In contrast, people who identify as independent have no such response to the political cue. Moreover, this result also holds when we estimate a model that includes only independents (results shown in Table A6.10 of the online appendix to this chapter).

have known since about the 1950s that a sizeable portion of the electorate votes for a certain candidate because of the convincing messages they receive from their friends (Berelson et al. 1954; Katz and Lazarsfeld 1955). Given the immense degree to which political parties rely on word-of-mouth marketing, the results we have presented thus far should be a cause for concern. Afraid of making poor impressions on others, people go so far undercover that they refuse to openly admit their partisan preference.

Calling oneself "independent" is just one consequence of striving to make a positive impression. Even if a person begrudgingly admits to a pollster that he is a partisan, this person may not be comfortable enough with his partisanship to engage in the types of activities that help parties to win elections. In our next set of analyses, we directly test whether people who care more about making positive impressions on others are more likely to avoid the types of political behaviors that make partisan affiliation obvious.

Relying on self-monitoring may pose a unique challenge here. People who are higher in self-monitoring generally want to present themselves in the most positive way possible. This need to make a positive impression has been shown to produce inflated self-reports of political action (Belli et al. 1999). In short, our higher self-monitors might be more motivated to misrepresent themselves by reporting that they took political actions when they actually did not do so.

Verba et al. (1995) consider a similar set of participatory actions. They note that over-reporting is most common for questions about voting but less common for other types of political actions. Furthermore, to the extent that people do report that they took an action (even when they actually did not do so in a particular year or campaign) it is simply reflective of their general tendency to take that action. More importantly, our theoretical predictions point the other way. We argue that people who are higher in self-monitoring should be less likely to participate in partisan politics. As a result, any tendency to misreport behavior on a survey should work against us, making our predictions more difficult to observe and, subsequently, making the tests presented here more conservative.

Finally, we address one additional concern. It is possible that any patterns we observe might be a function of disengagement from politics generally rather than a specific desire to avoid partisanship. To test this alternative explanation, we conduct our tests not only on the entire sample but also only on people who have a preexisting history of participation in politics. This allows us to show that even people who are politically active are not immune from the tendency to go undercover. We provide the details of these tests in Appendix A6.

We use these analyses to confirm whether the extent to which a person cares about making a positive impression has an effect on their political behavior. Again, what differentiates our approach from previous work is that we view going undercover much more broadly than existing political science research. Previous work focused on the fact that people hide from partisanship by identifying as independent, but we argue that the label "independent" is just one way in which people hide from partisanship. While some scholars have treated partisan identification (or lack thereof) as the most important outcome of a political disease, we believe it is one of a host of symptoms – and a more benign symptom at that. The desire to present a positive self-image can lead to more serious participatory consequences that scholars have missed while focusing on the label "independent."

6.5.1. Analyzing Behavior: Persuading Others

Some of the earliest work on American political behavior suggested that an individual's family and friends exert considerable influence over his or her political preferences (Berelson et al. 1954; Lazarsfeld et al. 1948). To be sure, individuals prefer to discuss politics with people who hold similar political beliefs (Mutz 2002), but "they also take what is available" (Huckfeldt and Sprague 1987). Furthermore, political discussions may arise in unexpected settings, leaving individuals exposed to a variety of perspectives they would never have sought out (Walsh 2004). As a result, expressing one's political opinions in public settings is one of the most important ways that we can transmit influential information about politics and parties. As Duncan Watts, professor of sociology and principal researcher at Microsoft Research, explains "potentially, anybody can influence somebody else." Organizations who seek to persuade fare better when they rely on ordinary people to do the persuasion, Watts advises.[19]

Given the significance of persuasive political discussion for electoral outcomes, the ANES asks the following of its respondents:

We would like to find out about some of the things people do to help a party or a candidate win an election. During the campaign, did you talk to any people and try to show them why they should vote for or against one of the parties or candidates?

The partisan nature of the activity – "*show them why they should vote for or against one of the parties or candidates*" – means that engaging in this type of discussion could betray one's own partisan preferences. Although it may theoretically be possible to persuade someone to support a particular party without appearing partisan, it is a difficult task. Research on interpersonal conversation shows that people readily form (often accurate) perceptions about the political preferences of their conversational partners (Eveland and Hutchens 2013). If a person wants to avoid partisanship because they are concerned with making a positive impression, then they may be more hesitant to engage in political persuasion at all. Thus, among those who are most concerned with making a positive impression, we should expect to find low levels of persuasive discussion. We return to our estimation model to consider this possibility, again controlling for the respondent's own partisan affiliation.

---

[19] Watts was speaking to a group of marketers at the SES Conference and Expo in 2011.

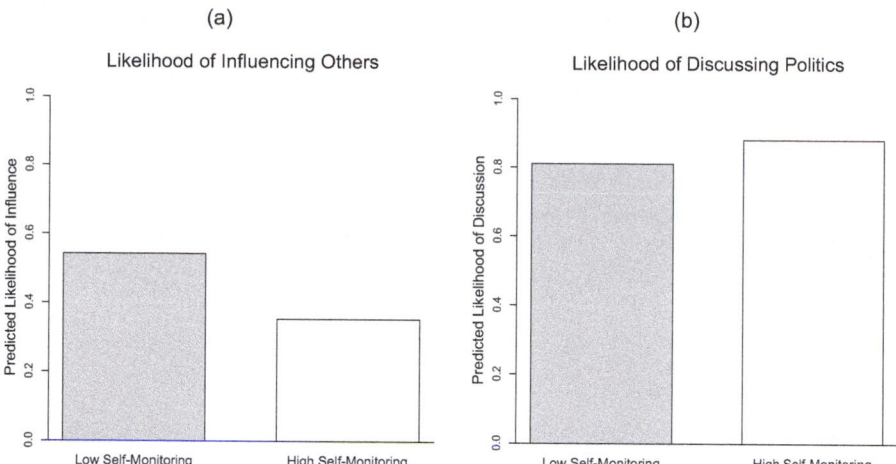

FIGURE 6.4. Effect of Self-Monitoring on Partisan and Nonpartisan Discussion Figure 6.4a Figure 6.4b.
Differences between high and low self-monitors significant at p<0.05 for Figure 6.4a, are not significant for Figure 6.4b. Estimates obtained when all other control variables set at means. All models included in the chapter appendix.

This discussion question is similar to the measure we use in Chapter 5, and immediately we see that increases in self-monitoring decrease the likelihood of engaging in this type of political discussion (full model estimates in Table A6.11 of Appendix A6). Focusing on the substantive effects of self-monitoring, our results demonstrate that as self-monitoring increases people become significantly less willing to persuade others to vote for or against a candidate (Z-score $= -2.37$, p-value $= 0.018$). When we directly compare people at the lower and higher ends of the self-monitoring scale the results are even more striking (Figure 6.4a). Driven by a need to make a positive impression, people who are higher in self-monitoring are nearly 20 percentage points less likely to engage in political persuasion as compared with low self-monitors. That is to say, among 100 individuals who are low self-monitors, more than half would have tried to persuade another person to vote for a certain candidate. In contrast, among 100 high self-monitors, the persuaders would be in the minority.

We must be sure that high self-monitors are avoiding *partisan politics* in particular and not just politics generally. If high self-monitors are merely avoiding politics – rather than avoiding *partisan* politics – they should be less likely to engage in any type of political discussion. In other words, not only should these people be less likely to try to influence others to support a particular party, but they should also be less likely to simply discuss politics with friends at all. We can test this using a survey question that asks ANES respondents, "Do you ever discuss politics with your family or friends?"

We rely on the same model to consider the extent to which self-monitoring affects people's willingness to simply talk about politics. The results point in a very different direction from what we saw in the case of *partisan* politics. When the discussion is simply political – rather than overtly partisan – we see little difference between high and low self-monitors. They are equally as likely to discuss politics with their friends and family (Figure 6.4b). Moreover, increases in self-monitoring do not produce significant changes in willingness to engage in political discussion (Z-score = –0.86, p-value = 0.391). These results are parallel to our findings in Chapter 5: to the extent that people care about making a positive impression, they avoid *partisan* behaviors. High self-monitors, it seems, do not simply avoid politics; they avoid partisanship – or, at the very least, partisan advocacy.[20]

6.5.2. Analyzing Behavior: Political Actions

The patterns in Figure 6.4 reflect the fact that individuals refrain from influencing others to support a party so as to conceal their own partisan identity. We can expect similar patterns when we look at other overtly partisan behaviors. People who are high in self-monitoring should be less likely to attend partisan rallies, to wear partisan buttons, to work for a campaign, or to donate to a party. As our next step, we consider whether engaging in these behaviors is similarly less frequent among respondents who are most concerned with making a good impression.

We can consider political action in two ways: first, does a person participate in at least one of these activities and, second, in how many activities does a person participate? In both cases we use the base model we have employed throughout this chapter, again controlling for whether the respondent identifies as an independent. In tracking the number of activities, however, we must rely on a different estimation approach (a poisson model) that is better suited to this particular outcome variable.[21]

The results for both types of outcomes point to a familiar conclusion (full estimates in Table A6.14 of the online appendix to this chapter). People who work hard to make a positive impression are, in fact, less likely to take overtly partisan actions. Indeed, people who are high in self-monitoring are less likely to participate in even one of these overtly partisan activities. Further, an increase in self-monitoring significantly decreases the overall number of overtly partisan activities in which people participate (Z-score = –1.83, p-value = 0.067).[22]

---

[20] Additional robustness checks included in Table A6.11 of the online appendix to this chapter; substantive results in Tables A6.12 and A6.13 of the same appendix.

[21] We include more information on this poisson, including discussions of over-dispersion and the appropriateness of the estimation approach in the online appendix to this chapter.

[22] In addition to these results, we also conduct a subsequent test to confirm that self-monitoring has a direct and substantively important effect on action that is distinct from the effect of merely identifying as independent. We elaborate on these tests in the appendix. Results are shown in Table A6.15 of the online appendix to this chapter.

As Americans grow more concerned with making positive impressions, they become less likely to take overtly partisan actions. We see this when we analyze the extent to which people attempt to influence others directly, and we also see this when we track the extent to which people participate in activities that might reveal their partisanship. More importantly, we do *not* see these results when we consider general political behaviors. People go undercover to avoid *partisanship*, not to avoid politics.

6.6. PARTISANS UNDERCOVER

As we were writing this book, a record number of Californians registered to vote without identifying a party preference – over 4 million people (or 23.6% of all registered voters in the state of California).[23] In Arizona, independents for the first time made up the largest bloc of voters – a rapid rise that led the Arizona secretary of state to launch a $400,000 effort to educate independents on their right to vote in primary elections.[24] Meanwhile, in the 2014 election, independents made up a plurality of voters in a number of the most competitive states. Exit polls show that 39 percent of Arkansas voters and 41 percent of Colorado voters reported that they were independent. In states where independents did not meet plurality, they were nonetheless dominant: in Iowa 31 percent of 2014 voters identified as independent and 28 percent did so in Georgia.[25] This pattern is emerging all over the country. And the consequences of so many Americans hiding undercover should terrify the parties.

Throughout this book, we have shown what happens when individuals avoid partisanship: widespread political inaction. Whether we blame the parties themselves or the incessant media coverage of partisan conflict, we can agree that partisanship is becoming a dirty word in politics. The increasingly popular response is to distance oneself from the party. One way to do this is to self-identify as independent. Another more consequential way is to disengage from campaigns and to avoid participating in politics when doing so means betraying a partisan identity.

Others have argued that identifying as an independent is inconsequential. Much as people want to hide their party, the argument goes, they will still vote for the party in the privacy of the ballot box. We do not disagree that when it comes to vote choice, independents tend to rely on their partisan preferences. What we suggest is that identifying as an independent is merely one symptom of a consequential habit of avoiding partisanship. Candidates and parties need ordinary people to influence their friends and spread the party's message to their

---

[23] Data from the Public Policy Institute of California.

[24] Yvonne Sanchez (August 23, 2014). "Independents' Primary Participation Surges." *The Arizona Republic*.

[25] Data based on exit poll surveys conducted and reported by CNN. Partisanship patterns based on exit poll reporting from Senate races.

networks. Candidates and parties succeed to the extent that ordinary voters are vocal, clear, and public in their support. Candidates and parties lose all of this when people try to avoid partisanship.

In this chapter, we use national survey data to show that when people want to make positive impressions on others, they avoid partisanship. Identifying as an independent on a survey is merely one small act. When Americans avoid partisanship, they may refuse to persuade their friends and family to support a party. They may be unwilling to attend partisan rallies, to wear partisan buttons, to work for a campaign, or to donate to a party. Does this avoidance matter for American parties? Yes. Can this avoidance actually have positive consequences for American parties? We turn to this question in Chapter 7.

7

The Myth of Partisan Compromise

"Bipartisanship is not the opposite of principle. One can be very conservative or very liberal and still have a bipartisan mindset."

— Richard Lugar, Republican Senator, Indiana, concession statement

Consider these two facts: (1) nearly 40 percent of Americans identify as political independents; (2) 58 percent of Americans believe that America needs a third party.[1] The conditions seem perfect for a third party to emerge onto the American political scene. At the very least, one might expect that Democrats and Republicans should embrace bipartisanship in hopes of appealing to so many disaffected Americans.

Yet in reality, the reverse is happening. Alternatives to the Republican and Democratic parties have declined dramatically over the past century (Tamas and Hindman 2014), as has voter support for third and minor parties (Hirano and Snyder 2007). Meanwhile, Democratic and Republican candidates are increasingly ideologically extreme (Großer and Palfrey 2014) and the American public often appears increasingly partisan, especially in their affect toward members of the opposing party (Iyengar et al. 2012; Mason 2014).[2]

How is it possible that an electorate in which nearly a plurality of people claim they are independent exists in this political climate? One of the greatest

[1] Jeffrey M. Jones (September 24, 2014) "Americans Continue to Say a Third Political Party is Needed." *Gallup.com*. Data based on the Governance Poll, conducted by Gallup in September 2014 with a sample of 1,017 adults.

[2] It is important to note that others have argued that the American public is much less ideologically polarized than these scholars suggest (Fiorina et al. 2008). The evidence we cite, however, speaks not simply to ideological polarization but to affective polarization. As Iyengar et al. (2012) and more recently Mason (2014) show, even if people are not as ideologically far apart as Abramowitz (2010) suggests, people increasingly harbor strong animosity toward members of the opposing party.

divides in American politics may well be the chasm between what we say and what we do.

Throughout this book, we have shown the degree to which negative perceptions of partisanship influence the way ordinary Americans relate to politics. From self-identifying as independent to withdrawing from political conversation, eschewing outwardly partisan forms of political participation, and avoiding partisan coworkers and neighbors, many Americans are going undercover and deliberately avoiding partisanship. Throughout these chapters, however, we have not addressed the elephant in the room. How is it that Americans are both anti-partisan and politically polarized?

In this chapter, we examine whether the people who reject partisanship are distinct from those who are polarized. Although undercover partisans may not actually be "independent" in the political sense of the word, perhaps they are so ashamed of parties that they have begun to seek compromise and hold their representatives accountable to bipartisan values. We explore what undercover partisans want from parties in two ways. First, we take people at their own word and we simply ask people who call themselves "independent" to tell us what they want from politics and from their representatives. Yet we also remain cautious that, as always, what people say may not always be indicative of their true underlying preferences. As a next step, we use an experimental approach to find out what people who are most likely to avoid partisanship *actually* want from their representatives.

We find that there is little overlap between what people say they want and what they actually want. Just because people preach bipartisanship does not mean that they are satisfied with bipartisan compromise. We find that even Americans whose distaste for partisan politics leads them undercover still want their preferred party to fight tooth and nail. In short, when push comes to shove the people who should be the greatest promoters of bipartisan compromise want neither bipartisanship nor compromise.

7.1 TALKING THE TALK

As President Barack Obama was preparing to take on Mitt Romney in his 2012 reelection bid for the White House, all eyes, as usual, turned to the independent voters.

"They're disappointed, disillusioned and in some cases, downright disgusted," reported Katie Couric to CBS viewers, "Independent voters are now the largest segment of the electorate, representing 40 percent of Americans."[3]

Couric took to the streets of Pennsylvania, a battleground state, to find out what makes independents tick. Independent voter Scott Barclay, a father of three, told her: "When I look at the political situation right now, all I really see

---

[3] Couric, Katie (October 14, 2010) "Independent Voters Could Decide Congress" CBSNews.com

is that the Democrats are against the Republicans. The Republicans are against the Democrats. And no one's really for America."

One by one, the independent voters with whom Couric spoke yearned for bipartisanship and civility. Couric summed up her interviews as follows, "Just as the founding fathers learned the art of compromise more than 220 years ago, these independent voters hope their elected officials will somehow meet them in the middle."

Couric's interviewees were not unusual. The people Linda Killian interviewed for her 2012 book *The Swing Vote: The Untapped Power of Independents* reported similar preferences. A self-proclaimed independent from Colorado, "sick of what he sees going on in Washington" told Killian that "there's no real compromise. It's like this tug-of-war match – it's not constructive. It's all a power play" (Killian 2012 p. 14). A fifty-two-year-old small business–owner from Virginia, Killian describes, echoed the same sentiments: "it was 'stupid' that the government almost shut down last year and says it just proved 'it's all about the parties' and that politicians aren't really working for the country" (Killian 2012 p.17).

Hearing from independents themselves through in-depth interviews with a small sample of people provides researchers with a valuable opportunity to better understand who they are and what they want. However, it is possible that the people more likely to speak to Couric and Killian are especially dissatisfied with the political process.[4] In contrast, national surveys of large, diverse sets of people rely on "closed-ended" questions (in which response categories are provided) to ease the logistics of data collection. This limits our ability to consider how people reason about politics (Geer 1991). In an ideal scenario, we could get the best of both worlds – a large survey that gives people an unconstrained ability to discuss how they feel about partisan politics.

In conducting research for this book, we were fortunate enough to access such a rarity in survey research: a large-scale survey of open-ended questions posed to both partisans and independents.[5] In this survey, identifying as independent is our best indicator of partisan avoidance. The dataset includes 2,915 Americans (including 896 self-identified independents) from around the country, each of whom was asked: "What word or short phrase would you use if you could send a personal message to President Obama?" The responses that poured in provide us with a unique opportunity to hear what Americans want

---

[4] It is important to note that Killian (2012) does spend time clarifying that the people she interviews are representative of ordinary Americans. With Couric's report, there is always the possibility that journalists are much more likely to speak to people who fit the goals of the story the journalist wants to write.

[5] These data were collected by the research survey group at Survey Monkey. The responses were collected from Survey Monkey Audience, an online panel recruited from the millions of diverse Survey Monkey surveys delivered every day in the United States. Since 2011, more than 4 million people have signed up to take surveys in exchange for a fifty cent contribution to a charity of their choice.

from the President in their own words and, as a result, how people feel about partisanship in general.

As we analyzed the nearly 3,000 messages people wrote to President Obama – messages that ranged from one- or two-word notes to thoughtful paragraphs, two unsurprising patterns emerged.[6] First, the vast plurality of people who picked "Republican" on the partisanship question (45 percent) sent Obama messages of criticism. "Please leave office!" implored one Republican respondent. Others were equally unsympathetic. "Worst President ever!" "You've failed."

On the other side of the aisle, a large plurality of self-identified Democratic respondents – over 40 percent – took the opportunity to praise the President for his hard work. "Thank you and keep up the good work! Don't be discouraged," said one Democratic respondent. Others provided notes of encouragement: "Chin up! You're doing great!" "Great job!" "Hang in there!"

After we account for Democrats' messages of encouragement, however, another pattern emerges. The Democratic respondents' second most popular message was for Obama to *fight*. "Stand up to bullies!" called one Democrat. "Don't back down!" was another common refrain. One said simply, "Get angry, Obama!"

"Fight harder!"
"Fight for us!"
"Fight back!"
"Fight!!"

The desire for their party to represent their needs *without* compromise is striking. Among Democrats, fewer than 2 percent of respondents sent Obama a message calling for more bipartisanship or suggesting he extend an olive branch to the Republicans. In survey after survey, Americans claim that they prefer bipartisanship and compromise (Harbridge et al. 2014). But while people are drawn to the term "compromise," they are much less enthusiastic about the idea of parties actually sacrificing any of their principles to produce real legislation (Harbridge et al. 2014).

In sharp contrast to partisans stood respondents who identify as independents. Rather than calling for fighting, cooperation and compromise were among the most popular messages independents hoped to send to the president. "Work across the aisle – accomplish more," pled one independent. "What happened to 'working together'?" asked another.

"Teamwork."
"Work together."
"Play nicely with others."
"Focus on compromise."

---

[6] All open-ended questions were coded to obtain the over-arching pattern of response. Coding is available in the online appendix to this chapter.

For independents, compromise was a central theme that ran through their messages to Obama. Indeed, this reflects exactly the types of responses Killian (2012) details in her book. One of Killian's interviewees even praised Democratic Senator Mark Warner because "he's willing to step out there and work with Republicans on the right way to tackle the deficit" (p. 17). These responses, at first glance, offer American politics an important new course. As people eschew partisanship they may become drawn to bipartisan compromise. At least, that is what they say.

7.1.1. The Promised Land of Compromise

By this point in our book, readers will surely expect that what people say is not always an accurate representation of what they mean. Independents, both in long interviews and a large national survey, call for compromise. But does this reflect a sincere preference?

By all accounts Americans – even partisans – want compromise in government. Just a month before the 2014 midterm election, for example, NBC News asked voters to name the most important issue to them in deciding how to vote. Later, on *Meet the Press*, host Chuck Todd reported that most voters identified not an issue but rather "an atmosphere." Said Todd, "Voters are most concerned about breaking the partisan gridlock in Washington."[7] Yet this ostensible desire for compromise is more complicated, scholars suggest.

Partisans love and hate compromise. They love the term compromise, they love to criticize politicians for a lack of compromise, but they dislike compromise in practice (Harbridge et al. 2014). A partisan's idea of a perfect bipartisan compromise seems to include the opposition simply giving up fighting while their own party passes the legislation it wanted to pass all along (Harbridge et al. 2014). This perception of "compromise" is, of course, tied to ideology and partisanship. Partisans do not want their party to make concessions because they believe in the party's ideological position. Indeed, it is possible that partisans are *more* dissatisfied when politicians push against long-held ideological principles (Carson et al. 2010).

But these are partisans. Independents, who have somehow shed their partisan ties, could be different. Even if independents are undercover partisans, the very fact that they have gone undercover may signal a strong dissatisfaction with the party, which may in turn translate to a greater willingness to accept compromise even if their (secretly) preferred party has to make concessions. This type of relationship would suggest that the motivations that lead people to hide their partisanship may also weaken the partisan attachments that produce political gridlock (Harbridge et al. 2014).

Can people who avoid partisanship live up to this promise?

---

[7] Airing of *Meet the Press*, October 26, 2014.

7.2 WALKING THE WALK

In the preceding chapters we have focused on what leads people to hide their partisanship and how these tendencies to go undercover manifest themselves politically. The consequences of undercover partisanship that we have revealed are not terribly positive. Indeed, we show that the motivation to avoid partisanship also leads people to limit their political participation out of the fear that participating means giving the impression that one is partisan. The topic of compromise, however, leads us to explore the more politically positive aspect of avoiding the party. If people avoid the party because they believe there are negative traits associated with partisanship, then perhaps these motivations lead them to be more open to compromise. Avoiding the party does not change ideological preferences (Chapter 3) but perhaps gives people the latitude to be more flexible in their expectations of parties.

To examine how people feel about political compromise we conducted an experiment on a large, national sample of Americans. Instead of asking our participants how they feel about *compromise* – a vague term often fraught with social desirability bias – we presented people with stories of legislators reaching a compromise in regard to an important bill. We focused on legislative compromise because Congress is the institution that most often represents partisanship in American politics (Levendusky 2009) and is most often implicated in arguments concerning the lack of compromise in politics. We can use this study to analyze how people who avoid (or are motivated to avoid) partisanship feel about different types of compromise across party lines.

7.2.1. Tracking the Preferences for Compromise

We recruited a nationally representative sample of 2,496 adults from across the country and invited them to participate in a survey (Study 7.1, demographics in Table A1.3). Forty-two percent of our participants identified as independents – an outcome consistent with polls and surveys conducted at around the same time as our study.[8] First, our participants answered a variety of questions about themselves, many of which were deliberately nonpolitical. Nestled within these nonpolitical questions were measures of partisanship and our now familiar measures of self-monitoring.

We then informed participants that the Democrats and Republicans in Congress were voting on an important economic bill. Although the precise nature of the bill was kept deliberately vague, we focused on the economy because it is an issue that people of all political stripes care about. In fact, polls show that both Democrats and Republicans refer to the economy when asked to identify the most important problem in our country.[9] They consistently

---

[8] Please see the appendix for details on our sample, experimental treatments, and measures.
[9] Gallup 2014 Study.

report that "the economy" should be the government's number one priority.[10]

The information that our participants received about the discussion surrounding this economic bill varied along two factors. In total, these two factors together produced eight experimental groups. As this is a larger experiment than the studies in previous chapters, we will describe the specifics of the design in three steps. We will first explain each of our two factors. We will then list the groups these factors form jointly. Finally, we will situate this design within the broader literature and explain why we presented our participants with these particular treatments.

The first factor in the study is the type of political discussion surrounding the bill. This is a two-level factor, meaning that participants could be randomly assigned to one of two conditions: (1) a condition in which the discussion of the bill between the two parties is described as acrimonious (the "disagreement" condition) or (2) a condition in which the parties' discussion of the bill is described as cooperative (the "unity" condition).

The second factor in the study is the *outcome* of the partisan discussion of the bill. In particular, here we vary whether the bill passed because the parties were able to reach a compromise or whether the bill failed because the parties could not reach a compromise. We also differentiate between the types of compromise: some participants read about the bill passing because their own party made disproportionate concessions in order to reach a compromise with the other party, while others read about the bill passing because the *other party* made the disproportionate concessions to reach a compromise.[11] In the control conditions, participants could be randomly assigned to read about the bill passing because of compromise by both parties or about the bill failing because the parties did not reach a compromise.

Combining both factors, then, our participants could have been randomly assigned to one of eight groups. Below, we list each condition and include a brief excerpt of the vignette read by the respondents assigned to that condition. We include the full wording of each vignette in Table A7.1 of the online appendix to this chapter.

- Group 1: Participant's party compromises following disagreement: "Legislators lobbed insults at each other and clashed head-on over nearly every sentence in the bill. The level of conflict suggested that there could be

---

[10] According to a Pew January 2014 survey, for example, 36 percent of respondents volunteered that economic issues (either jobs or the economy in general) are the most important problem facing the country.

[11] Respondents' preferred parties were determined by their self-identified partisanship, which they revealed early in the study. For independents, we relied on the party to which they lean in order to identify a preferred party. Those participants who reported that they were "pure" independents – meaning that they do not lean toward any party – were randomly assigned to either a case where the Democrats made disproportionate concessions or the Republicans made disproportionate concessions.

no compromise between the parties.... Compromise was due to a willingness by [participant's party] to sacrifice some of their priority programs."

- Group 2: Opposing party compromises following disagreement:
  "Legislators lobbed insults at each other and clashed head-on over nearly every sentence in the bill. The level of conflict suggested that there could be no compromise between the parties.... Compromise was due to a willingness by [not participant's party] to sacrifice some of their priority programs."

- Group 3: Participant's party compromises following unity:
  "Legislators listened to each other with open minds and calmly discussed nearly every sentence in the bill. The level of courtesy suggested there could be room for compromise between the parties.... Compromise was due to a willingness by [participant's party] to sacrifice some of their priority programs."

- Group 4: Opposing party compromises following unity:
  "Legislators listened to each other with open minds and calmly discussed nearly every sentence in the bill. The level of courtesy suggested there could be room for compromise between the parties.... Compromise was due to a willingness by [not participant's party] to sacrifice some of their priority programs."

- Group 5: No compromise following disagreement:
  "Legislators lobbed insults at each other and clashed head-on over nearly every sentence in the bill. The level of conflict suggested that there could be no compromise between the parties. Ultimately, the two parties did not manage to reach a compromise and did not pass the bill."

- Group 6: No compromise following unity:
  "Legislators listened to each other with open minds and calmly discussed nearly every sentence in the bill. The level of courtesy suggested there could be room for compromise between the parties. Ultimately, the two parties did not manage to reach a compromise and did not pass the bill."

- Group 7: Control with a compromise:
  "Recently, Democrats and Republicans in Washington voted on an important economic bill that was crucial for the government to continue to function. Prior to the vote, the party leaders stated clearly that Democrats and Republicans had vastly different goals and priorities for this bill.... Both parties eventually compromised and the bill eventually passed."

- Group 8: Control without a compromise:
  "Recently, Democrats and Republicans in Washington voted on an important economic bill that was crucial for the government to continue to function. Prior to the vote, the party leaders stated clearly that Democrats and Republicans had vastly different goals and priorities for this bill.... The bill did not pass."

Our design follows a framework developed by previous experimental studies of individual response to compromise (Harbridge and Malhotra 2011;

Harbridge et al. 2014). We vary the extent to which a party makes concessions because the policy-making process rarely produces compromises that reflect an even split between the two party positions. Rather, compromise often requires that a party give something up for the sake of moving legislation forward (Gutmann and Thompson 2010). The Tax Reform Act of 1986 – a bill lauded as a true example of bipartisanship – only passed because the Republicans agreed to a program that increased income taxes for the wealthy.[12] A compromise on a student loan bill that passed in the summer of 2013 meant that Democrats had to step back and allow the Republicans to increase interest rates on the government loans college students use to fund their tuition.[13] Indeed, successful legislative compromise is often messier and much less satisfying than the abstract promise of bipartisanship where both parties are able to reach a meaningful compromise with trivial concessions.

Our design also accounts for the possibility that our participants already have beliefs and assumptions about compromise and the legislative process. In particular, we account for these beliefs through our control groups. The first control group explains that compromise occurred, but we provide no information as to which party was the compromiser. The second explains that compromise did not occur. We rely on these two groups because simply informing participants that Congress is engaged in a debate – without mentioning whether or not they reached compromise – may lead some participants to believe that the parties are heading toward gridlock (Hibbing and Theiss-Morse 1995; Elving 1995). To avoid this possibility, we follow the approach developed by Harbridge et al. (2014).[14] We view these two groups as the most appropriate baselines from which to consider how the type of outcome and the type of debate affect individual perceptions of compromise.

After our participants read their assigned scenarios, we asked them a series of questions to measure their feelings about compromise and the political parties. These measures were designed to address how people evaluate this particular compromise, rather than how they feel about compromise in a more abstract sense.

7.2.2. Make Your Choice

Compromise – especially *bipartisan* compromise – comes with a price. It presupposes that the Republicans' and Democrats' goals may not be aligned, and, in order to come to an agreement, either one or both parties must sacrifice some

---

[12] The Republicans agreed to cut $30 billion in annual tax loopholes for those who are wealthy, which resulted in those with higher incomes paying more annual income taxes (Gutmann and Thompson 2010).

[13] (August 9, 2013). "US Student Loan Bill Signed into Law in Rare Show of Bipartisan Compromise." *Associated Press*, as included in *The Guardian*.

[14] What differentiates our approach from the approach used by Harbridge et al. (2014) is that they rely on numerical values to indicate how much each party compromised; we do not do so.

of their goals or ideas. Perhaps not surprisingly, people who strongly believe in their own party's positions are often dissatisfied with the outcome of compromise (Gutmann and Thompson 2010). Research shows that Democrats and Republicans are often frustrated when a bipartisan compromise comes at the expense of their own party's legislative goals (Harbridge et al. 2014).

Leveraging the different types of ways in which the parties reach compromise, our experiment aims to test the limits of participants' preferences for compromise over legislative gridlock.[15] The more strongly a person values compromise over the potential for gridlock, the more pleased this person should be with compromise even if a compromise means that his preferred party has to make concessions. In contrast, a person who values his party's position over compromise should be less satisfied with a compromise in which a partisan sacrifice is made, even if this sacrifice is necessary to avoid gridlock. Our goal is to measure whether people prefer that their party gets its way or that the parties achieve compromise. We put to the test the common refrain of people who avoid partisanship that any compromise is better than the likelihood of legislative gridlock (Killian 2012).

Our experimental structure will also allow us to consider the effect of either acrimonious debate (disagreement conditions) or peaceful debate (unity conditions) on response to compromise (or lack thereof). Tracking group differences both within and across political context, we will be able to observe whether context changes the way people respond to different compromise outcomes. In particular, we will track whether people respond differently when their party makes disproportionate concessions following a period of acrimonious debate than when the concessions come following a period of more peaceful debate.

To understand how people who avoid partisanship feel about compromise, we need to rely on indicators of partisan avoidance. One such indicator, as we have shown in previous chapters, is whether an individual reports that they are independent. We are not arguing that all people who identify as independent are undercover partisans, but rather we suggest that for many people who want to avoid partisanship the label "independent" is a convenient way of doing so. Following this logic, as a first step we will consider how people who call themselves independent feel about compromise.

Describing oneself as "independent," however, is not the only indicator of undercover partisanship. As we describe in Chapter 2, for example, the same motivations that lead people with clear partisan preferences to report that they are independent also lead them to avoid political participation that may be perceived as partisan. Indeed, as we show in Chapter 6, a person who does

---

[15] Research suggests that legislative gridlock is mainly a product of an unwillingness by the two parties to compromise. Further, there is a relationship between divided government and gridlock (Binder 1999). In turn, gridlock means a political stalemate – a decline in the passage of bills and, even more broadly, the potential that Congress cannot legislate on the important problems of the day (Binder 1999).

not identify as independent on a survey may still be engaged in other forms of partisan avoidance. Therefore, rather than relying on the partisanship question alone, we consider our results in another way. Focusing on the motivations that lead people to avoid public displays of partisanship, we identify the *types* of people who are most likely to be undercover partisans based on the patterns we have described in the previous chapters of this book.

As we show across a variety of different contexts and studies, people who are high self-monitors are more likely to go undercover. High self-monitors are people who are not only more concerned about the way they are perceived by others but also more willing to change their behaviors in hopes of making a more positive impression. As we demonstrate in Chapters 5 and 6, people who are higher in self-monitoring are more likely to avoid many publicly partisan behaviors when they believe that being partisan will make a poor impression on others. Given our previous patterns of findings, we consider how high self-monitors – the people most likely to go undercover – feel about partisan compromise. This approach allows us to analyze our study through a different lens, without relying on "independence" as an indicator.

7.2.3. Capturing Preferences for Compromise

We rely on a variety of measures to capture people's feelings about compromise. We first ask people to rank a set of six priorities for their political party from most to least important. These six priorities include: (1) reducing the deficit, (2) making sure to spend money to help those who need it, (3) proposing new legislation, (4) repealing legislation that is no longer working, (5) compromising with the other party, and (6) fighting for what the party believes in. These latter two priorities are the most pivotal for our study, as their ranking will allow us to track how people view compromise relative to party. In considering compromise we focus on the percentage of participants who rank fighting for a party's beliefs as either the number 1 or number 2 priority and the percentage of participants who rank compromising as either the number 1 or number 2 priority. We treat this as a measure of prioritization. In Appendix A7, we also consider this scale in different ways, including utilizing a non-parametric approach to capture the entire rank order at once.

We also want to know whether feelings about compromise spill over into feelings about the party. To measure this possibility we also ask people to evaluate their preferred party on a five-point approval scale. We then use the scale to consider the percentage of people who report that they approve of the work that their party is doing.

Given the number of groups in our experiment and the number of different comparisons we can make across these groups, we approach our analyses as follows. First, we focus only on the groups that read vignettes in which a compromise occurred and the bill was passed. We use the compromise control group (Group 7) as a baseline to consider how the nature of the compromise and the type of debate affected participants' attitudes toward the parties. Second, we expand our analysis to include the groups that read vignettes in which a compromise did not occur and the bill failed. We can then use these groups to analyze whether people would prefer a compromise that is costly to their own party to the alternative of gridlock (i.e., no compromise at all).

7.3 LEANING INDEPENDENTS AND RESPONSES TO COMPROMISE

In our first analysis, we look exclusively at those participants who first self-identify as independents and will only state a preferred party when asked: leaning independents. In fact, as we discuss in Chapter 2, previous research suggests that these people are the classic undercover partisans. How do these people react when their preferred party actually *does* compromise? Do they respond like the independents Killian and Couric interviewed and embrace the idea that compromise is superior to gridlock? Or do they behave more like partisans and prioritize victory in legislative battles?

We first consider how leaning independents feel about fighting and compromise in Figure 7.1 by examining only the groups in which the participants read that the parties reached compromise. In this figure we compare the percentage of leaning independents who place compromising with the other party in their top two political priorities and the percentage of leaning independents who rank fighting for a party's position as either their first or second priority. The first two bars show the patterns for the control group, while the remaining bars represent the treatment groups.

In the control group we see that more leaning independents prioritize compromise than prioritize fighting (33 percent to 19 percent). This result follows from the arguments in the first half of this chapter that independents want compromise. This is, however, the only compromise condition in which more leaning independents prioritize compromise than fighting. When told that legislative debate is characterized by acrimonious disagreement, leaning independents prioritize fighting to compromise. Even when the debate is not as contentious (unity condition), leaning independents are just as likely to want their preferred party to fight as to compromise.

We see the largest change in the prioritization of fighting when leaning independents are told that after much disagreement, the parties reached compromise because *their own* party made more concessions. Once participants learn that their own party gave in following acrimonious disagreement, nearly half of them report that their party's top priority should be fighting (47 percent). This is nearly a 30 percentage point increase in the prioritization of fighting ($p<0.01$) from the control. In contrast, only a fifth of leaning independents answer that the party should prioritize compromise (21 percent), about a 13 percentage point decrease ($p<0.1$) from the control group. The message here is clear: we favor compromise, as long as our party is not the one compromising.

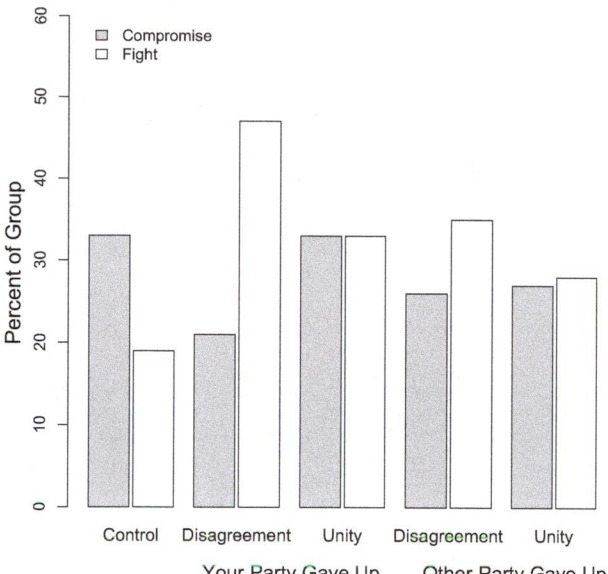

FIGURE 7.1. Prioritization of Compromise and Fighting, Leaning Independents. *Figure represents the percentage of participants who place compromising as either the first or second (of six) priorities for their party and participants who place fighting as either the first or second (of six) priorities for the party. The difference from control is significant for the condition in which the participant's party gave up under conditions of disagreement at $p < 0.01$ for prioritization of fighting, and at $p < 0.1$ for prioritization of compromise.*

We next consider whether these variations in compromise affect the way people evaluate the parties. Here we consider the percentage of participants who give their preferred party a positive evaluation. In Figure 7.2 we present the changes in evaluations of parties relative to the control group; negative values in this figure represent a decline in party evaluations. We see that leaning independents strongly punish their preferred party for compromising (Figure 7.2). Upon learning that their preferred party made concessions to compromise following partisan disagreement, the percentage of leaning independents who evaluate their party positively decreases by nearly 20 percentage points ($p < 0.05$) from the control group. In surveys and interviews, independents claim they dislike politics and parties because of a lack of compromise, but the leaning independents in our study *punish the party for attempting to end political gridlock.*

We also see no significant difference in how leaning independents evaluate their preferred party after a compromise is reached in the unity condition. These results suggest a strange circumstance for the parties. At worst, by

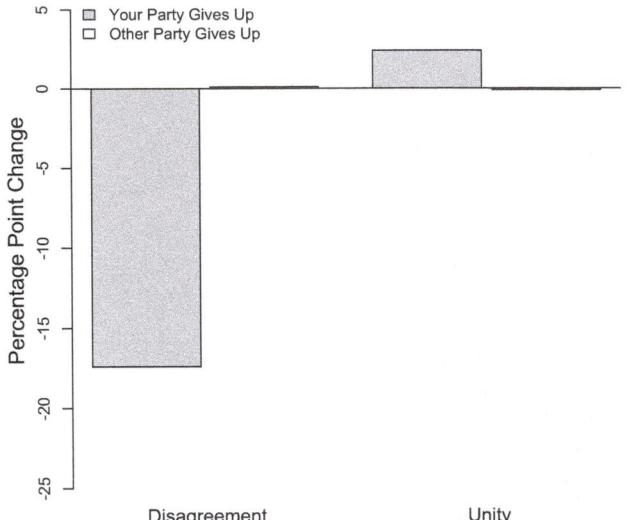

FIGURE 7.2. Change in Party Evaluations Relative to the Control Group.
Figure presents the change between the control condition and each of the treatment conditions. A negative value means a lower evaluation relative to the control. The difference from the control is significant for the condition in which the participant's party makes disproportionate concessions following disagreement; this difference from the control is significant at p<0.05.

compromising, parties risk losing support if the terms of the debate appear acrimonious. At best, a compromise will have no effect on party evaluations. Put another way, there appears to be no reward for compromise, only the potential for punishment.

What is also striking is that these leaning independents behave just like partisans. In analyses we present in the online appendix to this chapter (Figure A7.1), we find that both groups are likely to prioritize fighting, deprioritize compromise, and punish their party for sacrificing following an acrimonious debate. People who avoid the party may claim a desire for compromise, but when they encounter a realistic compromise scenario they behave just like the very partisans who told President Obama to keep fighting.

7.4. HIGH SELF-MONITORS AND RESPONSES TO COMPROMISE

As we theorize in Chapter 2 and show in the preceding chapters, one individual characteristic most associated with being an undercover partisan is high self-monitoring (a concern about self-presentation). Given our previous sets of

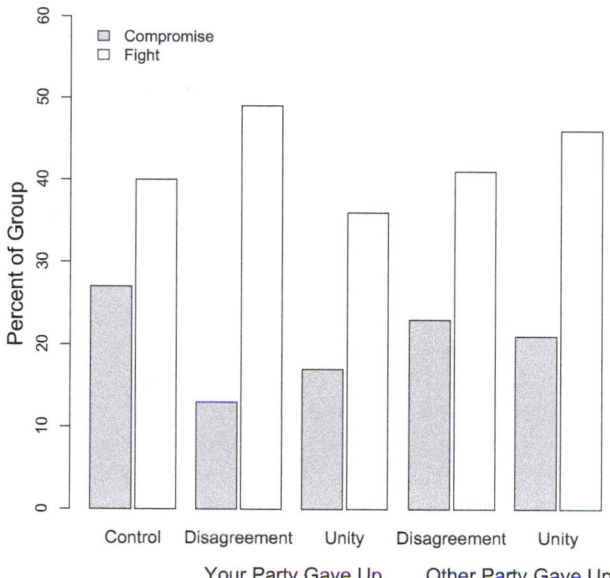

FIGURE 7.3. Prioritization of Compromise and Prioritization of Fighting, High Self-Monitors.

Figure represents the percentage of participants who place compromising as either the first or second (of six) priorities for their party and participants who place fighting as either the first or second (of six) priorities for the party. For the prioritization of compromise, the difference from the control group is significant for the condition in which the participant's party makes concessions under at $p < 0.01$. For prioritization of fighting, the difference from control is significant for disagreement, your party gave up at $p < 0.01$. Differences in preferences for compromise versus fighting are significant in all cases at $p < 0.05$.

results, we next consider how the people who are most likely to go undercover respond to compromise.[16]

Despite the fact that in our previous chapters high self-monitors were more likely to eschew partisanship, our present study demonstrates that high self-monitors, in fact, prefer that their party prioritizes fighting. We show these patterns in Figure 7.3, which, as in the previous section, only considers the five treatments where the parties reached a compromise. Focusing as we did before on the prioritization of compromise and the prioritization of fighting, we see

---

[16] One concern to keep in mind is that high self-monitors are inclined to misrepresent themselves to make a better impression on others and thus are likely to overstate their support for compromise, as that is the response that makes a more positive impression (Harbridge and Malhotra 2011). We will keep this pattern in mind as we consider our results, as this tendency will likely affect the patterns we observe.

that even in the control group more high self-monitors prioritize fighting than compromise. In fact, nearly 40 percent of high self-monitors report that fighting for its values should be their party's top priority compared to only 27 percent who suggest that the party prioritize compromise.

In fact, across all conditions, high self-monitors – the very people most likely to go undercover – are more likely to prioritize fighting than compromise. Regardless of which party made more concessions, fewer high self-monitors want to prioritize compromise in the treatment groups compared to the control group. The preference for fighting is especially high when acrimonious debate ended with the participant's party making more concessions to reach the compromise. About half of the participants who read about this type of compromise prioritize fighting – a nearly 10 percentage point increase from the control group. In contrast, only 13 percent prioritize compromise in this condition, a significant 14 percentage point decrease from the control (p<0.05).

Moreover, across all conditions, the high self-monitors behave much like low self-monitors, who, as we show in the previous chapters, are much less likely to hide their partisanship.[17] Indeed, this is the first set of results in this book in which these two groups of people behave in the exact same way. In analyses that we include in the online appendix to this chapter (Figure A7.2), we show that low self-monitors also prioritize fighting more than compromise when faced with a case in which their own party sacrifices following a period of acrimonious debate just like the high self-monitors.

Not only do people state that the parties should prioritize fighting over compromising, but they also explicitly punish parties who *do* compromise. We find that participants' evaluations of their *preferred* party significantly declines after their party compromises. In Figure 7.4 the bars represent the change in party evaluations between the control group and each treatment group. On the left side of the figure, we see how evaluations changed in the "disagreement" condition compared with the control condition. When participants' own party gave in for the sake of compromise, evaluations of that party decreased by approximately 9 percentage points. Even under unity, we see a 6 percentage point decline in rating, although it does not reach conventional levels of statistical significance.

When presented with scenarios of real compromise – rather than the abstract idea of compromise – high self-monitors are dissatisfied. In cases where party and compromise are at odds, high self-monitors seem to fall on the side of the party. Despite the fact that in every study in this book high self-monitors were the most likely to hide their partisan identities, their tendency to avoid partisanship does not translate to an unconditional support for compromise.

---

[17] All differences are relative to a baseline control point. We first compare the rate of prioritization of fighting. When the treatment is disagreement, your party gives up, the difference-in-difference (DID) for low and high self-monitors is not significant at p=0.59. For disagreement, other party gives up the DID is not significant at p=0.62.

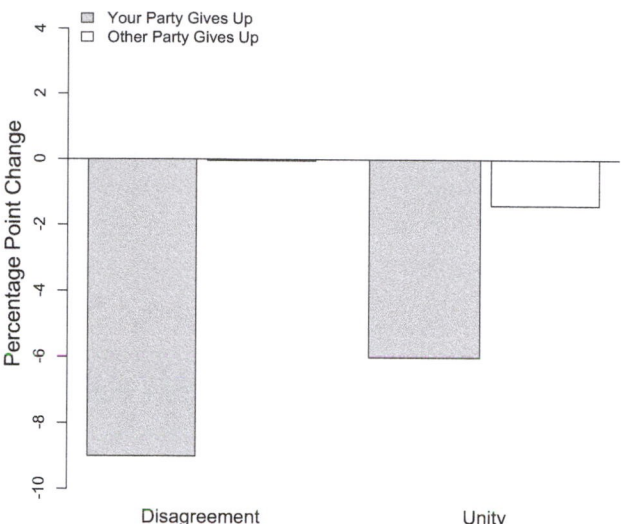

FIGURE 7.4. Change in Party Evaluations Relative To The Baseline Control Group. *Figure presents the change between the control condition and each of the treatment conditions. A negative value means a lower evaluation relative to the control. The difference from the control is significant for the condition in which the participant's party makes disproportionate concessions following disagreement. Difference from control is significant in disagreement; your party gives up condition at p<0.1.*

Rather, high self-monitors remain firm that their party's top priority should be fighting, as opposed to compromising. This preference is particularly strong when it is their own party that makes the greatest political concessions.

7.5. PURE INDEPENDENTS AND RESPONSES TO COMPROMISE

So far our results point to a tension. The very people who are most likely to hide from party labels and avoid any association with their preferred party are dissatisfied when their party sacrifices in order to reach a compromise. We can take our analysis, however, one step further and consider how pure independents – a group that few scholars have examined directly – feel about compromise. Most of the research that considers independents as undercover partisans focuses on leaners and leaves pure independents aside (e.g., Keith et al. 1992).

As we describe in the previous sections of this chapter, to consider how pure independents respond to partisan compromise, we modified our study. Given that pure independents do not report any party preference at all, we randomly assigned them to either read that the Republican Party made more concessions for the sake of compromise or that the Democratic Party did so. We cannot

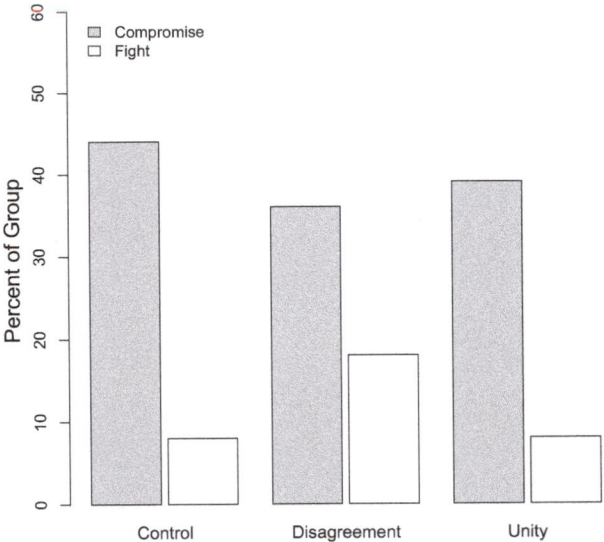

FIGURE 7.5. Prioritization of Compromise and Fighting, Pure Independents.
Figure represents the percentage of participants who place compromising as either the first or second (of six) priorities for their party and participants who place fighting as either the first or second (of six) priorities for the party. There is a significant difference in the prioritization of fighting between the control condition and the condition where compromise follows disagreement; this difference is significant at p<0.1.

directly consider how these people evaluate their preferred parties – because they have not disclosed any preference – but we can examine whether they believe parties should fight or should compromise.

In the control condition, we find that pure independents are in favor of compromise and much less supportive of fighting. Although pure independents' preference for fighting does increase when compromise is reached following acrimonious debate, these participants do maintain a preference for prioritizing compromise. Indeed, these results are the first to suggest that for people who fully eschew parties, any type of compromise is perceived positively (Figure 7.5).

These patterns are suggestive and we want to caution against using these results to draw the conclusion that those who are truly free of partisan attachments (i.e., pure independents) will help politics shift toward compromise and bipartisanship. Few individuals – both in our study and others – identify as pure independents. Indeed, the percentage of pure independents often hovers between 6 and 15 percent of any given survey sample. Even more importantly, pure independents have been on the decline over the last several decades.[18]

[18] Data from the American National Election Study, Cumulative data file.

Since 1980, the growth in independents has been a function of gains in leaning independents rather than pure independents. Put another way, the overall increases in independents often touted by media signal more people who may be dissatisfied with real compromise than people who welcome compromise in any form.

7.6 WHAT IF THERE IS NO COMPROMISE?

If people do not reward the party for compromising, then perhaps they punish the party for *not* compromising. To consider this possibility, we now turn to the remaining groups in our study – the groups in which the party did not compromise. Even if reading that their party sacrificed following acrimonious debate led participants to lower their evaluations of their party, it is possible that not compromising at all may produce even worse outcomes for that party. It is possible, for example, that by comparing our treatments to a control version of compromise rather than to a case where no compromise occurred, we are failing to observe a reward for reaching compromise.

First, we see that when leaning independents read about acrimonious debate (disagreement condition), they are quite forgiving of a failure to compromise. In fact, among leaning independents in the disagreement condition, evaluations of parties that do not compromise actually *increase* relative to the no compromise control group. This increase, however, does not reach statistical significance. Moreover, a failure to compromise following peaceful debate (unity condition) also does not lead people to punish the party more. Similar to the disagreement condition, we see no significant differences between the "no compromise" control group and the condition in which the parties fail to compromise following peaceful debate.

A more interesting comparison, however, is between cases where compromise happens and those where compromise does not happen. We consider this relationship by comparing evaluations of a party that compromised to those of a party that did not compromise. In these comparisons, we keep the context of the political debate constant, comparing compromise groups to non-compromise groups first in the disagreement conditions and then in the unity conditions.

Among leaning independents, the results follow a pattern: people evaluate parties that did *not* reach a compromise significantly more positively than parties that did compromise (Figure 7.6). When the debate is acrimonious (disagreement condition), the percentage of leaning independents who evaluate their party positively is nearly 20 percentage points lower when their party makes concessions to compromise than when their party does not compromise at all (Figure 7.6a). Although the participants are kinder to their party when they encounter a peaceful debate (unity condition), we still see no indication that compromising offers any kind of substantial reward for the party (Figure 7.6b). This is particularly true if compromise involves giving

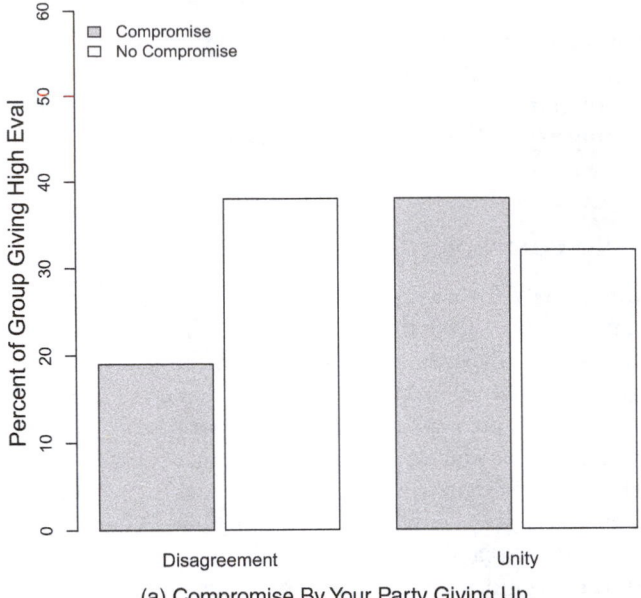

Your Party Gives Up to Compromise

(a) Compromise By Your Party Giving Up

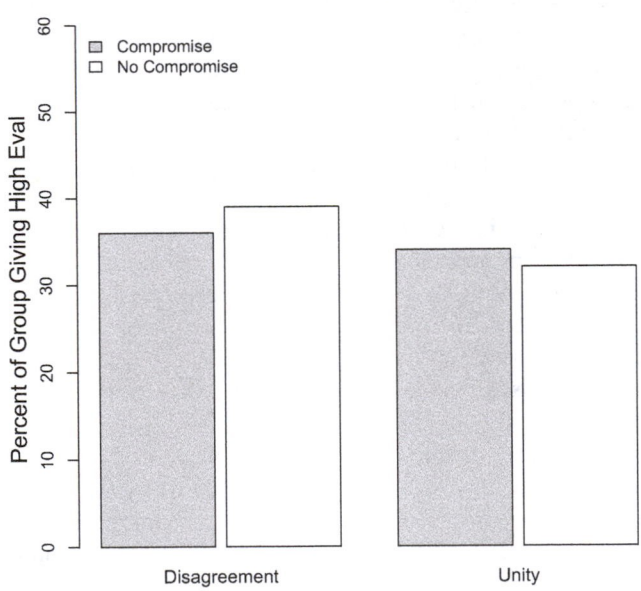

Other Party Gives Up to Compromise

(b) Compromise By Other Party Giving Up

FIGURE 7.6. Comparison of Compromising and Not Compromising (a): Compromise by Your Party Giving Up (b): Compromise by Other Party Giving Up.
Bars represent the percentage of group members who rate the party positively. Here we compare the treatment groups directly, without the control groups. The difference between compromise and no compromise is significant for leaning independents in the disagreement/your party gives up condition at $p < 0.05$.

something up, and quite often, real political compromise involves making some concession.

7.7. COMPROMISE OR MODERATION?

To this point we have shown that both people who are independent and people who are most likely to go undercover do not prioritize compromise. While they seem positively inclined toward compromise when it is presented as an abstract concept, these people quickly lose their enthusiasm when they are given additional information. Rather, the people who avoid partisanship behave much like the people who publicly identify as partisans. Parties, it seems, reap no benefit from sacrificing for the sake of compromise and, worse, may actually be punished for these types of efforts.

There remains the possibility that we have approached this question from the wrong direction. Maybe our undercover partisans do not simply want bipartisan compromise, where each party takes turns sacrificing for the sake of avoiding gridlock. Rather, the avoidance of partisanship may mean that people prefer political *moderation*. In other words, perhaps our undercover partisans want politicians to produce overall more moderate solutions to the day's most important issues. Maybe that is what they envision when they say "compromise." After all, when asked what they would say to President Obama, a sizeable proportion of respondents wanted the president to become more *moderate*.

We consider the desire for moderation by turning to individual ideology. To do so, we turn to a third dataset: a nationally representative survey of 2,119 Americans fielded in 2013.[19] If there is, indeed, a preference for moderation among those most likely to go undercover, we should observe that in their own ideological positioning. Traditionally, political scientists have sought to identify Americans' ideological preferences by asking a seemingly simple question: "When it comes to politics, do you usually think of yourself as liberal, moderate, or conservative?" Like many scholars who came before us, we asked our respondents to answer this very question. At first blush, it does indeed appear that people who identify as independent are more likely to identify as "moderate": 40 percent of them do so, as opposed to just 32 percent of Democrats and only 16 percent of Republicans.

But this, of course, is a muddy measure. If people identify as independent because they believe doing so will make for a positive impression, one could make the same argument about the label "moderate." Moreover, even without the role of impression-management, ideology is a complicated measure. Respondents may be considering different issues when they think of their ideology. Some, for example, may focus on social issues, like same-sex marriage and

---

[19] The survey in this study was administered by GfK to a general population of English-speaking adults over the age of 18 who reside in the United States. The survey was fielded between March 6 and 18, 2013.

reproductive rights. Others may instead consider economic issues, like taxes and government spending. Still others may weigh both social and economic issues equally.

We deal with these issues by splitting our measure of ideology into two separate dimensions – one for social issues and one for economic issues (Klar 2014c). This leaves us better able not only to uncover our respondents' true ideological positions but also to avoid the possibility that people use the label "moderate" to avoid revealing their overall political preferences. Indeed, people may be more forthcoming if they believe the questions reflect specific positions rather than an overall worldview. We therefore asked our respondents to identify themselves on these two ideological scales. The first we called "economic ideology" and we suggested that they think of things like taxes and the economy. The second we called "social ideology" and we suggested, in this case, that they consider issues like reproductive rights and same-sex marriage. Using these two scales, we can track whether the people who want moderation are actually themselves moderate.

We find that only 19 percent of independents identify as both economically moderate and socially moderate. By contrast, 14 percent identify as liberal on both scales, while 25 percent (the plurality) identify as conservative on both scales. That is to say that nearly 40 percent of self-identified independents are highly ideological when they are asked to consider specific policy dimensions. And the large majority of the remaining independents are ideological on at least one dimension. In short, despite a prevailing belief that independents value moderation and bipartisan compromise, our results suggest that this is not the case.

7.8. NOTHING MORE THAN FEELINGS

Despite their rhetoric and their reluctance to behave as partisans, it seems that *even voters who avoid parties* favor uncompromising rigidity.[20] In fact, when it comes to compromise, the people who avoid parties might behave much as we would expect partisans to behave. But does this mean that independents are a "myth"? Are they inconsequential? The answer is not so simple.

In the previous four chapters, we demonstrate that people see no social value in partisanship but rather place a broad social value on independence. We demonstrate not only a dislike of partisanship but also that people experience a physical repulsion from partisans. Given these results, it comes as no surprise that avoiding partisanship comes hand-in-hand with a self-professed preference for compromise. The open-ended survey data we report at the beginning of this chapter indicate that this is so. Indeed, the label "independent" suggests a

---

[20] In additional analyses, we examined how strong and weak partisans respond to each experimental stimulus – indeed we find that they oppose compromise and favor fighting for their preferred party's policies.

person who has risen above the two parties. If Americans are turned away from partisanship because of disagreement, then certainly compromise seems to be the best bait with which to lure them back.

What the experimental studies in this chapter demonstrate, however, is something much more complicated. Certainly, people who shy away from parties *report* an interest in compromise, yet for many people this interest in compromise is as much an exercise in impression management as is the label "independent." When learning about compromise between the two parties, the very same people who dislike parties *want their own party to fight harder*. When the debate is contentious, when sacrifices need to be made, the people who avoid parties actually punish their own party for compromising.

These people, be they independents or undercover partisans, are full of contradictions. On one hand, they refuse to identify with a partisan label or do anything to support a party they may secretly endorse. On the other hand, they are frustrated when their favored party compromises, wishing instead for a stronger fight. In some ways, these people lack the normatively positive aspects of partisans (for example, being politically participatory) while embracing the negative aspects of partisans (a stubborn dislike of compromise).

The people who avoid partisanship are a political candidate's worst nightmare. They do little to offer support, they refuse to admit their support publicly, and they are unlikely to convince their social networks to support a particular party position or policy. Meanwhile, they make grand overtures about partisan compromise yet grow increasingly frustrated when their party – the very same party they are ashamed to admit they prefer – bends in any way to the will of the opposition, even when this is the only way the political process can move forward. These voters want their party to engage in the very same behavior that (they claim) drove them away from partisanship in the first place.

8

The Partisan Underground in an Era of Polarization

"The greatest way to live with honor in this world is to be what we pretend to be."

– attributed to Socrates

On a Thursday in October of 2014, Steven Colbert, comedian and then-host of the satirical show *The Colbert Report*, made a confession to his audience: "For nine years now, I've been telling you I'm an independent conservative."

"But," Colbert paused, as the audience laughed, "that was a lie. Last night when I was coming out to my family as openly Republican, they said they always knew. They could tell."

Colbert said he wanted to "inspire" other "closeted Republicans" to join him in coming out. He had a particular person in mind: Bill O'Reilly. O'Reilly is not a comedian, and his show, *The O'Reilly Factor*, is not a satire. While *The Colbert Report* was broadcast by Comedy Central, *The O'Reilly Factor* airs on Fox News. While Colbert's personal political beliefs are somewhat ambiguous, most people place O'Reilly squarely on the Republican side of the political spectrum. Yet here was Colbert, showing clip after clip of O'Reilly proclaiming that he's an independent.

"I'm an independent, but I know both parties really well," O'Reilly informed guests on his show in one clip. "As you know, I'm an independent," O'Reilly told Republican Senator Marco Rubio in another clip. In a final clip, O'Reilly insisted, "I'm an independent! I'm an independent."

Colbert's response: "Whatever helps you sleep at night."

In 2014, Fred DuVal was a candidate for governor in Arizona. A same-sex marriage supporter, DuVal spent his campaign advocating for new programs to protect children from abuse and neglect. He argued in favor of funding education and wanted to "move Arizona forward."[1] Fred DuVal is a Democrat. Not only was he the most recent Democratic nominee for governor in Arizona, but since the 1980s DuVal has held leadership positions within the Democratic Party organization. He twice served on the Democratic National Committee, was the treasurer of the Democratic Governors Association, and worked for President Bill Clinton.

This is not information one would ever glean from DuVal's campaign materials. DuVal's Twitter and his Facebook made no mention of the fact that Fred DuVal is a Democrat. The "About Fred" page on his main website offered no hint of partisanship. In a paid campaign ad, the following information flashed to Arizona viewers over images of the Democratic nominee for governor: "Fred DuVal, Independent."

Bill O'Reilly, the talk-show host and Fred DuVal, the candidate for governor, have little in common besides the desire to share a common political label: "independent." What would motivate these two people with very clear (and opposing) political positions to share this ambiguous political label? O'Reilly and DuVal are different from the average person. They speak to a wider audience, and their political choices are more consequential. Their motivations, however, are rooted in the same place as those of other Americans: make the best impression possible. Throughout the previous seven chapters we have explored what happens when people come to believe that being frank about one's partisanship is no longer a means of making that positive impression. O'Reilly and DuVal are a testament to this phenomenon.

8.1 THE STATE OF PARTISANSHIP IN AMERICA

Over the past five decades, political scientists have taken different approaches to defining partisanship. In Chapter 2, we discussed the approach of *The American Voter* (also known as "the Michigan model"). This approach considers partisanship as a characteristic or self-description that shapes the way people view political issues. Since the introduction of the Michigan model in the 1960s, other traditions have emerged. One tradition considers partisanship as a sum of ideologies, issue positions, and political and economic events. According to this approach, individuals adjust their party identification in response to new political information (Fiorina 1981; Achen 1992, 2002). The second tradition, which we introduced in Chapter 2, takes a more psychological and sociological approach to understanding how partisanship shapes people's relationship with politics.[2]

---

[1] Wording from the Fred DuVal for Arizona Governor website.

[2] This second, more psychological tradition finds its roots in the Michigan model, whereas the first approach – often called the "tally" approach – finds its roots in a more rational approach to updating preferences.

This second tradition views partisanship as "a pervasive dynamic force shaping citizens' perceptions of, and reactions to, the political world" (Bartels 2002, p. 138) and brings to the forefront the idea that partisanship is akin to a social identity, a concept not unlike religion (Green, Palmquist, and Schickler 2002). Thinking about partisanship as an identity helps to explain why people's partisan preferences do not necessarily match their ideological views (Green et al. 2002) and why people may, in fact, hold similar ideological views to members of the opposing party yet still despise them (Iyengar et al. 2012; Mason 2014). Our work follows from the tradition that views partisanship as an identity, but we add a component that few scholars have previously considered – the *expression* of partisanship. As we show, people may hold on to stable partisan identities and preferences but fluctuate in the degree to which they are willing to express them. It is this difference between identity and expression that guides our work.

8.1.1. The Expression of Partisanship

In July of 2015 more than 40 percent of people reported that they were independents, a nationwide increase in the number of independents even from as recently as 2010.[3] In the four years between 2010 and 2014, in states that require party registration, the total number of people registered as either Democrats or Republicans has declined by 2,847,353. Many of these people, registration records suggest, would rather register as "unaffiliated" or "undeclared" than select a party. In fact, in a number of states that ask for partisan preferences, those selecting "unaffiliated" already form the plurality of active registered voters.[4]

Political pundits hail these changes as the dawn of a new American political reality, one in which politically untethered voters can be swayed by credible arguments from either of the two parties. Political scientists, on the other hand, as we explain in Chapters 1 and 2, dismiss the idea that these patterns have political consequences. Our goal in this book has been to challenge both of these notions.

Independents, we argue, are not "up for grabs" by either party, nor are they bastions of neutrality who weigh which options are best for American progress.

---

[3] Data based on the July 2015 Political Survey conducted by the Pew Research Center for the People & the Press, based on 2,002 telephone interviews. The percentage of independents is based on results that do not exclude participants who gave no party preference (4%) or refused to answer the question.

[4] Data is based on patterns reported by state websites. Data is based on states that require individuals to report a party, and if no party is reported classifies individuals as "unaffiliated" or "no party." Patterns based on states that report partisan registration. Data excludes Utah, Rhode Island and West Virginia. Data reported in the online appendix to this chapter. We use 2010 and 2014 as both periods contained midterm elections. Where possible we obtain results from September of the years.

Although some people who report they are independent may see themselves as ideologically and politically removed from both parties, many are quite connected to one of the two existing political parties. As we show in Chapter 7, for example, many people who identify as independent are unlikely to support a bipartisan compromise if that compromise comes at the expense of their preferred party's policies. Moreover, as we show in Chapters 3 and 6, even when people shift from stating that they are partisans to stating that they are independents, little else changes about them politically.

To return to the question we posed at the very beginning of this book: why do these people insist on calling themselves "independents" when by all other measures they are partisan? As we argue in Chapter 2, people want to make the best impression possible. The degree to which this concern shapes an individual's behavior can vary across people and across contexts. When people hear information that suggests there is insurmountable disagreement between the parties, or that partisans are angry and combative, they come to believe that there is nothing positive to calling oneself a partisan. As a result, Americans avoid partisanship and instead call themselves "independent."

Our empirical evidence tracks a series of mechanisms that research on undercover partisans and independents has heretofore ignored. We show in Chapter 3 that being independent makes the best impression possible, while being a strong partisan does the opposite. Independents are perceived as competent and attractive, as we show in Chapter 4, while partisans are unlikable and untrustworthy. As a result, Americans do not want to live near partisans, and when asked to visualize partisanship they imagine something negative and unpleasant. Moreover, as we show throughout this book, exposure to partisan disagreement exacerbates these beliefs. Even exposure to a presidential debate leads people to hide from partisanship. Notably it is the people who are most willing to change their behaviors to make a positive impression – the high self-monitors – who are most likely to avoid the party when they hear about disagreement.

The findings we present in Chapters 3 and 4 suggest that the label "independent" is not a function of noble political goals but rather of self-preservation. People want to be liked. They want others to form positive impressions of them. They want to have friends and supporters. In fact, some people want this so much that they are willing to misrepresent themselves if it means making a better impression. These people have considered the American political context and determined that being openly partisan is not the way to win admirers. In turn, they avoid public displays of partisanship even as they are privately frustrated when their preferred party gives up too much to reach a legislative compromise.

The fact that independents are "not real" does not mean that we agree with political scientists' conclusion that independents in America are politically inconsequential. Rather, as we argue in Chapter 2, the growing percentage of independents is an indicator of a broad and troubling phenomenon. If people believe that partisanship does not make for a positive impression, then they are likely to avoid other types of behaviors that may make their political affiliations known to others. Breaking with previous research, we show that the label "independent" is just one symptom of a bigger disease of partisan avoidance. Even people who are still willing to (grudgingly) call themselves Democrats or Republicans in an anonymous survey may nonetheless avoid being publicly partisan.

Indeed, people are avoiding partisanship in ways that are markedly more consequential than merely using the label "independent." Reconsidering decades of conventional wisdom on what it means to participate in politics, we show in Chapter 5 that when people hear about partisan disagreement, they are unwilling to reveal their partisan identities in social networks and are unwilling to wear partisan stickers. They are also unwilling to engage in partisan discussions. In Chapter 6, we demonstrate that people who worry about what others think are significantly less likely to take on participatory behaviors that may lead others to guess their partisan preferences. They are even unwilling to admit that they discuss politics with partisans. Independents, these findings suggest, are far from politically inconsequential. Although it is unlikely that independents are plotting an uprising to take down the American government, a large proportion of independents signals that Americans want to avoid the party.

8.2 GOING UNDERCOVER: REMAINING QUESTIONS

Contemporary American politics functions in an information-rich environment. Political elites may attempt to set the political agenda and tone, but their messages are more often than not filtered through and dissected by media. As Shanto Iyengar argues, "in reality unmediated candidate rhetoric is an increasingly endangered form of political communication.... Today, virtually all political speech is mediated, either by reporters or pundits" (2005, p. 4). This means that not only are people continuously receiving political information, but they are also being informed about the ways in which they can filter and interpret this new information. These forces create what Walter Lippmann famously described as the "pictures in people's heads" (Lippmann 1922, p. 3). These pictures, of course, may not reflect the true state of politics.

Our next step is to consider the two possible "pictures" that people may have formed about partisanship and American politics in general. First, we want to address the portrait of America as an increasingly partisan nation. Second, we want to consider the idea that political participation and political action have significantly increased over the last three decades. We focus on these two "pictures" because they may appear to be in contradiction with the arguments we make in this book. If people are eschewing partisanship then why does it seem like people are *more* partisan than ever? If people are avoiding public displays of partisanship, then why does political participation seem to be on the rise? In the section that follows we address each of these points. We argue that both of these ideas are at least in some part "pictures in people's heads," to return to

Lippmann's words. Certainly some people are more partisan and some people are more likely to participate than they were before, but the state of partisanship and participation is much more nuanced – and much more complementary to our argument – than these stark pictures may suggest.

8.2.1 Are Americans More Partisan?

Given the cacophony of partisan information that permeates the American media, it may be difficult to imagine that Americans are avoiding politics. On the contrary, it may seem like America is full of vocal partisans. The very notion that Americans are, in fact, retreating from partisanship may seem completely contrary to the images people see and the rhetoric people hear from political elites. The news media present angry partisans blaming each other for gridlock, and campaign rallies are filled with people who carry signs that sharply attack the other side. Anonymous comments on news articles bring polarization into sharp focus, and as more people join social media websites they may even come to see strong partisan disagreement among their friends. Even if we turn our lens away from politicians in Washington and focus on ordinary Americas, it can seem like partisans are everywhere.

In 2014, for example, the Pew Research Center undertook an extensive study of partisanship and ideology in America. The Pew researchers found that since 1994 "partisan animosity has increased substantially."[5] Across a variety of indicators, surveys showed that some people seemed to cling closer to their party than ever before. In turn, media coverage of the Pew report underscored the partisan divisions. Describing the state of American partisanship as "depressing," journalist and editor Ezra Klein highlighted the stark patterns found in the Pew data. Americans, Klein concluded, not only dislike the other party but also *fear* the other party, and he warned ominously that the partisan divide is going to get worse. Elsewhere articles headlined "The Divided States of America" and "A Long Division" trumpeted the report as new evidence of the intense partisan divides among Americans.[6] These articles, as we demonstrate in Chapter 2, are consistent with a media focus on partisan disagreement.

We are not going to discount all evidence suggesting that some Americans are becoming more partisan. The key, however, is that this applies to *some* Americans. Even as the Pew report on partisanship documents the ways in which people are more divided than ever, it issues an important caution: "these sentiments are not shared by all – or even most – Americans." Even more pivotally

---

[5] Pew Research Center Report (June 12, 2014). "Political Polarization in the American Public." Access at http://www.people-press.org/2014/06/12/political-polarization-in-the-american-public/.

[6] The article "Divided States of America" by Alan Murray, was published in *The Wall Street Journal* on June 12, 2014. "A Long Division" by Mark Murray, was published by *NBC News* on October 17, 2014.

the Pew report acknowledges that "the most ideologically oriented and politically rancorous Americans make their voice heard through greater participation in every stage of the political process." The reason it seems like America is
more partisan than ever is because the loudest political voices are the voices of
those who are most partisan. Moreover, these voices are consistently amplified
by what Morris Fiorina terms "the maw of the polarization narrative."[7]

Certain segments of the public may be more partisan than before, and certain segments of the public may dislike the opposing party more than they have
in the past. Indeed, these segments of the public may even be quite politically
consequential. Yet our work suggests that what seems like a growing display
of partisanship is, at least in part, a mirage. Some people are indeed public
about their partisanship, but many more are retreating undercover. Moreover,
the people who are most willing to be vocal about their partisanship, as we
argue in Chapter 2, are more often the people who are least concerned with
what others think. These people may continue to vocalize their preferences
openly, publicly, and without concern for the perceptions of others, creating
the image that partisanship is everywhere. As a consequence, patterns of partisan retreat and activism create an almost cyclical problem for parties. The high
volume of strongly partisan voices only increases the perception that there are
negative traits associated with partisanship. As more people go undercover, the
voices of disagreement appear to be even louder.

8.2.2. Are Americans More Politically Active?

Americans' attachment to their parties is commonly estimated by examining
the most obvious forms of participation: voter turnout. Regardless of how one
measures turnout (be it as a percentage of the voting age population or of
the voting eligible population), there appears to be some stability over time.
Although some scholars suggest that there has been a decline in overall turnout
(Gerber and Green 2000), by other accounts Americans have been voting at a
relatively constant rate over the past thirty-five years – the same time period
over which we see a rise in independents. Much like the argument of increasing partisanship, these patterns too may seem initially inconsistent with the
arguments in the preceding chapters. If partisanship is losing its luster and if
individuals prefer to portray themselves as independent rather than help their
own parties to garner ever-important votes, then how is it that the votes keep
coming in?

First, it is important to acknowledge that there is some scholarly disagreement about over time shifts in turnout, as well as political participation in general. While a number of scholars suggest that there have been no downward
trends in patterns of turnout (McDonald and Popkin 2001), others argue that

---

[7] Morris Fiorina (June 23, 2014). "Americans Have Not Become More Politically Polarized."
WashingtonPost.com *Monkey Cage Blog*.

turnout has been on the decline since the 1980s (Gerber and Green 2000; Blais and Rubenson 2013). Still, let us make the more conservative assumption for our argument, and assume that voter turnout has remained stable since the 1980s. Even if we make this assumption, most scholars agree that large groups of people are failing to cast their ballots. It is the presence of these non-voters that bridges the arguments in the preceding chapters with aggregate patterns of political participation.

The modern American election is a costly affair. Indeed, as the number of voters remains stable, the cost of an election rises each year, causing *The New York Times* to pronounce in 2010 that "one thing seems certain: votes are getting more expensive."[8] In 2012, the candidates spent a record amount of money to get their voters to the ballot box: approximately $14.95 per Obama voter and $16.28 per Romney voter. There are, of course, confounding factors that make it difficult to measure precisely how much one vote "costs." Perhaps most significantly, changes in campaign finance laws have allowed for substantially more money to pour into political campaigns.[9] As a result, we cannot definitively conclude that the massive increase in spending to mobilize roughly the same sized electorate is due only to sheer necessity. Nonetheless, it is notable that increasing amounts of campaign spending have *not* come hand-in-hand with equally large increases in voter turnout. This relationship between spending and turnout suggests that any stability in turnout is a puzzle: if parties (and numerous other groups) are pouring more and more money into elections, *why has voter turnout not increased*?

Moreover, even if we turn to characteristics that traditionally explain patterns of political participation, voter turnout still seems surprisingly *low*. Raymond Wolfinger and Steven J. Rosenstone famously identified two determinants of voter turnout that, as it happens, also tend to predict so many other outcomes in life: primarily, a high income and high education (Wolfinger and Rosenstone 1980). According to their analyses – and the voluminous amount of research on voter turnout that has since followed – these two factors are crucial in allowing individuals to overcome the costly burden of voting.

As per capita income has increased so has the percentage of Americans who have completed four years of college or received even more education (Figure 8.1), yet—even from the most optimistion perspective – *turnout remains stable*. This is especially surprising given that numerous states have enacted policies such as early voting, mail-voting, and same-day voter registration to reduce the burden of voting (Burden et al. 2014). In short, even assuming stability in voter turnout leads to a question: Why are *more* people not voting?

---

[8] Eduardo Porter. "The Cost of a Vote Goes Up." *New York Times*, November 6, 2010.
[9] In the 2010 case of *Citizens United v. Federal Election Commission*, for example, the Supreme Court ruled that the government could not restrict independent political expenditures by non-profit corporations, for-profit corporations, labor unions, and other associations.

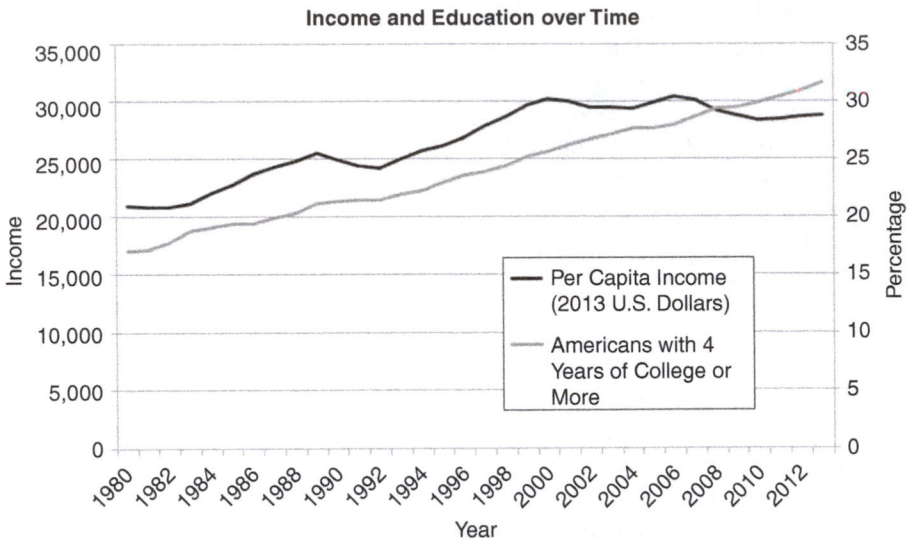

FIGURE 8.1. Income and Education over Time (1980–2013).
Income and educational data come from the U.S. Census Bureau.

We can pose similar questions about other forms of political participation. We examined data from four separate nationally representative surveys[10] and consistently found an aggregate decline since the 1990s of public willingness to support one's party through things like wearing a campaign sticker or trying to persuade someone else to support a particular candidate. This may be because people are engaging in different forms of participation. Much is written, for example, about political activism on social media – colloquially referred to as "slacktivism." According to a study by the Pew Research Center, 38 percent of all social media users report having "liked or promoted material related to political or social issues" online, leading to a 2013 report concluding that "notable shares of social network site users say their activity on the sites has prompted them to learn more about social or political issues and to take action around those issues."[11] Yet there is reason to believe that *partisan* politics are *not* overwhelmingly publicly supported on social media sites. A recent study revealed that, in fact, only 4 percent of adults who regularly log in to Facebook self-identify on their profile page with an ideological affiliation that is "interpretable" (Bakshy et al. 2015).

[10] The surveys in the American National Election Studies (ANES), the General Social Survey, the National Annenberg Election Survey, and the Civic Competence Study run by CIRCLE. Each shows a steady decline in political participation over the past decade, though the ANES is anomalous in demonstrating a brief increase in 2004, followed by a subsequent decline in the following years.

[11] Pew Center report available online at http://www.pewinternet.org/2013/04/25/civic-engagement-in-the-digital-age/ (Retrieved May 7, 2015).

We should not rejoice in finding stability in aggregate participation rates. Rather, the patterns in participation may actually *reinforce* the arguments we make in this book: Americans have become increasingly reluctant to support their own parties and, in turn, are avoiding parties by eschewing various forms of political participation. To this end, then, the forces we explore in this book can explain why partisan mobilization may be increasingly becoming a Sisyphean task, and why the very factors that should *reduce* the costs of participation have little effect on people's willingness to take political action. Indeed, as Leighley and Nagler (2013) demonstrate, what characterizes the modern non-participant is dissatisfaction with politics and an alienation from parties.

The great irony of these patterns is that if more people were more willing to admit their partisanship, parties may not need to spend as much money convincing other people to take actions. It is difficult to understate the political significance of open political communication between citizens. "When one citizen discusses politics with another citizen, the stage is set for the politics of one or both discussion parties to be affected" explained Huckfeldt and Sprague (1991, p. 122). Similarly, Gerber and Green (2000, 2008) demonstrate that direct citizen-to-citizen contact is the best form of mobilization. Not only that, but Gerber and Green (2008) argue that it is actually more cost-effective than other mobilization approaches. If parties cannot count on ordinary citizens to act as their salespeople (to return to James Stimson's [1990] point), parties have to settle for not only less effective forms of mobilization but also more expensive forms of mobilization.

As coverage of partisan politics becomes increasingly negative in tone, more Americans identify as independents, and fewer engage with politics. Contrary to what the media tend to report, most independents do hold secret partisan preferences, and they tend to support those parties. But contrary to most academic assumptions, independents are not, as a result, politically inconsequential. As the electorate moves undercover, the parties may be left with no proud supporters to lean on. Not only is the loss of the partisan salesperson a loss for parties, but it is a loss for the democratic norm of political participation as well.

8.3 WHERE HAVE ALL THE PARTISANS GONE?

Our story of American partisan politics begins with a simple idea: the image we project to the world is an amalgam of two components – who we are and who we want others to think we are. Who we are can be a function of our actual preferences, our identities, and the way we sort ourselves into existing political groups. How we want to be perceived, however, may be different from who we actually are. A person might identify as a Republican or a Democrat but might not consistently express this identity. When confronted with the possibility that their identity could make a poor impression on others, some will opt to hide behind a different label – a more positive (or at least more neutral) label. Someone who identifies as a Democrat is unlikely to call herself a Republican even for the sake of making a positive impression but may be quite willing to call herself an independent.

Even if one agrees with the idea that people generally want to make a positive impression, the idea that partisan disagreement is leading people to avoid expressing partisan identities may still catch them by surprise. Partisan identities, scholars argue, are persistent and are even immune to new information and new political events (Green et al. 2002; Groenendyk 2013). Our argument that people avoid partisanship may at first seem inconsistent with such a stable identity. We believe that these two arguments are, in fact, quite compatible. Partisanship, we agree, is stable. What *can* change is people's willingness to express their partisanship to others. Indeed, the changes in behavior we observe in Chapters 3, 5, and 6 are changes in willingness to *display* partisanship rather than changes in ideological positions or party preferences. This focus on the expression of partisanship distinguishes our work from previous scholarship.

Accounting for the way people express partisanship applies a different perspective to people's relationships to parties. Aiming to understand individual-level partisanship, the Michigan model measured the strength of partisan affiliations – are you a strong or a weak partisan? More recently, political scientists have focused on how strongly people feel about partisanship as an identity (Green et al. 2002) and how close they feel to their partisan group (Huddy et al. 2015). These approaches help clarify how people perceive politics and view their own political attachments.

We are also interested in partisan attachments, but we consider these attachments not only from the lens of the individual but also from the lens of the party. From this perspective, what matters is not only a person's internal connection to a partisan group but also his willingness to be open and public about this connection. Given a party's political needs, people who are willing to take on openly partisan behaviors are more valuable members than those people who are unwilling to do so. A reported group connection and an affective identity are important forces for explaining how people perceive politics, but warm feelings ring hollow if a person is unwilling to express them.

To consider the relationship between identity and expression we can briefly look to a part of America where aggregate partisanship has experienced the greatest shift: the American South (Green et al. 2002). Prior to the 1960s, the South was a stronghold for the Democratic Party. In the decades following the 1960s, however, Southern whites moved steadily toward the Republican Party – a shift that has been so thorough that over the past twenty years Southern states have become unambiguously red.

The transformation from blue to red state is in large part attributed to issues surrounding race (Green et al. 2002). Green et al. (2002) argue that the 1965 Voting Rights Act (VRA) launched the partisan shift in the South because the legislation brought blacks into the fold of the Democratic Party. This displeased white Southerners. Indeed, when we use the American National Election Study surveys to look at partisan identification between the years 1952 and 1968, we see an unusual pattern among Southern whites. As one may expect, the percentage of white Southerners who identify as Democrats decreases following the passage of the VRA. One may expect, then, that the parallel shift to this change in Democrats should be an increase in Republicans. This is not the case; rather, over the same time period the percentage of white Southerners who identify as Republicans remains fairly *constant*. White Southerners who left the party in the wake of the VRA did not immediately become Republicans. Instead, the pattern shows that they identified as independents.

The percentage of white Southerners who reported that they were independent ranged from 15 percent to 19 percent between 1952 and 1964 and then suddenly spiked to more than 30 percent by the 1970s.[12] This pattern at that time was unique to the South, as the percentage of independents remained stable over the same set of years among whites in the rest of the country. As the number of Southern independents dramatically grew, the vast majority identified as leaners. Between 1964 and 1968, the proportion of Southern whites who identified as leaning independents spiked by about 10 percentage points. We are not the first to identify this pattern. Indeed, tracking partisan identification in the South from 1952 to 1972, Beck (1977) writes "the most striking changes in the twenty-year interval were the increase in independents and the decrease in Democrats." (p. 479). Of course, as Beck (1977) notes, partisan changes in the South tell a complicated story, but these patterns suggest that at least to some extent Southern whites seemed hesitant to publicly express their partisan identities and instead self-identified as independent.

Such unwillingness to express one's identity is consequential. "Younger white Southerners are more Republican not because they are more conservative but because their attachments formed during a period when Republicans were more likely to be regarded as an attractive social group," Green et al. (2002) write (p. 161). The extent to which a party is "the attractive social group" is a function of expression. Not only does partisan socialization depend, at least in part, on messages from parents or other trusted adults about partisan groups (Niemi and Jennings 1991),[13] but also a party is only as attractive as the people willing to publicly express their support for it. If in the mid-1960s Southern whites began to hesitate about *expressing* their preferences for the Democrats, then new cohorts of Southern white voters would be less drawn to the Democratic Party. Over time, this decline in expression of support for the Democratic Party meant new voters were more open to Republican messages from the likes

---

[12] Given that we rely on the ANES we have data for presidential and midterm elections. As there were no midterm studies in certain years, we focus on presidential years of data to retain consistency.

[13] Although, importantly partisan identification is also shaped by the political events a person experiences during pivotal years (Niemi and Jennings 1991).

of Nixon and Reagan in the decades following the VRA. As Democratic voters began to slip undercover, in the long run the Democratic Party lost their support and ultimately their place in the South.

Decades after a declining willingness to express partisan preference exacerbated the Democrats' loss of their white Southern base, parties have come to depend even more on people's willingness to display their partisan identities. Modern parties depend on the "ground game" of ordinary people working to promote candidates. Although 2010 was by many accounts a poor electoral year for the Democrats, some party operatives argue that the races the Democrats did win were due to ground game efforts.[14] In one of the Democrats' few 2010 success stories, for example, Colorado Senator Michael Bennet, cut back on televised advertising in order to push voter-to-voter promotion. Democrats are not alone in their focus on ground-level efforts. In August of 2014, a leaked internal memo showed that Americans for Prosperity – a political advocacy group that funds conservative candidates for office – was concerned about recruiting more on-the-ground "activists," or people who would publicly support and promote the organization's cause.[15] With every passing campaign, parties depend more on promotion by ordinary people. Parties want people to share the partisan message with their social networks, to send emails, and to display bumper stickers. They depend on people to display pride in the party.

Even if one is unconcerned about the plight of the American political party, the retreat from public displays of partisanship stands to change the shape of modern American politics. Parties not only use "ground game" to win seats but also use factors like yard signs, social media posts, and registration records to understand the distribution of the public's partisan preferences. This means, as Green et al. (2002) write, "party identification...shapes the strategic context within which electoral competition and legislative politics occur" (p. 227). Party identification, Green et al. (2002) argue, is what forms the very terrain of American politics.

Over the last fifty years, formal membership in local party organizations has declined (Green et al. 2002). Rather, partisan identity and informal party organizations have maintained the party system (Masket 2009). This has been the paradox of the American political party: the survival of partisan identities in the face of declining means of formal membership (Green et al. 2002). Yet partisan identities persist because of the sheer fact that people are willing to *openly* place themselves into a particular partisan group. What we suggest in this book is that this willingness is declining. People may retain their identities,

---

[14] Molly Ball (August 24, 2014). "Inside the Democrats' Plan to Save Arkansas and the Senate." *The Atlantic.*

[15] Andy Kroll (August 12, 2014). "Confidential Memo: Former Koch Group Insider Fears the Tea Party Is Fading." *Mother Jones.*

but over time the reluctance to express them publicly is bound to upset the delicate equilibrium of partisanship in America. This may not mean a collapse of the partisan system as a whole, but it will mean profound changes in the way parties rely on citizens and the way parties view the political landscape, make political choices, and, ultimately, win elections.

Appendix

In this appendix we include supplemental information for the studies described in the main text. The first part of the appendix discusses the samples we used in our analyses. The second part presents the treatments we used in the studies. The final part presents a discussion of self-monitoring and its measurement.

In addition to the analyses presented in the main text of the chapters, we have completed numerous alternative analyses that test the robustness of our results as well as replications with additional samples under different conditions. We have also conducted numerous checks of the validity of our treatments, tests of random assignment within our experimental studies, and tests of measures. All of these additional tests – including coefficient estimates and alternative specifications of models presented in Chapter 6 – are available in our online chapter-by-chapter appendix. The chapter-by-chapter appendix also includes details on the content analyses included in the main chapters. The online appendix is located at the Cambridge University Press website.

A1: EXPERIMENTAL STUDIES AND SURVEY DATA

A1.1 Descriptions and Demographics of Experimental Samples

Our experimental studies deliberately rely on a variety of samples. The goal is to show that the results we find are not specific to one particular set of conditions but rather can replicate across different samples and different experimental contexts. Since we use similar types of samples across chapters, we describe each of our sample types below.

TABLE A1.1. *All Experimental Studies*

	Study Number	Description of Sample	Description of Result
	Chapter 3:		
1	Study 3.1*	National American, N = 330	Demonstrates that participants believe selecting "independent" makes a better impression.
2	Study 3.2	Internet, N = 127	Demonstrates that the belief that being independent makes a better impression persists after exposure to partisan debate.
3	Study 3.3*^‡	National American, N = 404**	Demonstrates that a combination of partisan disagreement and a need to make a positive impression lead people to be more likely to avoid partisanship.
	Chapter 4:		
4	Study 4.1‡	Internet, N = 156**	Demonstrates that partisan disagreement leads people to avoid even those partisans who agree with them politically.
5	Study 4.2	Internet-Skilled, N = 192**	Demonstrates that partisan disagreement leads to more negative visualizations of partisanship.
6	Study 4.3^	National American, N = 513	Demonstrates that partisan disagreement leads people to avoid neighborhoods with politically active residents.
7	Study 4.4	Internet, N = 163**	Demonstrates that people view partisans as less attractive, competent, trustworthy, and likable than independents.
	Chapter 5:		
8	Study 5.1*	Social Media Savvy, N = 128	Demonstrates that political disagreement makes people less likely to reveal political preferences on a social media website.
9	Study 5.2	Arizona Residents, N = 645	Demonstrates that political disagreement makes people less likely to take and display a partisan sticker.
10	Study 5.3	National American, N = 400**	Demonstrates that political disagreement leaves people less likely to participate in political discussions or join political websites.
	Chapter 7		
11	Study 7.1	National American, N = 2,496	Demonstrates that people most likely to be undercover partisans are dissatisfied when their preferred party makes concessions to reach compromise.

* Replication of study with different sample included in appendix to chapter
‡ Additional outcome measures included in appendix to chapter
^ Pre-tests of stimuli with different samples included in appendix to chapter
** Different parts of simultaneous study.

TABLE A1.2. *All Surveys*

Survey Name	Description of Survey	Description of Data Use
Chapter 1:		
Pew Politics Survey (2013)	Landline and cell-phone survey, 1,480 American adults; conducted July 17 to 21, 2013.	Descriptive patterns, independents and partisans.
Survey of Political Independents (2007)	Telephone interviews with 2,140 randomly selected American adults. Oversample of 1,014 respondents who identify as independent. Survey conducted May 3 to June 3, 2007. Survey is a collaboration between *The Washington Post*, Kaiser Family Foundation, and Harvard University.	Descriptive patterns of independents' demographics and reasons individuals offer for identifying as independent.
SSI Open-Ended Survey (2014)	Internet survey conducted specifically for this project in July 2014. Sample collected by Survey Sampling International.	Descriptive open-ended responses about reasons for selecting a partisan identification.
Chapter 3:		
Pew, People-Press Surveys	14 surveys from a series of Pew studies; all studies listed in online appendix.	Comparisons of proportions of independents in national survey samples pre– and post–Todd Akin's comments in 2012.
Chapter 6:		
American National Election Study, 2004 and 2006	Telephone sample of American adults, 2004 and 2006. A subset of 2004 participants was re-interviewed in 2006.	Estimates of the effect of self-monitoring on indicators of party avoidance.
Chapter 7:		
Survey Monkey Audience Survey, 2014	Internet survey of 2,915 Americans who are part of the Survey Monkey Audience panel.	Patterns in open-ended responses of "messages" to President Obama.
GfK General Population Survey, 2013	Survey 2,193 Americans, fielded online between March 6 and 13, 2013.	Patterns of identification across social and economic ideological positions.

A1.1 National Adult Samples

We rely on national adult samples recruited by different types of survey companies: Research Now (Study 3.1), Survey Sampling International (SSI) (Study 4.3, Study 7.1) and YouGov (Study 3.3, Study 5.3). The goal of these studies is to recruit a sample that is nationally representative – meaning that it matches the characteristics of the national population.

The Research Now recruitment process begins with a large panel of people who have already agreed to take part in surveys. The members of this panel are then sampled for participation in particular studies. Study samples are based on the specification requested by a particular researcher. Since our goal is to produce a sample that best matches the characteristics of the general population of American adults, Research Now relies on intra-panel recruitment techniques targeting those panel members who are older than eighteen. One of the benefits of Research Now is that the company deliberately attempts to reach population groups that are difficult to recruit for study participation. Although Research Now is a non-probability sample, it is a sample that is designed to match national demographic characteristics.

Two of our experimental samples and our sample of open-ended resposnes about identifying with a party come from Survey Sampling International (SSI). SSI is similar to Research Now, although SSI has conducted more academic studies, while Research Now has largely worked on consumer-preference surveys. Like Research Now, SSI recruits individuals to join their panel via opt-in recruitment methods online. Subsequently, within-panel samples are produced to approximate a target sample of registered voters based on age, race/ethnicity, gender, educational attainment, geographic region, annual household income, homeownership, and marital status. Although SSI samples are not as representative as national probability samples, they are more diverse than many types of convenience samples. Data collected through SSI have been used in a variety of political science studies, ranging from research by the Brookings Institute on the success or failure of Obamacare (Dropp et al. 2013) to research on experimental and survey methods (Berinsky et al. 2014).

The YouGov approach is also based on a panel of participants who are then randomly invited to take part in various studies – both political and nonpolitical. This panel includes over 2 million Americans, and YouGov relies on a process called "sample matching" to obtain nationally representative samples from this panel (see Rivers 2006 for a description). Research suggests that the YouGov technique produces samples of similar or higher quality to traditional telephone surveys (Berrens et al. 2003; Sanders et al. 2007). As a result, numerous scholars (Barabas and Jerit 2010; Brooks 2011) and surveys such as the Cooperative Congressional Election Study and the Cooperative Campaign Analysis Project (Jackman and Vavreck 2009) have relied on YouGov.

We present the demographic characteristics of the Research Now, SSI, and YouGov samples relative to the 2012 American National Election Study

TABLE A1.3. *Samples Comparisons, National Adult*

	SSI	Research Now	YouGov	ANES 2012 Web	ANES 2012 FTF	Pew 2014[1]	U.S. Census[2]
% female	51.42%	60.8%	51.56%	52.1%	52.01%	51.08%	50.8%
% 18 to 25	12.41%	11.20%	6%	9.44%	12.39%	13.33%	7.2%
% over 65	12.95%	25.6%	17.62%	19.93%	18.20%	17.26%	14.6%
$75,000+	32.49%	29.20%	–	–	–	27.60%	34.5%
BA+[3]	28.17%	25.58%	25.45%	30.37%	29.07%	27.10%	29.7%
Democrats	39.55%	32.48%	33.91%	37.41%	35.74%	33.35%	–
Republicans	23.14%	24.61%	23.88%	30.42%	25.77%	22.90%	–

[1] January 2014 Political Survey; results are weighted.
[2] Based on the 2013 American Community Survey Estimates.
[3] Those twenty-five and over given Census data.

(ANES), the U.S. Census, and Pew in Table A1.3. The 2012 ANES was conducted both via the Internet and face-to-face (FTF); we present comparisons between our samples and both the web and FTF versions of the 2012 ANES. We use these samples for comparison as they are often considered the "gold standard" of sampling. Our samples are quite comparable to the U.S. Census, ANES, and Pew.

The main difference is that there are more women in the Research Now sample relative to the other samples. We use the Research Now sample in Study 3.1, and previous research does not suggest that the test used interacts with gender characteristics. Moreover, we replicate the same result shown in Study 3.1 using a sample that contains a slight oversample of *men* (Mechanical Turk, see discussion in Section A1.2), suggesting that the greater percentage of women in the Research Now sample is not responsible for the observed outcomes.

A1.2 Internet Samples

Our Internet samples were recruited via the crowdsourcing website Amazon Mechanical Turk. Mechanical Turk is an online web-based platform for recruiting and paying people to perform tasks. These samples have been used widely across the social sciences (Berinsky et al. 2012; Kriner and Shen 2012; Doherty 2013; Huber and Paris 2013; Mattes and Redlawsk 2014). Although Mechanical Turk samples are not nationally representative, they provide a diverse group of participants and a new context in which we are able to test hypotheses. Moreover, recent research has shown that Mechanical Turk participants behave much like participants in national adult samples (Leeper and Mullinix 2014; Mullinix et al. 2014). Furthermore, to the extent that Mechanical Turk participants behave unlike other types of participants, they are most likely to do so in studies that require them to place an extensive amount of trust in the

TABLE A1.4. *Samples Comparison, Internet Samples*

	Study 3.2	Internet Savvy (Studies 4.2 and 4.3)	ANES 2012 Web	ANES 2012 FTF	Pew 2014	U.S. Census
% Female	51.38%	42.94%	52.1%	52.01%	51.08%	50.8%
% 18 to 25	26.70%	25.47%	9.44%	12.39%	13.33%	7.2%
% over 65	2.18%	3.73%	19.93%	18.20%	17.26%	14.6%
$75,000+	21.04%	24.83%	–	–	27.60%	34.5%
BA+	28.58%	27.87%	30.37%	29.07%	27.10%	29.7%
Democrats	31.74%	48.22%	37.41%	35.74%	33.35%	–
Republicans	23.08%	16.75%	30.42%	25.77%	22.90%	–

researcher (Krupnikov and Levine 2014), something which we are not asking our participants to do.

Since 2010, numerous articles have analyzed the effects of political information on individual preferences using Mechanical Turk. This subject population has been used to analyze topics such as cognitive biases (Arceneaux 2012), the role of negative advertising (Dowling and Wichowsky 2015), ambiguity in campaign appeals (Hersh and Schaffner 2013), and the effects of party reputation and brand (Butler and Powell 2013), as well as many other topics.

Our reliance on this sample, however, is also deliberate given the tasks we are asking our participants to complete in certain studies. In particular, in Study 4.2 we ask participants to search for Internet images and provide us with the URL. This means that we must ensure that all of our participants are equally adept at using the Internet in this way, as systematic differences in Internet skill would confound our results. As a result, this particular subject population offers us the best means of ensuring that all participants are at a certain Internet use baseline. In particular, in Study 4.2 we even conduct an additional check to ensure that all our participants are Internet-savvy enough to complete the task. Although we do not require such a check in Study 4.3, this study nonetheless does ask people to categorize faces by moving images. Again, this requires some familiarity with the Internet, therefore again, this particular sample is particularly beneficial. We present the demographics of this sample in Table A1.4.

Compared to our national adult samples, the Mechanical Turk samples – which we term "Internet" samples for ease of discussion – are somewhat demographically different. This is, however, to be expected. Given that participating in Turk requires some Internet skill, it follows that these samples skew younger. For example, according to recent U.S. Census records, 78.7 percent of people aged eighteen to thirty-four years access the Internet from their homes. In contrast, of people who are more than sixty-five years of age, only 48.7 percent access the Internet from their own home. Overall, 51 percent of people aged sixty-five or older reported accessing the Internet from either a home or non-home location. In contrast, 86 percent of people aged 18 to 34 reported that they had accessed the Internet from some location.[4] As a result, when our goal is to obtain a sample that is familiar with the Internet, it is reasonable to expect that it would be weighted more heavily toward those in the younger category and have comparatively fewer people in the 65 and older category.

Age aside, our Internet convenience samples recruited through Mechanical Turk are similar to our comparison samples. The convenience sample recruited for Study 3.2 is similar in gender and educational attainment to the Census sample. While the participants recruited for studies 4.2 and 4.3 – the Internet savvy samples – do skew more Democratic, this skew would only have made it more difficult for us to show the results we did. In fact, we see similar patterns across all parties in that sample.

A1.3 Face-to-Face Samples

Our final category is face-to-face samples. These, by definition, are samples from studies that relied on people directly interacting with researchers or research assistants. For the sake of categorization, we also include samples in which the initial interaction between the researcher and the participant occurred face-to-face – even if the bulk of the participation occurred over the internet. The samples in this category are by necessity geographically limited. As a result, they are less diverse than the samples in our national Internet studies.

Especially different is the sample that we use in our social media study. As we discuss in Chapter 5, the participants in this study were selected because of their familiarity with social media and the fact that they already formed a type of "network." Furthermore, these participants were all members of an undergraduate class. As a result, this is the least diverse sample of all the samples we use. The characteristics of this sample allow us to retain the internal validity of the study (participants who are familiar with social media websites and networks). Moreover, this study also retains a baseline of external validity as many users of social media are quite similar to our participants. The sample demographics are shown in Table A1.5. We do not have income characteristics for these samples. The members of our social media sample are students, meaning their income levels would not be reflective of their actual socioeconomic positions. These participants completed the entire study online at their own time rather than in a lab. We include them in this category because the initial instruction to these participants occurred in a face-to-face manner.

Our adult Tucson sample, however, was approached on the street, and income was not asked to retain privacy and trust between the interviewer and the participant.

---

[4] Data from the U.S. Census Bureau, Current Population Survey, 2012. Internet release on January 2014.

TABLE A1.5. *Samples Comparison, Face-to-Face Samples*

	Social Media	Tucson Sample	ANES 2012 Web	ANES 2012 FTF	Pew 2014	U.S. Census
% Female	52.25%	53.98%	52.1%	52.01%	51.08%	50.8%
% 18 to 25	100.00%	19.53%	9.44%	12.39%	13.33%	7.2%
% over 65	–	1.86%	19.93%	18.20%	17.26%	14.6%
$75,000+	–	–	–	–	27.60%	34.5%
BA+	–	26.58%	30.37%	29.07%	27.10%	29.7%
Democrats	29.63%	23.95%	37.41%	35.74%	33.35%	–
Republicans	29.63%	21.02%	30.42%	25.77%	22.90%	–

These types of face-to-face samples are common in political science experiments. For example, Brader (2006) relies on face-to-face studies with Massachusetts residents for his advertising experiments. Taber and Lodge (2006), Lodge and Taber (2013) rely on face-to-face studies of undergraduate students to analyze the role of cognitive biases. Further, although undergraduate student samples have garnered criticism in the past (Sears 1986), recent research suggests that they can be useful (Druckman and Kam 2011) and often perform as well as national samples (Krupnikov and Levine 2014; Leeper and Mullinix 2014).

A2: TREATMENTS USED IN EXPERIMENTAL STUDIES

Study 3.1 Treatments
Group 1: Participants who were instructed to make the worst impression were told, "For the next question, please select the answer you believe will make the WORST impression on others – even if this answer does not actually describe your true feelings."

Group 2: Participants who were instructed to make the best impression were told, "For the next question, please select the answer you believe will make the BEST impression on others – even if this answer does not actually describe your true feelings."

Study 3.2 Treatments
This study asked people to either make the best or worst impression using the same wording as the treatments in Study 3.1. Prior to this treatment, all participants received the following text from a presidential debate (the text was taken from the *New York Times* transcript of the debate):

Transcript from the 2nd Presidential Debate between President Barack Obama and Governor Mitt Romney October 16, 2012

ROMNEY: In the last four years, you cut permits and licenses on federal land and federal waters in half.

OBAMA: Not true, Governor Romney.

ROMNEY: So how much did you cut (inaudible)?

OBAMA: Not true.

ROMNEY: How much did you cut them by, then?

OBAMA: Governor, we have actually produced more oil –

ROMNEY: No, no. How much did you cut licenses and permits on federal land and federal waters?

OBAMA: Governor Romney, here's what we did. There were a whole bunch of oil companies.

(CROSSTALK)

ROMNEY: No, no, I had a question and the question was how much did you cut them by?

OBAMA: You want me to answer a question –

ROMNEY: How much did you cut them by?

OBAMA: I'm happy to answer the question.

ROMNEY: All right. And it is –

OBAMA: Here's what happened. You had a whole bunch of oil companies who had leases on public lands that they weren't using. So what we said was you can't just sit on this for ten, twenty, thirty years, decide when you want to drill, when you want to produce, when it's most profitable for you. These are public lands. So if you want to drill on public lands, you use it or you lose it.

ROMNEY: OK, (inaudible) –

OBAMA: And so what we did was take away those leases. And we are now reletting them so that we can actually make a profit.

ROMNEY: And production on private – on government land –

OBAMA: Production is up.

ROMNEY: – is down.

OBAMA: No, it isn't.

ROMNEY: Production on government land of oil is down 14 percent.

OBAMA: Governor –

ROMNEY: And production on gas –

(CROSSTALK)

OBAMA: It's just not true.

ROMNEY: It's absolutely true. You'll get your chance in a moment. I'm still speaking.

Study 3.3 Treatments

We designed our treatments to appear as short news briefs. They are similar in word count and structure.

Control Group: "Every February, Americans wait for Groundhog Phil in the little town of Punxsutawney, Pa. According to folklore, Phil's sighting of his own shadow means there will be 6 more weeks of winter. If Phil does not see his shadow, it means "there will be an early spring." The official website of

Punxsutawney Phil, perhaps not impartial, claims the Groundhog has issued a correct forecast 100% of the time."

Unity Group: "As President Barack Obama begins his second term, the Democrats and Republicans in Washington appear to be more unified than ever. Political experts predict that Americans can expect a new era of bipartisanship in Washington. The profound debate that has raged between the two parties appears to be settling. The next two years may very well bring progress towards two parties cooperating in Washington."

Disagreement Group: "As President Barack Obama begins his second term, the Democrats and Republicans in Washington appear to be as divided as ever. Political experts predict that Americans can expect even more of the partisan bickering that has characterized Washington in recent years. The profound debate that has raged between the two parties has not been settled in the least. The next two years may very well bring a continuous cycle of two parties battling it out in Washington."

Study 4.1 Treatments
We designed our treatments to appear as short news briefs. They are similar in word count and structure.

Control Group: "Every February, Americans wait for Groundhog Phil in the little town of Punxsutawney, Pa. According to folklore, Phil's sighting of his own shadow means there will be 6 more weeks of winter. If Phil does not see his shadow, it means "there will be an early spring." The official website of Punxsutawney Phil, perhaps not impartial, claims the Groundhog has issued a correct forecast 100% of the time."

Unity Group: "As President Barack Obama begins his second term, the Democrats and Republicans in Washington appear to be more unified than ever. Political experts predict that Americans can expect a new era of bipartisanship in Washington. The profound debate that has raged between the two parties appears to be settling. The next two years may very well bring progress towards two parties cooperating in Washington."

Disagreement Group: "As President Barack Obama begins his second term, the Democrats and Republicans in Washington appear to be as divided as ever. Political experts predict that Americans can expect even more of the partisan bickering that has characterized Washington in recent years. The profound debate that has raged between the two parties has not been settled in the least. The next two years may very well bring a continuous cycle of two parties battling it out in Washington."

Following treatment, participants answered a series of distractor questions about airline policy. We asked the distractor questions between the treatments and the key outcome questions to ensure that people would not attempt to guess the goals of the study and adjust their responses accordingly. After the distractor tasks, we asked participants a series of questions that follow from Iyengar et al. (2012). The questions were as follows:

Coworker question: "Imagine that there is a new coworker at your job. This coworker voted prefers the same candidate as you for President. This coworker also frequently discusses politics. How happy or unhappy would you be about this new coworker?"

[Scale of 1 (very unhappy) to 10 (very happy)]

Lawn-signs question: "Imagine that you have a neighbor who likes to display political signs promoting candidates on his or her lawn during electoral campaigns. How happy or unhappy would you be about this neighbor?"

[Scale of 1 (very unhappy) to 10 (very happy)]

Study 4.2 Treatments

Study 4.2 introduces a new treatment designed to eliminate the alternative explanation that our results are a function of people imagining politicians, rather than partisanship. This new treatment describes partisan disagreement at the mass level, rather than the elite level. The control treatment matched the treatment used in Study 3.3. The disagreement and unity treatments remained largely the same as those used in Study 3.3 with one change. The treatments in Study 3.3 began with "As President Obama begins his second term." The treatments in Study 4.2 were adjusted to state "With President Obama well into his second term." The adjustment is made to reflect the dates on which this study was fielded. The additional, mass partisanship treatment was as follows:

With President Barack Obama well in to his second term, the Democrats and Republicans in Washington appear to be as divided as ever. Political experts predict that the partisan bickering which has characterized Washington in recent years will also spill over to ordinary Americans. The next year may very well bring a continuous cycle of bitter partisan disagreement among the American public.

In order to capture the images, our participants were given the following instructions:

We are interested in the kinds of images that come to mind when you think of the term "political partisan." Using Google Image Search (image.google.com) or another website of your preference, please find an image that you think BEST fits your vision of a "political partisan." Please paste the full URL (including http) for that image in the space below. (Opening a new browser window or browser tab will not disrupt this study).

Then, they were given a text box for the URL; the text box was adjusted such that the response had to start with http, thus limiting non-URL responses.

Study 4.3 Treatments
These treatments were shown prior to the neighborhood images:

Unity Treatment: "With President Barack Obama well in to his second term, the Democrats and Republicans in Washington are showing signs of being more unified. Political experts predict that Americans can expect a new era of bipartisanship in Washington. The profound debate that has raged between the two parties appears to be settling. The next year may very well bring progress towards two parties cooperating in Washington."

Disagreement Treatment: "With President Barack Obama well in to his second term, the Democrats and Republicans in Washington appear to be as divided as ever. Political experts predict that the partisan bickering which has character-ized Washington in recent years will also spill over to ordinary Americans. The next year may very well bring a continuous cycle of bitter partisan disagreement among the American public."

Individuals rated the quality of the two neighborhoods on a 1–10 scale using the following instructions:

Please rate the overall quality of the neighborhoods above on a scale from 1 to 10 – where 1 means a low quality neighborhood, and 10 means a high quality neighborhood.

They were then given two scales next to each other. One scale was labeled Neighborhood A, and the other was labeled Neighborhood B. The appropriate ends of the scale were labeled as "low quality" and "high quality." The images of the neighborhoods remained on-screen while the participants did the ratings.

Participants rated the extent to which they would want to live in the neigh-borhoods on a 1 to 10 scale using the following instructions:

Please rate your overall willingness to live in the neighborhoods above on a scale from 1 to 10 – where 1 means that you would not want to live in this neighborhood, and 10 means that you would want to live in this neighborhood.

Again, the two ends of the scale were appropriately labeled, and we used sep-arate scales for each neighborhood.

Finally, our measure of willingness to attend an event with residents of each neighborhood was measured as follows:

Would you rather attend an event where most other attendees live in Neighborhood A or an event where most other attendees live in Neighborhood B?

Participants could then select either Neighborhood A or Neighborhood B.

Study 5.3 Treatments
Our treatments were designed to appear as short news briefs and are similar in word count and structure.

Control Group: "Every February, Americans wait for Groundhog Phil in the little town of Punxsutawney, Pa. According to folklore, Phil's sighting of his own shadow means there will be six more weeks of winter. If Phil does not see his shadow, it means "there will be an early spring." The official website of Punxsutawney Phil, perhaps not impartial, claims the Groundhog has issued a correct forecast 100% of the time."

Unity Group: "As President Barack Obama begins his second term, the Democrats and Republicans in Washington appear to be more unified than ever. Political experts predict that Americans can expect a new era of bipartisanship in Washington. The profound debate that has raged between the two parties appears to be settling. The next two years may very well bring progress towards two parties cooperating in Washington."

Disagreement Group: "As President Barack Obama begins his second term, the Democrats and Republicans in Washington appear to be as divided as ever. Political experts predict that Americans can expect even more of the partisan bickering that has characterized Washington in recent years. The profound debate that has raged between the two parties has not been settled in the least. The next two years may very well bring a continuous cycle of two parties battling it out in Washington."

In this study we relied on behavioral outcome measures. The measures were as follows:

[Introductory text, all subjects]

"Although the 2012 campaign is over, there are still ways in which you can be politically engaged. Are you interested in receiving more information about the types of issues the Democrats and Republicans will be working on in the coming year?

"If you select yes, at the end of this study you will be taken to a website that asks for your email address. *You will not be able to complete this study without visiting this website.*"

Study 7.1 Treatments

We develop our treatments to signal both political context and compromise. This allows us to consider the tension between the two. The treatments test the idea that people who avoid partisanship are the least favorable to political gridlock. The treatments are shown in Table A7.1.

The outcome measures we use in this study focus on evaluating perceptions of compromise and perceptions of parties. These are:

What do you think should be [participant's party's] most important priorities in Congress? Please the rank the following items from one (most important) to six (least important).

Response options (randomized): (1) Fighting for what they believe in, (2) Compromising with the [not participant's party], (3) Making sure to spend money to help those who need it, (4) Proposing new legislation, (5) Repealing existing legislation, (6) Reducing the deficit.

TABLE A7.1. *Treatments for Compromise Study (Study 7.1)*

Compromise Treatments

Baseline Control (N = 218)	"Recently, Democrats and Republicans in Washington voted on an important economic bill that was crucial for the government to continue to function. Prior to the vote, the party leaders stated clearly that Democrats and Republicans had vastly different goals and priorities for this bill. In many cases, Democratic goals were sharply at odds with Republican goals. Both parties eventually compromised and the bill eventually passed."
Disagreement, Your Party Sacrifices (N = 245)	"Recently, Democrats and Republicans in Washington voted on an important economic bill that was crucial for the government to continue to function. Prior to the vote, the party leaders stated clearly that Democrats and Republicans had vastly different goals and priorities for this bill. In many cases, Democratic goals were sharply at odds with Republican goals. When it came time to debate the bill, Democrats and Republicans voiced their disagreements on the Congressional floor. Legislators lobbed insults at each other and clashed head-on over nearly every sentence in the bill. The level of conflict suggested that there could be no compromise between the parties. Ultimately, the two parties did manage to reach a compromise and pass the bill. This compromise was due to a willingness by the [participant's party] to sacrifice some of their priority programs, and giving in to [not participant's party] preferences."
Disagreement, Other Party Sacrifices (N = 229)	"Recently, Democrats and Republicans in Washington voted on an important economic bill that was crucial for the government to continue to function. Prior to the vote, the party leaders stated clearly that Democrats and Republicans had vastly different goals and priorities for this bill. In many cases, Democratic goals were sharply at odds with Republican goals. When it came time to debate the bill, Democrats and Republicans voiced their disagreements on the Congressional floor. Legislators lobbed insults at each other and clashed head-on over nearly every sentence in the bill. The level of conflict suggested that there could be no compromise between the parties. Ultimately, the two parties did manage to reach a compromise and pass the bill. This compromise was due to a willingness by the [not participant's party] to sacrifice some of their priority programs, and giving in to [participant's party] preferences."
Unity, Your Party Sacrifices (N = 265)	"Recently, Democrats and Republicans in Washington voted on an important economic bill that was crucial for the government to continue to function. Prior to the vote, the party leaders stated clearly that Democrats and Republicans had vastly different goals and priorities for this bill. In many cases, Democratic goals

TABLE A7.1 *(continued)*

	were sharply at odds with Republican goals. When it came time to debate the bill, Democrats and Republicans voiced their disagreements on the Congressional floor. Legislators listened to each other with open minds and calmly discussed nearly every sentence in the bill. The level of courtesy suggested there could be room for compromise between the parties. Ultimately, the two parties did manage to reach a compromise and pass the bill. This compromise was due to a willingness by the [participant's party] to sacrifice some of their priority programs, and giving in to [not participant's party] preferences. "
Unity, Other Party Sacrifices (N = 267)	"Recently, Democrats and Republicans in Washington voted on an important economic bill that was crucial for the government to continue to function. Prior to the vote, the party leaders stated clearly that Democrats and Republicans had vastly different goals and priorities for this bill. In many cases, Democratic goals were sharply at odds with Republican goals. When it came time to debate the bill, Democrats and Republicans voiced their disagreements on the Congressional floor. Legislators listened to each other with open minds and calmly discussed nearly every sentence in the bill. The level of courtesy suggested there could be room for compromise between the parties. Ultimately, the two parties did manage to reach a compromise and pass the bill. This compromise was due to a willingness by the [not participant's party] to sacrifice some of their priority programs, and giving in to participant's party] preferences."

No Compromise Conditions

Control, No Compromise (N = 215)	"Recently, Democrats and Republicans in Washington voted on an important economic bill that was crucial for the government to continue to function. Prior to the vote, the party leaders stated clearly that Democrats and Republicans had vastly different goals and priorities for this bill. In many cases, Democratic goals were sharply at odds with Republican goals. The bill did pass."
Disagreement, No Compromise (N = 273)	"Recently, Democrats and Republicans in Washington voted on an important economic bill that was crucial for the government to continue to function. Prior to the vote, the party leaders stated clearly that Democrats and Republicans had vastly different goals and priorities for this bill. In many cases, Democratic goals were sharply at odds with Republican goals. When it came time to debate the bill, Democrats and Republicans voiced their disagreements on the Congressional floor. Legislators lobbed insults at each other and clashed head-on over nearly every sentence in the bill. The level of conflict suggested that there could be no compromise between the parties. Ultimately, the two parties did not manage to reach a compromise and did not pass the bill."

(continued)

TABLE A7.1 (*continued*)

Unity, No Compromise (N = 251)	"Recently, Democrats and Republicans in Washington voted on an important economic bill that was crucial for the government to continue to function. Prior to the vote, the party leaders stated clearly that Democrats and Republicans had vastly different goals and priorities for this bill. In many cases, Democratic goals were sharply at odds with Republican goals. When it came time to debate the bill, Democrats and Republicans voiced their disagreements on the Congressional floor. Legislators listened to each other with open minds and calmly discussed nearly every sentence in the bill. The level of courtesy suggested there could be room for compromise between the parties. Ultimately, the two parties did not manage to reach a compromise and did not pass the bill."

Do you approve or disapprove of the job [participant's party] is doing in Congress?

Strongly Approve, Somewhat Approve, Neither Approve nor Disapprove, Somewhat Disapprove, Strongly Disapprove

Detailed descriptions of original analyses, as well as information about treatment validation, replications of results and more information on the studies, are included in the online chapter-by-chapter appendix.

A3. SELF-MONITORING

The measures of self-monitoring we use originate in previous research that relies on this characteristic (Terkildsen 1993, Feldman and Huddy 2005; Berinsky and Lavine 2012). These come from a shortened scale initial developed in psychology (Snyder 1979). Self-monitoring is based on the way people adapt to their outside environment and is a concept distinct from other individual characteristics such as the need for cognition or evaluation (Cacioppo et al. 1996).

In most of our experimental studies we use both the five-point versions of the self-monitoring questions (Berinsky and Lavine 2012) and the true-false versions of the questions (Terkildsen 1993; Feldman and Huddy 2005). We use the shortened version of the scale validated by Berinsky and Lavine (2012). Although Berinsky and Lavine (2012) argue that the five-point version is a stronger measure, we use both of the versions to ensure robustness, as previous experimental results rely on the true/false version of the scale. We also discuss the extent to which our results are robust to both versions of the scale when appropriate. There is one case where we obtain very slightly different results depending on the scale, and this case is when we rely on observational data rather than experimental data.

The five-point version of the scale is as follows:

1. When you are with other people, how often do you put on a show to impress or entertain them?
   Always
   Most of the time
   Some of the time
   Once in a while
   Never
2. When you are in a group of people, how often are you the center of attention?
   Always
   Most of the time
   Some of the time
   Once in a while
   Never
3. How good or poor of an actor would you be?
   Excellent
   Good
   Fair
   Poor
   Very poor

The true- false version is as follows:

1. I would probably make a good actor. [True/False]
2. In groups of people, I am rarely the center of attention. [True/False]
3. I guess I put on a show to impress or entertain people. [True/False]

We treat self-monitoring as an individual trait and do not expect that it would be affected by our treatments. Nonetheless, in the studies in which we include measures of self-monitoring, we measure self-monitoring prior to treatment exposure.

References

Aarts, Henk, and Ap Dijksterhuis (2003). "The Silence of the Library: Environment, Situational Norm and Social Behavior." *Journal of Personality and Social Psychology* 84(1): 18–28.

Abramowitz, Alan I. (2010). *The Disappearing Center: Engaged Citizens, Polarization and American Democracy*. New Haven, CT: Yale University Press.

Abrams, Samuel J., and Morris P. Fiorina (2014). "Are Leaning Independents Just Deluded or Dishonest Weak Partisans?" Working Paper. Sarah Lawrence College and Stanford University.

Abramson, Paul R., John H. Aldrich, and David W. Rohde (1983). *Change and Continuity in the 1980 Elections. (Rev. ed)*. Washington: C.Q. Press.

Achen, Christopher H. (1992). "Breaking the Iron Triangle: Social Psychology, Demographic Variables and Linear Regress in Voting Research." *Political Behavior* 14(3): 195–211.

Achen, Christopher H. (2002). "Parental Socialization and Rational Party Identification." *Political Behavior* 24(2): 141–170.

Ahn, T. K., Robert Huckfeldt, Alexander K. Mayer, and John Barry Ryan (2013). "Expertise and Bias in Political Communication Networks." *American Journal of Political Science* 57(2): 357–373.

Aldrich, John H. (1995). *Why Parties? The Origin and Transformation of Party Politics in America*. Chicago: University of Chicago Press.

American Political Science Association Committee on Political Parties (1950). "Toward a More Responsible Two-Party System: A Report." Supplement to the *American Political Science Review* 44(3), Part 2.

Ansolabehere, Stephen, and Shanto Iyengar (1995). *Going Negative: How Attack Ads Shrink and Polarize the Electorate*. New York: Free Press.

Arceneaux, Kevin (2012). "Cognitive Biases and the Strength of Political Arguments." *American Journal of Political Science* 56(2): 271–285.

Bailey, Michael, Daniel J. Hopkins, and Todd Rogers (2014). "Unresponsive and Unpersuaded: The Unintended Consequences of Voter Persuasion Efforts" (May 26, 2014). Available at SSRN: http://ssrn.com/abstract=2307631

Bakshy, Eytan, Solomon Messing, and Lada Adamic (2015). "Exposure to Ideologically Diverse News and Opinion on Facebook." *Science* 348: 1130–1132.

Banning, James H. (1996). "Bumper Sticker Ethnography: Another Way to View the Campus Ecology." *The Campus Ecologist* 14(3): 1–4.

Barabas, Jason, and Jennifer Jerit (2010). "Are Survey Experiments Externally Valid?" *American Political Science Review* 104(2): 226–242.

Bartels, Larry (2002). "Beyond the Running Tally: Partisan Bias in Political Perceptions." *Political Behavior* 24(2): 117–150.

Bashir, Nadia, Penelope Lockwood, Alison L. Chasteen, Daniel Nadolny, and Indra Noyes (2013). "The Ironic Impact of Activists: Negative Stereotypes Reduce Social Change Influence." *European Journal of Social Psychology* 43(7): 614–626.

Baumeister, Roy F., Ellen Bratslavsky, Catrin Finkenauer, and Kathleen Vohs (2001). "Bad Is Stronger than Good." *Review of General Psychology* 5(4): 323.

Beck, Paul Allen (1977). "Partisan Dealignment in the Postwar South." *American Political Science Review* 71(2): 477–496.

Beck, Paul Allen (2002). "Encouraging Defection: The Role of Personal Discussion Networks in Partisan Desertions to the Opposition Party and Perot Votes in 1992." *Political Behavior* 24(4): 309–338.

Beck, Paul Allen, Russell Dalton, Steven Greene and Robert Huckfeldt (2002). "The Social Calculus of Voting: Interpersonal, Media and Organizational Influences on Presidential Choices." *American Political Science Review* 96(1): 57–73.

Beck, Paul Allen, and M. Kent Jennings (1975). "Parents as 'Middlepersons' in Political Socialization." *The Journal of Politics* 37(1): 83–107.

Beck, Paul Allen, and M. Kent Jennings (1979). "Political Periods and Political Participation." *American Political Science Review* 73(3): 737–750.

Belli, Robert F., Michael Traugott, Margaret Young, and Katherine A. McGonagle (1999). "Reducing Vote Overreporting in Surveys: Social Desirability, Memory Failure, and Source Monitoring." *Public Opinion Quarterly* 63(1): 90–108.

Berelson, Bernard R., Paul F. Lazarsfeld, and William N. McPhee (1954). *Voting: A Study of Opinion Formation in a Presidential Election*. Chicago: University of Chicago Press.

Berinsky, Adam J. (1999). "The Two Faces of Public Opinion." *American Journal of Political Science* 43(4): 1209–1230.

Berinsky, Adam J. (2002). "Political Context and the Survey Response: The Dynamics of Racial Policy Opinion." *The Journal of Politics* 64(2): 567–584.

Berinsky, Adam (2004). "Can We Talk: Self-Presentation and the Survey Response." *Political Psychology* 25(4): 643–659.

Berinsky, Adam J., Gregory A. Huber, and Gabriel S. Lenz (2012). "Evaluating Online Labor Markets for Experimental Research: Amazon.com's Mechanical Turk." *Political Analysis* 20(3): 351–368.

Berinsky, Adam J., and Howard Lavine (2012). "Self-Monitoring and Political Attitudes." *Improving Public Opinion Surveys: Interdisciplinary Innovation and the American National Election Studies* (John Aldrich and Kathleen M. McGraw, eds.), Princeton, NJ: Princeton University Press, 27–45.

Berinsky, Adam, Michelle Margolis, and Michael W. Sances (2014). "Separating the Shirkers from the Workers? Making Sure Respondents Pay Attention on Self-Administered Surveys." *American Journal of Political Science* 58(3): 739–753.

Berrens, Robert P., Alok Bohara, Hank Jenkins-Smith, Carol Silva, and David L. Weimer (2003). "The Advent of Internet Surveys for Political Research: A Comparison of Telephone and Internet Samples." *Political Analysis* 11(1): 1–22.

Binder, Sarah (1999). "The Dynamics of Legislative Gridlock." *American Political Science Review* 93(3): 519–533.

Bishop, Bill (2008). *The Big Sort: Why The Clustering of Like-Minded America Is Tearing Us Apart.* New York: Houghton Mifflin Harcourt.

Bishop, George, Robert G Meadow, and Marilyn Jackson-Beeck (1978). *The Presidential Debates: Media, Electoral and Policy Perspectives.* New York: Praeger

Blais, Andre, and Daniel Rubenson (2013). "The Source of Turnout Decline: New Values or New Contexts?" *Comparative Political Studies* 46(1): 95–117.

Bond, Robert M., Christopher J. Fariss, Jason J. Jones, Adam D. I. Kramer, Cameron Marlow, Jaimie E. Settle, and James H. Fowler (2012). "A 61-Million-Person Experiment in Social Influence and Political Mobilization." *Nature* 489: 295–298.

Boydstun, Amber (2013). *Making the News: Politics, the Media and Agenda Setting.* Chicago: University of Chicago Press.

Brader, Ted (2006). *Campaigning for Hearts and Minds: How Emotional Appeals in Political Ads Work.* Chicago: University of Chicago Press.

Brader, Ted, Nicholas Valentino, and Elizabeth Suhay (2008). "What Triggers Public Opposition to Immigration? Anxiety, Group Cues, and Immigration Threat." *American Journal of Political Science* 52(4): 959–978.

Briggs, Stephen R., Jonathan M. Cheek, and Arnold H Buss (1980). "An Analysis of the Self-Monitoring Scale." *Journal of Personality and Social Psychology* 38(4): 679.

Brooks, Deborah Jordan (2011). "Testing the Double Standard for Candidate Emotionality: Voter Reactions to the Tears and Anger of Female and Male Politicians." *Journal of Politics* 73(2): 597–615.

Brown, Jonathon D., and Frances M. Gallagher (1992). "Coming to Terms with Failure: Private Self-Enhancement and Public Self-Effacement." *Journal of Experimental Social Psychology* 28(1): 3–22.

Brown, Jonathon D., Rebecca L. Collins, and Greg W. Schmidt (1988). "Self-Esteem and Direct Versus Indirect Forms of Self-Enhancement." *Journal of Personality and Social Psychology* 55(3): 445–453.

Bryce, James. (1921). *Modern Democracies*, Vol. 1. New York: Macmillian.

Burden, Barry C., David T. Canon, Kenneth R. Mayer, and Donald P. Moynihan (2014). "Election Laws, Mobilization, and Turnout: The Unanticipated Consequences of Election Reform." *American Journal of Political Science* 58(1): 95–109.

Butler, Daniel M., and Eleanor Neff Powell (2013). "Understanding the Party Brand: Experimental Evidence on the Role of Valence." *The Journal of Politics* 76(2): 492–505.

Cacioppo, John T, Richard E. Petty, Jeffrey A. Feinstein, and W. Blair G. Jarvis (1996) "Dispositional Differences in Cognitive Motivation: The Life and Times of Individuals Varying in Need for Cognition." *Psychological Bulletin* 119(2) 197–253.

Campbell, Angus, Philip E. Converse, Warren E. Miller, and Donald E. Stokes (1960). *The American Voter.* Chicago: John Wiley & Sons, Inc.

Campbell, Bruce A. (1979). *The American Electorate: Attitudes and Action.* New York: Holt, Rinehart and Winston.

Campbell, David E. (2004). "Acts of Faith: Churches and Political Engagement." *Political Behavior* 26(2): 155–179

Carmines, Edward G., Jessica C. Gerrity, and Michael W. Wagner (2008). "Did the Media Do It? The Influence of News Coverage on the 2006 Congressional Elections." *Fault Lines: Why the Republicans Lost Congress* (Jeffery Mondak and Dona-Gene Mitchell, eds.) New York: Routledge, 22–41.

Carson, Jamie, Gregory Koger, Matthew Lebo, and Everett Young (2010). "The Electoral Costs of Party Loyalty in Congress." *American Journal of Political Science* 54(3): 598–616.

Carter, Travis J., Melissa J. Ferguson, and Ran R. Hassin (2011). "A Single Exposure to the American Flag Shifts Support toward Republicanism up to 8 Months Later." *Psychological Science* 22(8): 1011–1018.

Cialdini, Robert B., and Noah J. Goldstein (2004). "Social Influence: Compliance and Conformity." *Annual Review of Psychology* 55: 591–621.

Cohen, Jacob (1988). *Statistical Power Analysis for the Behavioral Sciences*. Hillsdale, NJ: Lawrence Erlbaum Associates, Publishers.

Craig, Stephen C., Richard G. Niemi, and Glenn E. Silver (1990). "Political Efficacy and Trust: A Report on the NES Pilot Study Items." *Political Behavior* 12(3): 289–314.

Darr, Joshua, and Matthew S. Levendusky (2014). "Relying on the Ground Game: The Placement and Effect of Campaign Field Offices." *American Politics Research* 42(3): 529–548.

Dennis, Jack (1988). "Political Independence in America, Part I: On Being an Independent Partisan Supporter." *British Journal of Political Science* 18(1): 77–109.

Dennis, Jack (1992). "Political Independence in America, Part III: In Search of Closet Partisans" *Political Behavior* 14(3): 261–296.

Doherty, David (2013). "To Whom Do People Think Representatives Should Respond: Their District or the Country?" *Public Opinion Quarterly* 77(1): 237–255.

Dowling, Conor M., and Amber Wichowsky (2015). "Attacks without Consequence? Candidates, Parties, Groups, and the Changing Face of Negative Advertising." *American Journal of Political Science* 59(1): 19–36.

Dropp, Kyle, Molly C. Jackman, and Saul Jackman (2013). "The Affordable Care Act: An Experiment in Federalism?" Brookings Institution Research Paper.

Druckman, James N. (2004). "Priming the Vote: Campaign Effects in a US Senate Election." *Political Psychology* 25(4): 577–594.

Druckman, James N., Don P. Green, Jim H. Kuklinski, and Arthur Lupia (eds.) (2011). *Cambridge Handbook of Experimental Political Science*. New York: Cambridge University Press.

Druckman, James N., and Cindy D. Kam (2011). "Students as Experimental Participants: A Defense of the 'Narrow Data Base'." In *Cambridge Handbook of Experimental Political Science* (James Druckman, Don P. Green, Jim H. Kuklinski, and Arthur Lupia, eds.) New York: Cambridge University Press, 41–57.

Druckman, James N and Thomas J. Leeper (2012) "Learning More from Political Communication Experiments: Pretreatment and Its Effects." *American Journal of Political Science* 56(4) 875–896.

Effron, Daniel A., Jessica S. Cameron, and Benoit Monin (2009). "Endorsing Obama Licenses Favoring Whites." *Journal of Experimental Social Psychology* 45(3): 590–593.

Elving, Ronald D. (1995). *Conflict and Compromise: How Congress Makes the Law.* New York: Simon and Schuster.

Enos, Ryan D., and Eitan D. Hersh (2015). "Party Activists as Campaign Advertisers." *American Political Science Review* 109(2): 252–278.

Eveland, William P., and Myiah J. Hutchens (2013). "The Role of Conversation in Developing Accurate Poliftical Perceptions: A Multilevel Social Network Approach." *Human Communication Research* 39(4): 422–444.

Faucheux, Ron (ed.) (2003). *Winning Elections: Political Campaign Management, Strategy, and Tactics.* Lanham, MD: Rowman & Littlefield.

Feldman, Stanley, and Pamela J. Conover (1983). "Candidates, Issues and Voters: The Role of Inference in Political Perception." *The Journal of Politics* 45(4): 810–839.

Feldman, Stanley, and Leonie Huddy (2005). "Racial Resentment and White Opposition to Race-Conscious Programs: Principles or Prejudice?" *American Journal of Political Science* 49(1): 168–183.

Fiorina, Morris P., (1981). *Retrospective Voting in American National Elections.* New Haven, CT: Yale University Press.

Fiorina, Morris P. (2012). "If I Could Hold a Seminar for Political Journalists…" *The Forum* 10(4): 2–10.

Fiorina, Morris P., Samuel A. Abrams, and Jeremy C. Pope (2005). *Culture War? The Myth of a Polarized America.* New York: Pearson Longman.

Fiorina, Morris P., Samuel A. Abrams and Jeremy C. Pope (2008) "Polarization in the American Public: Misconceptions and Misreadings. " *Journal of Politics* 70(2): 556–560.

Fowler, James, and Cindy Kam (2007). "Beyond the Self: Social Identity, Altruism, and Political Participation." *The Journal of Politics* 69(3): 813–827.

Fowler, James (2006). "Altruism and Turnout." *The Journal of Politics* 68(3): 674–683.

Fowler, Tim, and Doug Hagar (2013). "'Liking' Your Union: Unions and New Social Media during Election Campaigns." *Labor Studies Journal* 38(3): 201–228.

Franklin, Charles H. (1984). "Issue Preferences, Socialization, and the Evolution of Party Identification." *American Journal of Political Science* 28(3): 459–478.

Franklin, Mark N. (2004). *Voter Turnout and the Dynamics of Electoral Competition in Established Democracies since 1945.* New York: Cambridge University Press.

Gangestad, Steven W, and Mark Snyder (2000). "Self-Monitoring: Appraisal and Reappraisal." *Psychological Bulletin* 126(4): 530–555.

Gans, Herbert J. (1979). *Deciding What's News: A Study of CBS Evening News, NBC Nightly News, Newsweek, and Time.* Evanston, IL: Northwestern University Press.

Geer, John (1991). "Do Open-Ended Questions Measure 'Salient' Issues?" *Public Opinion Quarterly* 55(3): 358–368.

Gerber, Alan S., and Donald P. Green (2000). "The Effects of Canvassing, Telephone Calls, and Direct Mail on Voter Turnout: A Field Experiment." *American Political Science Review* 94(3): 653–663.

Gilens, Martin, Paul M. Sniderman, and James H. Kuklinski (1998). "Affirmative Action and the Politics of Realignment." *British Journal of Political Science* 28(1): 159–183.

Goffman, Erving (1959). *The Presentation of Self in Everyday Life.* New York: Anchor Books.

Goffman, Erving (1967). *Interaction Ritual: Essays on Face-to-Face Behavior.* New York: Anchor Books.

Goldstein, Noah J, Robert B. Cialdini, and Vladas Griskevicius (2008). "A Room with a Viewpoint: Using Social Norms to Motivate Environmental Conservation in Hotels." *Journal of Consumer Research* 35(3): 472–482.

Green, Donald P (1988). "On the Dimensionality of Public Sentiment toward Partisan and Ideological Groups" *American Journal of Political Science* 32(3): 758–780.

Green, Donald P., and Alan S. Gerber (2008). *Get Out the Vote: How to Increase Voter Turnout*, Second Edition. Washington, DC: Brookings Institution Press.

Green, Donald P., Alan S. Gerber, and David W. Nickerson (2003). "Getting Out the Vote in Local Elections: Results from Six Door-to-Door Canvassing Experiments." *The Journal of Politics* 65(4): 1083–1096.

Green, Donald, Bradley Palmquist, and Eric Schickler (2002). Partisan Hearts and Minds: Political Parties and the Social Identities of Voters. New Haven, CT: Yale University Press.

Groenendyk, Eric (2013). *Competing Motives in the Partisan Mind: How Loyalty and Responsiveness Shape Party Identification and Democracy.* New York: Oxford University Press.

Großer, Jens, and Thomas R. Palfrey (2014). "Candidate Entry and Political Polarization: An Antimedian Voter Theorem." *American Journal of Political Science* 58(1): 127–158.

Gutmann, Amy, and Dennis Thompson (2010). *The Spirit of Compromise: Why Governing Demands It and Campaigning Undermines It.* Princeton, NJ: Princeton University Press.

Hajnal, Zoltan, and Taeku Lee (2010). *Why Americans Don't Join the Party: Race, Immigration and the Failure (of Political Parties) to Engage the Electorate.* Princeton, NJ: Princeton University Press.

Harbridge, Laurel (2015). *Is Bipartisanship Dead? Policy Agreement and Agenda-Setting in the House of Representatives.* New York: Cambridge University Press

Harbridge, Laurel, and Neil Malhotra (2011). "Electoral Incentives and Partisan Conflict in Congress: Evidence from Survey Experiments." *American Journal of Political Science* 55(3): 494–510.

Harbridge, Laurel, Neil Malhotra, and Brian F. Harrison (2014). "Public Preferences for Bipartisanship in the Policymaking Process." *Legislative Quarterly* 39(3): 327–355.

Hardy, Bruce, and Kathleen Hall Jamieson (2005). "Can a Poll Affect Perception of Candidate Traits?" *Public Opinion Quarterly* 69(5): 725–743.

Heerwig, Jennifer A., and Brian J. McCabe (2009). "Education and Social Desirability Bias: The Case of a Black Presidential Candidate." *Social Science Quarterly* 90(3): 674–686.

Hendry, David J., Robert A. Jackson, and Jeffery J. Mondak (2008). "Abramoff, Email, and the Mistreated Mistress." *Fault Lines: Why the Republicans Lost Congress* (Jeffery Mondak and Dona-Gene Mitchell, eds.) New York: Routledge Press, 84–110.

Hersh, Eitan D., and Brian F. Schaffner (2013). "Targeted Campaign Appeals and the Value of Ambiguity." *The Journal of Politics* 75(2): 520–534.

Hibbing, John R., and Elizabeth Theiss-Morse (1995). *Congress as Public Enemy: Public Attitudes toward American Political Institutions.* New York: Cambridge University Press.

Hibbing, John R., and Elizabeth Theiss-Morse (2002). *Stealth Democracy.* New York: Cambridge University Press.

Hillygus, D. Sunshine, and Simon Jackman (2003). "Voter Decision Making in Election 2000: Campaign Effects, Partisan Activation, and the Clinton Legacy." *American Journal of Political Science* 47(4): 583–596.

Hirano, Shigeo and James M. Snyder (2007) "The Decline of Third-Party Voting in the United States" *Journal of Politics* 69(1): 1–16.

Holbrook, Allyson L., and Jon A Krosnick (2010). "Social Desirability Bias in Voter Turnout Reports Tests Using the Item Count Technique." *Public Opinion Quarterly* 74(1): 37–67.

Holbrook, Allyson L., Melanie C. Green, and Jon A. Krosnick (2003). "Telephone Versus Face-to-Face Interviewing of National Probability Samples with Long Questionnaires: Comparisons of Respondent Satisficing and Social Desirability Response Bias." *Public Opinion Quarterly* 67(1): 79–125.

Holtgraves, Thomas (1992). "The Linguistic Realization of Face Management: Implications for Language Production and Comprehension, Person Perception, and Cross-Cultural Communication." *Social Psychological Quarterly* 55(2): 141–159.

Hoskinson, Kevin (2001). "Ray Bradbury's Cold War Novels." *Ray Bradbury* (Harold Bloom, ed.). Philadelphia: Chelsea House Publishers, 125–140.

Hosmer, David W., and Stanley Lemeshow (2000). *Applied Logistic Regression*. New York: Wiley.

Huber, Gregory A., and Celia Paris (2013). "Assessing the Programmatic Equivalence Assumption in Question Wording Experiments: Understanding Why Americans Like Assistance to the Poor More Than Welfare." *Public Opinion Quarterly* 77(1): 385–397.

Huckfeldt, Robert, Paul E. Johnson, and John D. Sprague (2004). *Political Disagreement: The Survival of Diverse Opinions within Communication Networks*. New York: Cambridge University Press.

Huckfeldt, Robert, and John D. Sprague (1987). "Networks in Context: The Social Flow of Political Information." *American Political Science Review* 81(4): 1197–1216.

Huckfeldt, Robert, and John D. Sprague (1991). "Discussant Effects on Vote Choice: Intimacy, Structure, and Interdependence." *The Journal of Politics* 53(1): 122–158.

Huckfeldt, Robert, and John D. Sprague (1992). "Political Parties and Electoral Mobilization: Political Structure, Social Structure, and the Party Canvass." *American Political Science Review* 86(1): 70–86.

Huckfeldt, Robert, and John D. Sprague (1995). *Citizens, Parties, and Social Communication: Information and Influence in an Election Campaign*. New York: Cambridge University Press.

Huddy, Leonie, Joshua Billig, John Bracciodieta, Lois Hoeffler, Patrick Moynihan, and Pat Pugliani (1997). "The Effects of Interviewer Gender on the Survey Response." *Political Behavior* 19(3): 197–220.

Huddy, Leonie, Lilliana Mason, and Lene Aarøe (2015). "Expressive Partisanship: Campaign Involvement, Political Emotion, and Partisan Identity." *American Political Science Review* 109(1): 1–17.

Hur, Misun, Jack L. Nasar, and Bumseok Chun (2010). "Neighborhood Satisfaction, Physical and Perceived Naturalness and Openness." *Journal of Environmental Psychology* 30(1): 52–59.

Iyengar, Shanto (2005). "Speaking of Values: The Framing of American Politics." *The Forum* 3(3): Article 7.

Iyengar, Shanto, Gourav Sood, and Yptach Lelkes (2012). "Affect, Not Ideology: A Social Identity Perspective on Polarization." *Public Opinion Quarterly* 76(3): 405–431.

Iyengar, Shanto, and Sean J. Westwood (2014). "Fear and Loathing across Party Lines: New Evidence on Group Polarization." *American Journal of Political Science* 59(3): 690–707.

Jackman, Simon, and Paul M. Sniderman (2006). "The Limits of Deliberative Discussion: A Model of Everyday Political Arguments." *The Journal of Politics* 68(2): 272–283.

Jackman, Simon, and Lynn Vavreck (2009). *The 2007–8 Cooperative Campaign Analysis Project*. Palo Alto, CA: Polimetrix.

Jacobson, Gary C. (2009). "The Effects of the George W. Bush Presidency on Partisan Attitudes." *Presidential Studies Quarterly* 39(2): 172–209.

Kane, Emily, and Laura J Macaulay (1993). "Interviewer Gender and Gender Attitudes." *Public Opinion Quarterly* 57(1): 1–28.

Katz, Elihu (1957). "The Two-Step Flow of Communication: An Up-to-Date Report on an Hypothesis." *Public Opinion Quarterly* 21(1): 61–78.

Katz, Elihu, and Paul. F. Lazarsfeld (1955). *Personal Influence: The Part Played by People in the Flow of Mass Communications*. New York: The Free Press.

Katz, Richard (1979). "The Dimensionality of Party Identification: Cross-National Perspectives." *Comparative Politics* 11(2): 147–164.

Keeter, Scott, Cliff Zukin, Moly Andolina, and Krista Jenkins (2002). "Improving the Measurement of Political Participation." Presented at the Annual meeting of the Midwest Political Science Association. Chicago (April 25–28, 2002).

Keith, Bruce E., David B. Magleby, Candice J. Nelson, Elizabeth Orr, Mark C. Westlye, and Raymond E. Wolfinger (1992). *The Myth of the Independent Voter*. London: University of California Press

Killian, Linda (2012). *The Swing Vote: The Untapped Power of Independents*. New York: St. Martin's Press.

Kinder, Donald R., Mark D. Peters, Robert P. Abelson, and Susan T. Fiske (1980). "Presidential Prototypes." *Political Behavior* 2(4): 315–337.

Klar, Samara (2014a). "Partisanship in a Social Setting." *American Journal of Political Science* 58(3): 687–704.

Klar, Samara (2014b). "Identity Importance and Political Engagement among American Independents." *Political Psychology* 35(4): 577–591.

Klar, Samara (2014c). "A Multidimensional Study of Ideological Preferences and Priorities among the American Public." *Public Opinion Quarterly* 78 (Special Issue): 344–359.

Klein, Richard A., Kate Ratliff, Michelangelo Vianello, Reginald B. Adams, Stepan Bahník, Michael J Bernstein,...Brian A. Nosek (2014). "Investigating Variation in Replicability: A "Many Labs" Replication Project." *Social Psychology* 45(3): 142–152.

Konda, Thomas M., and Lee Sigelman (1987). "Public Evaluations of the American Parties, 1952–1984." *The Journal of Politics* 49(3): 814–829.

Kraus, Sidney (2000). *Televised Presidential Debates and Public Policy* (2nd ed.). Mahwah, N.J.: Lawrence Erlbaum.

Kriner, Douglas L., and Francis X. Shen (2012). "How Citizens Respond to Combat Casualties: The Differential Impact of Local Casualties on Support for the War in Afghanistan." *Public Opinion Quarterly* 76(4): 761–770.

Krupnikov, Yanna (2011). "When Does Negativity Demobilize? Tracing the Conditional Effect of Negative Campaigning on Turnout." *American Journal of Political Science* 55(4): 797–813.

Krupnikov, Yanna, and Adam Seth Levine (2010). "Measuring People's Willingness to Engage in Political Action." *Sourcebook for Political Communication Research: Methods, Measures, and Analytical Techniques.* (Eric P. Bucy and Lance Holbert, eds.). New York: Routledge 149–164.

Krupnikov, Yanna, and Adam Seth Levine (2014). "Cross-Sample Comparisons and External Validity." *Journal of Experimental Political Science* 1(1): 59–80.

Krupnikov, Yanna (2014). "How Negativity Can Increase and Decrease Voter Turnout: The Effect of Timing." *Political Communication* 31(3): 446–466.

Krysan, Maria (1998). "Privacy and the Expression of White Racial Attitudes: A Comparison across Three Contexts." *Public Opinion Quarterly* 62(4): 506–544.

Kuklinski, James H., Michael D. Cobb, and Martin Gilens (1997). "Racial Attitudes and the 'New South'." *The Journal of Politics* 59(2): 323–349.

Ladd, Everett Carll (1985). "On Mandates, Realignments, and the 1984 Presidential Election." *Political Science Quarterly* 100(1): 1–25.

Laband, David N., Ram Pandit, John P. Sophocleus, and Anne M. Laband (2009). "Patriotism, Pigskins, and Politics: an Empirical Examination of Expressive Behavior and Voting." *Public Choice* 138(1–2): 97–108.

Lavine, Howard, and Mark Snyder (1996). "Cognitive Processing and the Functional Matching Effect in Persuasion: The Mediating Role of Subjective Perceptions of Message Quality." *Journal of Experimental Social Psychology* 32(6): 580–604.

Layman, Geoffrey, Thomas M. Carsey, and Juliana Menasce Horowitz (2006). "Party Polarization in American Politics: Characteristics, Causes, and Consequences." *Annual Review of Political Science* 9: 83–110

Lazarsfeld, Paul F., Bernard Berelson, and Hazel Gaudet (1948). *The People's Choice.* New York: Columbia University Press.

Lazer, David, Brian Rubineau, Carol Chetkovich, Nancy Katz, and Michael Neblo (2010). "The Coevolution of Networks and Political Attitudes." *Political Communication* 27(3): 248–274.

Lee, Frances (2009). *Beyond Ideology: Politics, Principles and Partisanship in the US Senate.* Chicago: University of Chicago Press.

Leeper, Thomas J., and Kevin J. Mullinix (2014). "To Whom, and With What Effect? Parallel Experiments on Framing." Presented at the *Annual Meeting of the American Political Science Association.* Washington, DC (August 28–August 31, 2014).

Leighley, Jan E., and Jonathan Nagler (2013). *Who Votes Now? Demographics, Issues, Inequality, and Turnout in the United States.* Princeton, NJ: Princeton University Press.

Levendusky, Matthew (2009). *Partisan Sort: How Liberals Became Democrats and Conservatives Became Republicans.* Chicago: University of Chicago Press.

Lippa, Richard (1978). "Expressive Control, Expressive Consistency, and the Correspondence between Expressive Behavior and Personality." *Journal of Personality* 46(3): 438–461.

Lippmann, Walter (1922). *Public Opinion.* New York: Harcourt, Brace, and Co.

Lodge, Milton, and Charles Taber (2013). *The Rationalizing Voter.* New York. Cambridge University Press.

Long, J. Scott (1997). *Regression Models for Categorical and Limited Dependent Variables.* Thousand Oaks, CA: Sage Press.

Lupia, Arthur, and Mathew D. McCubbins (1998). *The Democratic Dilemma: Can Citizens Learn What They Need to Know.* New York: Cambridge University Press.

Luskin, Robert C., James P. McIver, and Edward G. Carmines (1989). "Issues and the Transmission of Partisanship." *American Journal of Political Science* 33(2): 440–458.

Magleby, David B., Candice J. Nelson, and M. C. Westlye (2011). "The Myth of the Independent Voter Revisited." *Facing the Challenge of Democracy: Explorations in the Analysis of Public Opinion and Political Participation* (Paul Sniderman and Benjamin Highton, eds.). Princeton, NJ: Princeton University Press, 238–263.

Makse, Todd, and Anand E. Sokhey (2014). "The Displaying of Yard Signs as a Form of Political Participation." *Political Behavior* 36(1): 189–213.

Masket, Seth (2009). *No Middle Ground: How Informal Party Organizations Control Nominations and Polarize Legislatures.* Ann Arbor: University of Michigan Press.

Mason, Lilliana (2014). "I Disrespectfully Agree: The Differential Effects of Partisan Sorting on Social and Issue Polarization." *American Journal of Political Science* 59(1): 128–145.

Mattes, Kyle, and David P. Redlawsk (2014). *The Positive Case for Negative Campaigning.* Chicago: University of Chicago Press.

McClendon, Gwyneth H. (2014). "Social Esteem and Participation in Contentious Politics: A Field Experiment at an LGBT Pride Rally." *American Journal of Political Science* 58(2): 279–290.

McDermott, Rose (2011). "Internal and External Validity." *Cambridge Handbook of Experimental Political Science* (James Druckman, Don P. Green, Jim H. Kuklinski, and Arthur Lupia, eds.). New York: Cambridge University Press, 27–40.

McDonald, Michael P., and Samuel L. Popkin (2001). "The Myth of the Vanishing Voter." *American Political Science Review* 95(4): 963–974.

Mendelberg, Tali (2001). *The Race Card.* Princeton, NJ: Princeton University Press.

Messing, Solomon, Annie Franco, Arjun Wilkins, Dustin Cable, and Matthew Warshauer (2014). "Campaign Rhetoric and Style on Facebook in the 2014 U.S. Midterms." Facebook Research Note. October 10, 2014: https://www.facebook.com/notes/10152581594083859/.

Middleton, Joel A., and Donald P. Green (2008). "Do Community-Based Mobilization Campaigns Work Even in Battleground States? Evaluating the Effectiveness of MoveOn's 2004 Outreach Campaign." *Quarterly Journal of Political Science* 3(1): 63–82.

Miller, Warren E., and J. Merrill Shanks (1997). *The New American Voter.* Cambridge, MA: Harvard University Press.

Monson, J. Quin (2004). "Get on Television versus Get on the Van: G.O.T.V. and the Ground War in 2002." *The Last Hurrah? Soft Money and Issue Advocacy in the 2002 Congressional Elections* (David B. Magleby and J. Quin Monson, eds.) Washington, DC: Brookings Institution Press, 90–116.

Mullinix, Kevin J., James N. Druckman, and Jeremy Freese (2014). "The Generalizability of Survey Experiments." *Institute for Policy Research, Northwestern University, Working Paper.*

Mutz, Diana C. (2002). "The Consequences of Cross-Cutting Networks for Political Participation." *American Journal of Political Science* 46(4): 838–855.

Mutz, Diana, and Byron Reeves (2005). "The New Videomalaise: Effects of Televised Incivility on Political Trust." *American Political Science Review* 99(1): 1–15.

Nall, Clayton, and Jonathan Mummolo (2014). "Why Partisans Don't Sort: How Quality Concerns Trump Americans' Desire for Like-Minded Neighbors." Presented at the Annual Meeting of the Midwest Political Science Association. Chicago (April 3–6, 2014).

Nicholson, Stephen P., and Gary M. Segura (2012). "Who's the Party of the People? Economic Populism and the U.S. Public's Beliefs about Political Parties." *Political Behavior* 34(2): 369–389.

Niemi, Richard, and M. Kent Jennings (1991). "Issues and Inheritance in the Formation of Party Identification." *American Journal of Political Science* 35(4): 970–988.

Norpoth, Helmut (1987). "Under Way and Here to Stay: Party Realignment in the 1980s?" *Public Opinion Quarterly* 51(3): 376–391.

Oltmanns, Thomas F., Marci E. J. Gleason, E. David Klonsky, and Eric Turkheimer (2005). "Meta-Perception for Pathological Personality Traits: Do We Know When Others Think That We Are Difficult?" *Consciousness and Cognition* 14(4): 739–751.

Oosterhof, Nikolaas, and Alexander Todorov (2009). "Shared Perceptual Basis of Emotional Expressions and Trustworthiness: Impressions from Faces." *Emotion* 9(1): 128–133

Paivio, Allan, and Kalman Csapo (1971). "Short-Term Sequential Memory for Pictures and Words." *Psychonomic Science* 24(2): 50–51.

Panagopoulos, Costas (2009). "Partisan and Nonpartisan Message Content and Voter Mobilization: Field Experimental Evidence." *Political Research Quarterly* 62(1): 70–76.

Petersen, Michael B., and Lene Aarøe (2013). "Politics in the Mind's Eye: Imagination as a Link between Social and Political Cognition." *American Political Science Review* 107(2): 275–293.

Pomper, Gerald (1976). "Impacts on the Political System." *American Electoral Behavior: Change and Stability.* (Samuel Kirkpatric, ed) Beverly Hills: Sage Publications. 137–143.

Pope, Jeremy C. (2012). "Voting vs. Thinking: Unified Partisan Voting Does Not Imply Unified Partisan Beliefs." *The Forum* 10(3): Article 5.

Price, Vincent, Joseph N. Cappella, and Lilach Nir (2002). "Argument Repertoire as a Reliable and Valid Measure of Opinion Quality: Electronic Dialogue during Campaign 2000." *Political Communication* 19(1): 73–93.

Prior, Markus (2012). "Who Watches Presidential Debates? Measurement Problems in Campaign Effects Research." *Public Opinion Quarterly* 76(2): 350–363.

Prior, Markus (2014). "Visual Political Knowledge: A Different Road to Competence?" *The Journal of Politics* 76(1): 41–57.

Pronin, Emily (2009). "The Introspection Illusion" *Advances in Experimental Social Psychology, Vol. 41* (Mark Zanna, ed.). Burlington. VT: Elsevier Press, 1–67.

Ranney, Austin (ed.) (1979). *The Past and Future of Presidential Debates.* Washington DC: American Enterprise Institute for Public Policy Research.

Reeves, Keith (1997). *Voting Hopes or Fears? White Voters, Black Candidates, and Racial Politics in America.* New York: Oxford University Press.

Rivers, Douglas (2006). "Sample Matching: Representative Sampling from Internet Panels." Polimetrix White Paper Series.

Rodriguez-Bailon, Rosa, Miguel Moya, and Vincent Yzerbyt (2000). "Why Do Superiors Attend to Negative Stereotypic Information about Their Subordinates? Effects of

Power Legitimacy on Social Perception." *European Journal of Social Psychology* 30: 651–671.

Rolfe, Meredith (2012). *Voter Turnout: A Social Theory of Political Participation*. New York: Cambridge University Press.

Rosenstone, Steven, and John M. Hansen (1993). *Mobilization, Participation, and Democracy in America*. New York: MacMillan.

Rowatt, Wade C., Michael Cunninghan, and Perri B. Druen (1998). "Deception to Get a Date." *Personality and Social Psychology Bulletin* 24(11): 1228–1242.

Roy, Robin E., Kristin S. Weibust, and Carol T. Miller (2007). "Effects of Stereotypes about Feminists on Feminist Self-Identification." *Psychology of Women Quarterly* 31(2): 146–156.

Ryan, John Barry (2013). "An Experimental Study of Persuasive Communication." *Political Communication* 30(1): 100–116

Sanders, David, Harold D. Clarke, and Marianne Stewart (2007). "Does Mode Matter for Modeling Political Choice? Evidence from the 2005 British Election Study." *Political Analysis* 15(3): 257–285.

Saramäki, Jari, E. A. Leicht, Eduardo López, Sam Roberts, Felix Reed-Tsochas, and Robin Dunbar (2014). "Persistence of Social Signatures in Human Communication." *Proceedings of the National Academy of Sciences* 111(3): 942–947.

Schattschneider, E. E. (1942). *Party Government: American Government in Action*. New York: Holt, Rinehart and Winston.

Scheufele, Dietram A. (2002). "Examining Differential Gains from Mass Media and Their Implications for Participatory Behavior." *Communication Research* 29(1): 46–65.

Schlenker, Barry R., and Michael F. Weigold (1989). "Goals and the Self-Identification Process: Constructing Desired Identities." *Goal Concepts in Personality and Social Psychology* (Pervin, ed.) Hillsdale, NJ: Erlbaum, 243–290.

Schlenker, Barry R., and Michael F. Weigold (1992). "Interpersonal Processes Involving Impression Regulation and Management." *Annual Review of Psychology* 43: 133–168.

Sears, David O. (1969). "Political Behavior." *Handbook of Social Psychology, Vol. 5, Second Edition* (Lindzey and Aronson, eds.) Reading, MA: Addison-Wesley, 315–458.

Sears, David O. (1986) "College Sophomores in the Laboratory: Influences of a Narrow Databse on Psychology's View of Human Nature" *Journal of Personality and Social Psychology* 51(3) 515–530.

Settle, Jaime, Robert M. Bond, Lorenzo Coviello, Christopher J. Farriss, James H. Fowler and Jason J. Jones (forthcoming) "From Posting to Voting: The Effects of Political Competition on Online Political Engagement." *Political Science Research and Methods*. FirstView Article.

Shadish, William R., Thomas D. Cook, and Donald T. Campbell (2001). *Experimental and Quasi-Experimental Designs for Generalized Causal Inference*. Boston: Houghton Mifflin.

Shaffer, Leigh S. (1983). "Toward Pepitone's Vision of a Normative Social Psychology: What Is a Social Norm?" *Journal of Mind and Behavior* 4(2): 275–293.

Shaw, Daron (2004). "Erratum for 'The Methods behind the Madness: Presidential Electoral College Strategies, 1989–1999.'" *The Journal of Politics* 66(2): 611–615.

Shea, Daniel M., and Michael John Burton (2006). *Campaign Craft: The Strategies, Tactics, and Art of Political Campaign Management*, 3rd edition. Westport, CT: Praeger.

Sinclair, Betsy (2012). *The Social Citizen: Peer Networks and Political Behavior.* Chicago: University of Chicago Press.

Sinclair, Betsy, Margaret McConnell, and Melissa R. Michelson (2013). "Local Canvassing: The Efficacy of Grassroots Voter Mobilization." *Political Communication* 30(1): 42–57.

Sirgy, M. Joseph, and Terri Cornwell (2002). "How Neighborhood Features Affect Quality of Life." *Social Indicators Research* 59(1): 79–114.

Smidt, Corwin D. (2014). "Dynamics in Partisanship during American Presidential Campaigns." *Public Opinion Quarterly* 78(S1): 303–329.

Smith, Aaron, and Lee Rainie (2008). "The Internet and the 2008 Election." Pew Internet and American Life Project.

Sniderman, Paul M., and Edward G. Carmines (1997). "Reaching Beyond Race." *PS: Political Science & Politics* 30(3): 466–471.

Snyder, Mark (1974). "Self-Monitoring of Expressive Behavior." *Journal of Personality and Social Psychology* 30(4): 526–537.

Snyder, Mark (1979). "Cognitive, Behavioral, and Interpersonal Consequences of Self-Monitoring." *Advances in the Study of Communication and Affect: Perception of Emotion in Self and Others* (Patricia Pliner, Kirk Blankstein, and Irwin M. Spiegel, eds.) New York: Plenum Press, 181–202.

Snyder, Mark (1987). *Public Appearances, Private Realities: The Psychology of Self-Monitoring.* New York: W.H. Freeman/Henry Holt & Co.

Snyder, Mark, Steve Gangestad, and Jeffry A. Simpson (1983). "Choosing Friends as Activity Partners: The Role of Self-Monitoring." *Journal of Personality and Social Psychology* 45(5): 1061–1072.

Snyder, Mark and Jeffry A. Simpson (1984). "Self-Monitoring and Dating Relationships." *Journal of Personality and Social Psychology* 47(6): 1281–1291.

Stieglitz, Stefan, Tobias Brockmann, and Ling Dang-Xuan (2012). "Usage of Social Media for Political Communication." Pacific Asia Conference on Information Systems 2012 Proceedings. Paper 22.

Stimson, James A. (1990). "A Macro Theory of Information Flow." *Information and Democratic Processes* (James Kuklinski and John Ferejohn, eds.) Champaign, IL: University of Illinois Press, 345–368.

Stimson, James A. (1993). "The Myth of the Independent Voter (Review)." *American Political Science Review* 87(2): 494–495.

Strahan, Erin J., Anne E. Wilson, Kate E. Cressman, and Vanessa Buote (2006). "Comparing to Perfection: How Cultural Norms for Appearance Affect Social Comparisons and Self-Image." *Body Image* 3(3): 211–227.

Streb, Matthew J., Barbara Burrell, Brian Frederick, and Michael A. Genovese (2008). "Social Desirability Effects and Support for a Female American President." *Public Opinion Quarterly* 72(1): 76–89.

Tamas, Bernard, and Matthew Dean Hindman (2014). "Ballot Access Laws and the Decline of American Third-Parties." *Election Law Journal: Rules, Politics, and Policy* 13(2): 260–276.

Taber, Charles S., and Milton Lodge (2006). "Motivated Skepticism in the Evaluation of Political Beliefs." *American Journal of Political Science* 50(3): 755–769.

Terkildsen, Nayda (1993). "When White Voters Evaluate Black Candidates: The Processing Implications of Candidate Skin Color, Prejudice, and Self-Monitoring." *American Journal of Political Science* 37(4): 1032–1053.

Valentino, Nicholas A., Vincent L. Hutchings, and Ismail K. White (2002). "Cues that Matter: How Political Ads Prime Racial Attitudes during Campaigns." *American Political Science Review* 96(1): 75–90.

Vavreck, Lynn (2007). "The Exaggerated Effects of Advertising on Turnout: The Dangers of Self-Reports." *Quarterly Journal of Political Science* 2(4): 287–305.

Verba, Sidney, Kay. L. Schlozman, and Henry Brady (1995). *Voice and Equality: Civic Voluntarism in American Politics*. Cambridge, MA: Harvard University Press.

Wallack, Grace, and John Hudak (2014). "How Much Did Your Vote Cost? Spending Per Voter in the 2014 Senate Races" FixGov Blog, Brookings Institute. http://www.brookings.edu/blogs/fixgov/posts/2014/11/07-spending-per-voter-2014-midterm-senate-wallack-hudak

Walsh, Katherine Cramer (2004). *Talking about Politics: Informal Groups and Social Identity in American Life*. Chicago: University of Chicago Press.

Wattenberg, Martin P. (1986). *The Decline of American Political Parties: 1952–1954*. Cambridge, MA: Harvard University Press.

Weber, Christopher, and Christopher Federico (2013). "Moral Foundations and Heterogeneity in Ideological Preferences." *Political Psychology* 34(1): 107–126.

Weber, Christopher, Howard Lavine, Leonie Huddy, and Christopher Federico (2014). "Placing Racial Stereotypes in Context: Social Desirability and the Politics of Racial Hostility." *American Journal of Political Science* 58(1): 63–78.

Weisberg, Herbert F. (1980). "A Multidimensional Conceptualization of Party Identification." *Political Behavior* 2(1): 33–60.

Weisberg, Herbert (1993). "*The Myth of the Independent Voter*. By Bruce E. Keith; David B. Magleby; Candice J. Nelson; Elizabeth Orr; Mark C. Westlye; Raymond E. Wolfinger (Review)." *Public Opinion Quarterly* 57(3): 428–430.

Wolfinger, Raymond E. (1995). "The Promising Adolescence of Campaign Surveys." *Campaigns and Elections American Style* (James A. Thurber and Candice J. Nelson, eds.) Boulder, CO: Westview, 181–191.

Wolfinger, Raymond E. and Steven J. Rosenstone (1980). *Who Votes?* New Haven, CT: Yale University Press.

Zaccaro, Stephen J., Roseanne Foti, and David A. Kenny (1991). "Self-Monitoring and Trait-Based Variance in Leadership: An Investigation of Leader Flexibility across Multiple Group Situations." *Journal of Applied Psychology* 76(2): 308–315.

Zaller, John (ed.) (1992). *The Nature and Origins of Mass Opinion*. New York: Cambridge University Press.

Zaller, John, and Stanley Feldman (1992). "A Simple Theory of the Survey Response: Answering Questions versus Revealing Preferences." *American Journal of Political Science* 36(3): 579–616.

Zhang, Weiwu, Thomas J. Johnson, Trent Seltzer, and Shannon L. Bichard (2010). "The Revolution Will Be Networked: The Influence of Social Network Sites on Political Attitudes and Behaviors." *Social Science Computer Review* 28(1): 75–92.

Zimbardo, Philip G. (2007). *The Lucifer Effect: Understanding How Good People Turn Evil*. New York: Random House.

Index

CPSIA information can be obtained
at www.ICGtesting.com
Printed in the USA
LVHW081347271118
598409LV00015B/400/P

9 781316 500637